No! I am not prepared that...

...an attendant level, one...

such a progress, state...

...the prince; no doubt

...glad to be of use

caution, and not...

hamlyn history

LITERATURE

Publishing Director Laura Bamford

Editor Trevor Davies

Assistant Editor Tarda Davison-Aitkins

Art Director Keith Martin

Executive Art Editor Mark Stevens

Designer Martin Topping

Picture Research Wendy Gay

Production Controller Julie Hadingham

First published in Great Britain in 1998 by Hamlyn
an imprint of Reed Consumer Books Limited
Michelin House, 81 Fulham Road, London SW3 6RB
and Auckland, Melbourne, Singapore and Toronto

Copyright © 1998 Reed Consumer Books Limited

ISBN 0 600 59408 4

A catalogue record for this book is available from the British Library

Produced by Toppan

Printed in China

Page 1: St Cuthbert Praying in the Sea from the *Life and Miracles of St. Cuthbert*.

Opposite: Alice and the Dodo from *Alice's Adventures in Wonderland*.

Contents: Roman writers Virgil, Horace and Variusin in conversation.

Page 6: Orson Welles as Harry Lime in Graham Greene's *The Third Man* (1949).

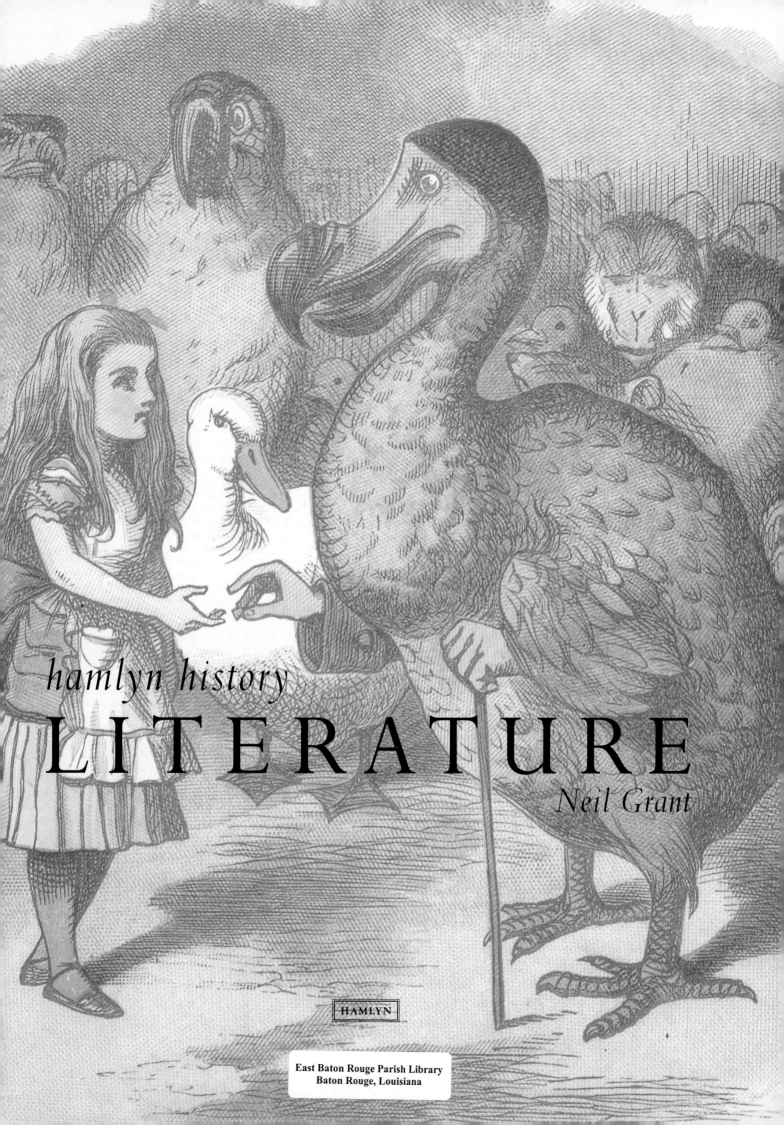

hamlyn history

LITERATURE

Neil Grant

HAMLYN

CONTENTS

INTRODUCTION

Human beings have probably been telling stories for as long as they have had language, and they started writing them down as soon as they developed a form of writing. Although the earliest writing seems to be Sumerian grocery lists (how much grain in the barn, etc.), the Mesopotamian epic of Gilgamesh is about 4,000 years old, and similarities with the Hebrew Old Testament suggest that both derive from a common, ancient source, just as the Iliad and the Odyssey, written about the 8th century B.C., undoubtedly derive from much older oral tradition.

However, the overwhelming mass of what we regard as literature was written within about the past 500 years or so, since the invention of printing with movable type in Europe. In that period Europe dominated and therefore European languages, and for the past 200–300 years, the influence of the British Empire, followed by the world dominance of the U.S.A., has ensured that the English language has played a leading role, becoming, like Latin in the Middle Ages, a universal language. A history of world literature, therefore, is inevitably centred on English literature and backed up by the literature of other European languages of international scope, notably French and Spanish. The literature of other, often more ancient, societies, in Asia particularly, tends to be neglected except inasmuch as it connects with the Western tradition. We should remind ourselves that, one thousand years ago, one of the greatest protonovels was being written by a lady of the Japanese court.

Since Britain ceased to be a great power, 'English literature' has been increasingly superseded by 'literature in English', and countries where writers use the English language are less and less wedded to the traditional canon of English literature – Chaucer, Shakespeare, Wordsworth, Dickens, etc. Many Indian schoolchildren, still learn Shakespeare, but since even British schoolchildren find it hard going, how long will Shakespeare last in a country where he has far less cultural relevance? In America, heir to the English canon, feminists, Afro-Americans and others are questioning the old literary hierarchy of, predominantly, white males.

Most of us still sometimes read for pleasure, in spite of the marvels of electronic entertainment, but do we read literature? What is literature anyway? The word originally meant all written language. We still sometimes use it in that sense, to describe printed information on a certain subject, as when we ask a travel agent for 'the literature on the Bahamas'. More formally, literature is defined, according to one dictionary, as 'writings in which expression and form, in connection with ideas of permanent and universal interest, are characteristic or essential features, as poetry, romance, history, biography, essays, etc.' Not all good books are literature, but all literature is good – interesting, significant, well-written, etc. – and the people who decide that it is good are the people who read it. It is entirely a subjective matter.

In any case, the vast majority of people read what they like, regardless of whether it is 'literature' or not. So far as modern fiction is concerned, there is a wide gulf between those who read literature and those who read popular novels. The former are interested in the many remarkable modern experiments in extending the form of the novel, the greater number read only for entertainment – a despicable reason in the view of many literary scholars – and prefer the traditional rules of character and narrative.

CHAPTER ONE
CLASSICAL
LITERATURE

Most of the many forms of literature characteristic of Western civilization would have been familiar to a citizen of Athens in the 5th century B.C. Although only a small proportion of the writings of the ancient Greeks has survived, it is mostly of the highest quality, and you do not have to be a classical scholar to read it with pleasure although, for most of us nowadays, that means in translation. Until recently most Western literature was written by people who were familiar with the works of the Greeks and could safely assume that their readers were too. Ignorance of the classical (i.e. Greek and Roman) tradition, and of the mythology that forms the subject matter of most Greek poetry and drama, not only leads to missing out on a great experience, but also raises problems in understanding the allusions of writers active over 2,000 years later.

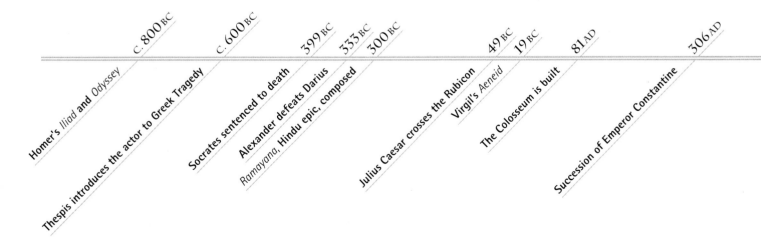

c. 800 BC — Homer's *Iliad* and *Odyssey*

c. 600 BC — Thespis introduces the actor to Greek Tragedy

399 BC — Socrates sentenced to death

333 BC — Alexander defeats Darius

300 BC — *Ramayana*, Hindu epic, composed

49 BC — Julius Caesar crosses the Rubicon

19 BC — Virgil's *Aeneid*

81 AD — The Colosseum is built

306 AD — Succession of Emperor Constantine

ANCIENT CIVILIZATIONS

A form of writing called 'cuneiform', with symbols representing objects and concepts, developed in ancient Mesopotamia (roughly, modern Iraq) about 3100 B.C. Cuneiform means 'wedge-shaped', so called because such symbols were easy to make on the clay tablets that served as paper. Writing was at first used for things like grocery lists – how much corn in the barn, etc. The earliest surviving epic, *Gilgamesh*, which tells of the adventures of a kind of super-hero, was first written down in cuneiform script about 1,000 years later.

Meanwhile the Egyptians had invented a better material than clay tablets for writing, made from pressed sheets of papyrus reed. Their hieroglyphic script, like Chinese, developed from picture-symbols. By about 2000 B.C. they were writing text books, poems and even stories.

THE FOUNDATIONS OF WESTERN LITERATURE

We can be certain that people told stories almost as soon as they learned how to speak, but stories could not be recorded until they could be written down. Pictures came before writing – the cave paintings at Altamira are nearly 20,000 years old – and pictures, like words, are a form of communication. Marks that identified objects are at least as old, although a full system of writing did not develop until about 5,000 years ago.

Above: **Sir Lawrence Alma-Tadema, A Reading from Homer, c.1835. Originally, of course, all literature was oral verse, intended to be sung or chanted, and reading, when it became possible, was not a solitary occupation but group entertainment.**

A full writing system requires an alphabet, providing a sign for every sound in the language. Along with other eastern Mediterranean people, including the Arabs and the Hebrews, the Phoenicians had a syllabic system before 1000 B.C., with signs for the different syllables, and the alphabet followed on from that. The Greeks borrowed this system and made the final step of dividing consonants from vowels and writing each one separately, thus inventing the modern alphabet. All alphabets were derived from theirs.

HOMER

In the late 8th century B.C., Greek literature began to be written down. As in other ancient literatures, the subjects concerned gods and heroes: the religious myths that people invent to explain phenomena for which they have no scientific explanation, and the exploits of famous men. They too are largely mythical though perhaps based more closely on real events than we can be sure of now. Archaeology has shown, for example, that the story of the siege of Troy was almost certainly based on an actual war between the Mycaeneans, forerunners of the Greeks, and their neighbours. These were stories that were, in one form or another, well known, having been repeated orally for many generations. They were brought together in two magnificent works of epic poetry, Homer's *Iliad* and *Odyssey*.

These works formed the basis, almost the 'Bible', of Greek culture, and if any one person can be called the founder of Western literature, it is Homer. But was Homer one person? Tradition says he was a blind bard, who recited his epic verse at social gatherings, but there are no facts about him and most scholars believe that the *Iliad* and the *Odyssey* were written or reworked to varying degrees by different people. The structure changes, and there are signs of additions, and odd discrepancies: the author of the *Odyssey* seemed to like dogs, but the author of the *Iliad* did not.

The *Iliad* relates events during the ten-year siege of Troy, originally provoked by the abduction of the beautiful Helen by the Trojan prince Paris, and in particular the incidents arising from the wrath of Achilles, the premier Greek hero who was antagonized by the commander, Agamemnon. It ends with the capture of the city by Greek warriors smuggled into Troy in a wooden horse. The deviser of the wooden horse was Odysseus, a hero with brains as well as brawn, and the *Odyssey* is the story of his return home, a journey that lasted even longer than the siege and included encounters with the one-eyed giant Polyphemus, the enchantress Circe, the Lotus eaters, the Sirens, the monsters Scylla and Charybdis and others whose names are part of our culture.

Every educated person in ancient Greece grew up with Homer, regarded as the greatest of all poets. Being in Greek, his tales were not read in medieval Europe, but regained immense popularity in the 19th century. The British statesman W. E. Gladstone, among others, wrote several books on him.

THE ARCHAIC PERIOD

Homer was not of course the only writer in Archaic Greece (roughly 8th–6th centuries

'Zeus had spoken. His Messenger [Hermes] obeyed at once and bound under his feet the lovely sandals of untarnishable gold that carried him with the speed of the wind over the water or the boundless earth; and he picked up the wand which he can use at will to cast a spell upon our eyes or wake us from the soundest sleep. With this wand in his hand . . . he swooped down on the sea, and skimmed the waves like a sea-mew [gull] drenching the feathers of its wings with spray as it pursues the fish down desolate gulfs of the unharvested deep. So Hermes rode the unending waves . . .'
Homer, *Odyssey*, v. (prose translation by E.V. Rieu).

Below: **The earliest forms of writing were usually either carved or painted. Cuneiform, as in this clay tablet of the Sumerian Lamentation on the Ruins of Ur, c.2000 B.C., contained no curves.**

B.C.). Ionia produced the first Greek philosophers and scientists (as well as, possibly, Homer himself). On the island of Lesbos, the mysterious Sappho wrote her poems about love. The beginnings of Greek drama appeared in Attica, and distinctive forms of verse, notably lyric poetry, established their identities. Excluding Homer, the best-known writer of the period is Hesiod, who seems to have lived soon after him. He was the first Greek poet to find his subject matter in sources other than mythology. His 'Works and Days' reflected his knowledge of farming and provided practical advice for peasants, as well fascinating information on rural life of the time.

By the end of the Archaic period, there were signs that literary traditions were becoming centred on Athens. Athens's leading role in the Persian Wars, in which the Greek city states successfully defended their independence against the Persian empire, opened a glorious period of expansion and prosperity, with such a flowering of literature and the arts as has perhaps never since been equalled. Although defeat in the Peloponnesian War (431–04 B.C.) ended Athenian dominance, its literary creativity continued until the end of the Classical era, conveniently marked by the Macedonian conquest of 338 B.C.

CLASSICAL ATHENS

THE PHILOSOPHERS

Almost every type of literary composition with which we are familiar can be traced back to the Greeks. The most noted is probably tragic drama (see pages 14–15), but epic poetry and history are close behind, while in philosophy the Greeks created the foundation on which virtually all subsequent Western thought has been based. Western philosophy, it has been said, is essentially a series of footnotes to Plato.

The Athenian form of direct democracy, in which all citizens participated, not only encouraged public speaking, but also promoted the arts of oratory and rhetoric. At the highest level, there was intense debate on questions of morality and ethics. Against this background, Socrates appeared. His probing discussions with the bright young men of Athens turned philosophy from a somewhat fruitless speculation on the nature of the universe into the study of human society and moral values.

One of the most influential thinkers in history, Socrates didn't write a word. His teaching is known to us through his disciples, in particular Plato, who, himself, was no mere reporter, but an original thinker, at least the equal of Socrates, who turned philosophical dialogue into an art form. He was the author of the seductive theory of the ideal: that there is a perfect essence of any concept which represents the truth. (A crude example: all tables are imperfect approximations of the essence of tableness.)

Aristotle, a pupil of Plato and a thinker of limitless range, looked for reality in particulars rather than in essentials. He was to remain the supreme authority on most subjects (excluding religion) throughout the Middle Ages, and one of the hardest tasks of the thinkers of the

Above: **Homer's tale of the wooden horse in the *Iliad* has always been appreciated by illustrators, and Troy has been conceived in many ways, here a fanciful French Gothic town.**

Right: **A reconstruction of the Acropolis of Athens, topped by the Parthenon which contained the giant statue of Athena, as it might have looked at the time of the Peloponnesian War.**

European Renaissance was to gain credence for ideas that ran contrary to Aristotle's teaching. There were also famous schools of philosophy, such as the Stoics whose ideas, seriously misrepresented by the word 'stoical', were remarkably similar to those of Christianity and had a profound influence on Christian thinkers.

THE HISTORIANS

There are earlier examples of 'historical' writing in the chronicles of ancient Egypt and Mesopotamia and in the Book of Genesis, but history as a matter of recorded fact began with the Greeks. Herodotus, the 'father' of history, who wrote about the Persian Wars, was the first to break away from myth and legend in pursuit of facts. He was certainly not a scientific historian: his plentiful and fascinating digressions included highly improbable episodes, although he was usually careful to say that they were things he had been told, rather than things that were true.

Herodotus makes interesting and informative reading, but Thucydides is considered the greater historian. His history of the Peloponnesian War is one of the great classics of historiography. He was writing contemporary history, having held a high command in the war himself, and he employed both documentary and oral sources, but he used them with discrimination, assessing them for accuracy, looking for causes as well as relating events, and displaying shrewd judgment of what was significant and what was not. Like his successors, he was essentially concerned with human behaviour, its influence on history, and the conclusions about human nature that may be drawn from history. The fact that he was also a marvellous writer explains why some people, even now, know more about a civil war in Greece 2,400 years ago than they do about the far greater conflicts of their own era.

THE POETS

Besides Homer, only fragments of epic poetry survive from before the 6th century B.C. Lyric poetry, originally poetry sung to the lyre and written in a variety of metres, was then coming into its own, in drinking songs and songs of love and personal feeling. Lesbos, the island of Sappho, seems to have been its place of birth.

The greatest lyric poet was Pindar, unusually not an Athenian, but a native of Boeotia. After Pindar's death (*c.*440 B.C.), the finest lyric poetry was to be found in the works of dramatists. As in so many subjects, the great expert on poetry was Aristotle, whose *Poetics* is the origin of the dramatic unities, a particular influence on French Classical drama of the 17th century.

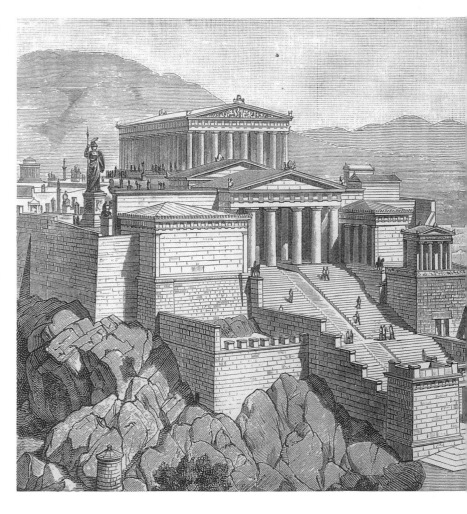

'So little trouble do men take in the search after truth, they prefer to accept whatever comes first to hand. Yet anyone who, upon the evidence which I have given, arrives at some such conclusion as my own about those ancient times, would not be far wrong. He must not put more reliance in the exaggerated embellishments of the poets, or in the tales of chroniclers who composed their work to please the ear rather than to speak the truth.'
Thucydides, *The Peloponnesian War*, i, 20–21, (trans. Jowett, rev. Brunt).

Drama represented the peak of Greek civilization and has remained a huge influence on the Western tradition. Anyone who comes to Greek tragedy with prior knowledge of, for example, Shakespeare will find it strikingly familiar.

Greek drama originated as a religious ritual performed at festivals such as the Athenian festival of Dionysus, consisting mainly of songs sung by a chorus. (Music was an important part of Classical drama, but no legacy survives today.) Through the work of the three great tragic playwrights, it evolved into a new art. The subject matter remained traditional religious myths, but was reinterpreted to engender a profound investigation of human fate and the relationship

GREEK THEATRE

'Now let the bloodstained god of war Whose savage music I hear Though no swords clash or shields ring, Be driven from our city, where the only song Is the groan of the dying, the whimper of fear. Rout him, the man-slayer, let him fly In disorder, let him hide his head In some bleak Thracian bay, Or ease himself in Amphitrite's bed. Now, whoever survives the night Dies at first light. Great Father Zeus, you who punish with fire, Incinerate the god of war Before we all lie dead.' Sophocles, *Oedipus Rex*, (trans. for the B.B.C. by Don Taylor, 1986).

Above: **A range of actors' masks from Greek drama. They are said to have been introduced by Thespis, the first prize-winning Athenian dramatist, and they remind us of the ritualistic character of Classical drama.**

between gods and human beings. Several plays were performed in one evening, including comedies, which were sometimes extremely coarse.

The greatest author of comedies was Aristophanes (died *c.*380 B.C.), equally adept at crude jokes and heavenly lyric poetry. The 'new comedy' of Menander and others in the late 4th century is the direct ancestor of the 'comedy of manners'. Drama was extremely popular among most classes. As Arthur Miller noted, the Greek theatre at Syracuse could hold 14,000 people.

AESCHYLUS

The first of the great tragic triumvirate, Aeschylus was born near Athens in 525 B.C. and fought in the Persian Wars. He wrote nearly 100 plays, including satyrs (comedies about satyrs, not necessarily 'satires' in the modern sense). Seven complete plays have survived, including *Persians*, *Seven Against Thebes* and the *Oresteia* trilogy about the doomed House of Atreus, which won the last of his many drama prizes in 458 B.C. Regarded as the founder of Greek tragedy, he introduced individual actors and dramatic dialogue, adopted stage costume and 'special effects', and, although Sophocles is said to have first introduced it, he seems to have used scenery. His themes are grand and solemn, dealing with destiny and the irresistible working of fate. His language is vivid, and as a lyric poet he is unsurpassed. Legend has it he was killed when an eagle dropped a tortoise on his head.

SOPHOCLES

A generation younger than Aeschylus, Sophocles (*b*.496 B.C.), lived throughout the greatest years of Athenian prosperity and through its defeat in the Peloponnesian War. He wrote even more plays than Aeschylus, but only seven (all tragedies) have survived. *Antigone*, *Oedipus Rex*, *Oedipus at Colonnus* (first produced after his death by his grandson, another Sophocles) and *Electra* are all still frequently performed.

Sophocles, who first won the drama prize in 468 B.C., defeating Aeschylus amid great popular excitement, was responsible for important developments in drama, including the introduction of a third actor and greater exploitation of scenery. He gave up the tradition of compiling plays as part of a trilogy, writing each one as complete in itself. He generally gave greater weight to human will, rather than the will of the gods, who were more remote, though no less respected, and action tended to grow from character rather than arbitrary events. Sophocles is thus the founder of the concept of the tragic hero, a great man ruined by his faults. *Oedipus Rex* is perhaps the most influential play ever written. Aristotle took it as the model tragedy in his *Poetics*. Sigmund Freud found in it the basis of his famous theory of the 'Oedipus complex'.

Sophocles was a handsome, charming and popular man. Though neither a politician nor a soldier, his fame brought him high office in Athens, and after his death at the age of 90 he was recognized as semi-divine.

EURIPIDES

Though no less successful, Euripides, born in 480 B.C., was a less genial, more reclusive figure

Above: The stage of a Greek theatre, with the Chorus in full flow and a predominantly female audience, from a ceiling painting in a Vienna theatre by Franz von Matsch (1861–1942).

than Sophocles. He wrote at least 80 plays, of which 18 have survived more or less intact. Among those still performed today are *Medea*, *Trojan Women*, *Orestes*, *Iphigenia at Aulis*, *Iphigenia in Tauris*, *Andromache* and *Electra*. His work is closer to everyday life than that of his two great predecessors, and was more controversial, for Euripides was prepared to question traditional morality as well as contemporary society. His lyric verse, especially his descriptions of nature, is more charming than grand in the manner of Aeschylus. His plays tend to show people in the grip of powerful and conflicting passions, but his language is more natural, less high-flown. Even more than Sophocles, he excelled in portraits of women, whether heroines or villains.

Like Aeschylus and Sophocles, Euripides came in for some amusing mockery at the hands of Aristophanes (for instance in *The Frogs*), but he was generally regarded with immense respect. Plutarch related several stories of his popularity; for instance, that the Spartan generals about to destroy Athens in 404 B.C. were dissuaded by someone singing the first chorus from *Electra*. Euripides spent his last years at the Macedonian royal court and died a victim, according to legend, of some misguided hunting dogs.

THE ROMANS

At the Roman Games in 240 B.C., Livius Andronicus presented two plays, a tragedy and a comedy. This event is sometimes seen as marking the formal beginning of Latin (Roman) literature. Significantly, the plays were adaptations of Greek originals, and Andronicus was probably a Greek himself. From the beginning, Roman culture was permeated by Greek influence. The literary genres of the Romans, like other arts, were derived from the Greeks, and Roman writers habitually compared themselves with the Greeks, if only to demonstrate how they differed from them. The 'golden age' of classical Latin literature was comparatively short, roughly a century, covering the last years of the Republic and the reign of the Emperor Augustus, who died in A.D. 14.

THE EARLY PERIOD

From the earlier Republican period, we have some good epic poetry and plays by two great playwrights, Plautus (*d*.184 B.C.) and Terence (*d*.159 B.C.). The surviving plays of Plautus, which influenced Shakespeare and his contemporaries, were adapted from earlier Athenian comedies by writers such as Menander, although Plautus, a labourer by trade, displayed wide knowledge and sympathy with the Roman lower classes. Terence was a former slave and apparently an African (born in Carthage). He died young, though six plays survive. They too were mostly based on Menander, but Terence, though less original than Plautus, surpassed him in characterization. His humour was less broad, pitched at a more cultivated audience. His plays, surprisingly acted by nuns in medieval England, influenced Restoration comedy, as well as the Elizabethans.

THE GOLDEN AGE

The first great figure of the golden age is that exemple of Roman virtue, Cicero (106–43 B.C.). Primarily a statesman and orator, he turned to literature and philosophy in later life, but is chiefly remembered for his published speeches, models of Latin prose, and his remarkable letters. They cover almost every conceivable subject though the most interesting, especially in the candid and intimate letters to Atticus, is Cicero himself. Cicero's contemporaries included Lucretius, the philosophical poet whose *De Rerum Natura* ('On the Nature of Things') advanced that the universe was a combination of atoms, and the lyric poet Catullus whose work, immensely varied in mood, was published posthumously.

Catullus had a profound influence on his contemporaries, including Horace (65–8 B.C.), the finest poet of his day after Virgil who, besides his *Odes* and *Satires*, wrote an influential book on poetry, *Ars Poetica*. Horace had a pervasive influence on English poetry: he was translated by Milton, adapted by Pope and Shelley among others, and anthologies of literary quotations find Horace a fruitful source of apt phrases. His genial temperament and good sense contributed to his popularity among contemporaries. Among lesser poets of the golden age were the elegists Tibullus, a friend of Horace and the subject of one of Horace's most charming Epistles, and Propertius, who was inspired, like so many, by his love for a woman, Cynthia.

VIRGIL

The poet Virgil (70–19 B.C.) was overall the most widely read – by generations of schoolboys not always willingly – poet in the Western world up to the 19th century. He was of Celtic origin, a farmer's son and himself owner of a farm in Mantua, where he wrote most of the pastoral *Eclogues*, which established his popularity, and the *Georgics*, influenced by Hesiod and certainly the finest poem on farming ever written. Reclusive and inclined to self-doubt, Virgil spent the last decade of his life writing the *Aeneid*, the work on which his reputation as 'the Latin Homer' rests. The subject of this epic is the greatness of Rome, and Virgil can be regarded as the first 'national' poet. Aeneas was a Trojan prince, whom legend recorded as the founder of Rome, and the theme recalls both the *Odyssey* and the *Iliad*. The first six books recount the hero's search for a home, while the last six deal with war and reconciliation between Trojans and Latins. For some readers, Virgil's imagery, especially in the *Georgics*, is supreme, while the music of his elegant hexameters is universally admired: 'the stateliest measure', said Tennyson, 'ever moulded by the lips of man'.

Virgil died with the *Aeneid* unfinished. His express wish that it be destroyed was fortunately vetoed by the Emperor Augustus.

OVID

The most felicitous of poets, Ovid (43 B.C.–A.D. 17) was a sophisticated social creature, the toast of fashionable Rome until, after antagonizing Augustus (partly by his manual of courtship and sex *The Art of Love*), he was banished to the Black Sea and died in exile. Of his surviving works, the best known is *Metamorphoses*, brilliant reworkings of the old myths in a more sceptical era, in which love, Ovid's greatest subject, is seen as the great agent of change. It was extremely popular in the Middle Ages and, it is said, was read more than any other book except the Bible.

'"Painters and poets alike have always had license to dare anything." We know that, and we claim and allow to others in their turn the same indulgence.'
Horace, *Ars Poetica.*

Opposite: Virgil, a 16th–century bust. His contemporary biographer states that Virgil was tall and dark, with the look of the farmer.

Above: Harvesting grapes, from the 4th–century A.D. mosaics in the church of Santa Constanza, Rome. Virgil, who never felt at home in Rome, was essentially a poet of the Italian countryside.

Although Augustus was an authoritarian ruler, he was careful to preserve republican traditions and exercised his power with moderation. After his death, old fears of imperial rule proved justified. The accession of Caligula in A.D. 37 introduced flagrant abuses, cruelty and immorality, resulting in the Emperor's murder. The decline in the quality of classical literature during the so-called Silver Age seems to reflect the political decline. Freedom of expression tended to be more limited, and there was more rhetoric, less wit and passion.

LATIN: THE SILVER AGE

THE SILVER AGE

Nevertheless, the post-Augustan period was not without its own literary giants. The Spanish-born Lucan (A.D. 39–65) was the author of the *Pharsalia*, generally regarded as the finest epic after the *Aeneid*, before he fell foul of the Emperor Nero and committed suicide at Nero's command. Seneca (4 B.C.–A.D. 65), the outstanding dramatic tragedian of the age, narrowly avoided death under Caligula, later becoming Nero's tutor. His tragedies are adaptations from the Greek and were highly influential in the Renaissance, when Greek speakers were few in comparison with Latin. Writers of prose included Pliny the Younger (c.62–c.113), the nephew of the Pliny the Elder, whose massive work, *Historia Naturalis*, was published in A.D. 77. The younger Pliny is chiefly remembered for his *Letters*, some written to the Emperor when he was a provincial governor. They contain a memorable description of the eruption of Vesuvius (A.D. 79) in which his uncle died while pursuing his research too assiduously. There were also outstanding achievements in the fields of satire and history. The most popular classical writer during the Renaissance was Plutarch (died c.125), a Greek, whose *Lives*, in the translation by Sir Thomas North (1579), were the chief source for Shakespeare's Roman plays.

SATIRE

Although there were satirical elements in some Greek comedy, satire is the one literary genre whose creation is credited to the Romans, in particular to Gaius Lucilius, who lived in the 2nd century B.C. He wrote a series of 'sermons' in verse, commenting adversely on public figures and social customs. His work is mostly lost, but he seems to have inspired Horace's mockery of public folly and vulgarity in his own lively *Satires*.

The greatest satirists, Martial and Juvenal, lived in the 1st–2nd centuries A.D. The Spanish-born Martial was a professional poet who grew disillusioned with city life and retired to the country. His *Epigrams* were published towards the end of the 1st century and consisted of short poems devoted to a single notion, sometimes obscene, sometimes flattering, often mocking.

times. Livy was highly regarded by Tacitus, the great historian of the Silver Age. Tacitus (died c.116), son-in-law of the famous Roman governor of Britain, Agricola, had the benefit of wider political and military experience, and was a famous orator. What survives of his work demonstrates extraordinary perception of character and motivation, and a crisp, vivid style. He was deeply affected by the brutal rule of Domitian (reigned A.D. 81–96) and became strongly anti-imperialist, imparting a hostile bias to his account of imperial government.

LATIN

The Roman Empire was the basis of European civilization; for over a thousand years after it had fallen, Europeans were fondly trying to restore it, or something like it. The name of the Holy (i.e. Christian) Roman Empire reflected the eagerness of the Ottonian German kings, like Charlemagne before them, to reclaim the greatness of the past, although, by most measurements of 'civilization', the Roman achievement was not surpassed until the modern era. Latin remained the standard language of educated people in Europe and provided an international cultural bond more powerful than a common market or a single currency. Thus Latin literature can be said to have lasted 1,500 years after Juvenal's death (A.D. 130), although it was no longer 'Roman', later writers being described as 'Christian', if appropriate, or by some other term.

Juvenal, who was much admired by the English satirists of the late 17th–18th century, was his younger contemporary and friend, but a far more savage writer. His bitter irony, ferocious invective, and hatred of the rich were directed, so the poet claimed, at an earlier generation, but it is obvious that this was mere form. He paints a grim picture of life for the non-rich in the Rome of the cultured Emperor Hadrian.

HISTORY

The great historians of republican Rome were Sallust (86–35 B.C.), who made a fortune as a provincial governor under Julius Caesar, retiring to become a historian in the tradition of Thucydides, and Livy (59 B.C.–A.D. 17). Livy came from north Italy and, unusually, seems never to have held political office. In spite of favouring the Republic, he found favour with Augustus and began publishing his great history of Rome (142 books, of which many are lost) in about 25 B.C. Though not always totally reliable, and heavily biased by his patriotic sympathies, Livy presents the finest account of ancient Rome from mythological

Above: Classical mythology provided endless inspiration for poets and artists. This painting from Roman Pompeii, shows the nature god Pan fleeing from a Hermaphrodite.

Right: Another wall painting from Pompeii shows a scene, dramatized by Euripides, in which Iphigenia is prepared for sacrifice, with her father's reluctant consent, to appease Artemis (Diana).

Hee

hateful t...
And thus...
ffor it w...

CHAPTER TWO
THE MIDDLE AGES

As the Roman Empire declined and 'civilised' Greco-Roman culture was overcome by a diversity of 'barbarian' counter culture, so literature was lost to what has become known as the 'Dark Ages'. With the end of classical culture European thought had lost its central focus of Rome and scholarship was left to the many emerging monasteries.

The Dark Ages is seen as a cultural step backwards, however this was a time of gradual fusion between the largely Christian Roman civilisation and heathen practices. Despite the lack of literary profusion during the Middle Ages a strong oral tradition was maintained and stories from these mysterious times have inspired many writers. Eventually works from all over Europe did emerge and had a great influence on the evolution of literature with the writings of such luminaries as Chaucer and Dante still being studied in schools today.

c. 700 — Beowulf

c. 1000 — The Lady Murasaki writes *The Tale of Genji*

1095 — Pope Urban II preaches first Crusade

1110 — Earliest record of a miracle play performed in Dunstable, England

1215 — King John signs *Magna Carta*

1314 — Jacques de Molay, the last leader of the Knights Templars is burned at the stake.

1321 — Dante completes the *Divinia Commedia*

1347 — 'Black death' sweeps through Europe

1400 — Geoffrey Chaucer dies

The decline of the Roman Empire was an immensely long and complicated process. In spite of the name sometimes given to the succeeding centuries, not all knowledge of Roman civilization was lost in the 'Dark Ages', and the Empire itself survived in Byzantium, in a form increasingly alienated from the West. But Rome itself fell into ruins and large parts of the former Roman Empire were occupied by tribes who were not only pagans but also illiterate. Among them were the Germanic tribes known as the Anglo-Saxons who occupied lowland Britain, extinguishing the culture of the Romano-Celts, despite the efforts of the legendary King Arthur and his knights.

ANGLO-SAXON LITERATURE

OLD ENGLISH

Anglo-Saxon, or Old English, is the oldest form of our language. Modern readers, unless they have studied it, cannot read it any more than they can read classical Greek, but the language is not the only problem. It is much easier to relate to the ancient Greeks than to the Anglo-Saxons with their grim gods and bloody, beleaguered heroes. Life in an Anglo-Saxon village is more remote to us than life in classical Athens. We would feel more at home dining in some comfort in an Attic villa while a bard recites Homer than we would in the draughty hall of some Saxon chief, or even in the cloisters of a Benedictine abbey listening to the Latin chants of the monks.

BEOWULF

Beowulf, the first English epic, dates from the 7th century and runs to about 3,000 lines. It relates the adventures of a Scandinavian hero and his conflicts with several ghastly monsters, the last of which proves fatal. Though in verse, it depends more on alliteration rather than rhyme and, like all early poetry, was designed to be recited – intoned even. It is slow-moving, largely due to the rhetorical trick of describing every object by a metaphorical synonym. Homer of course always referred to the sea (for instance) as 'the wine-dark sea' (actually a mistranslation, but a happy one), but in *Beowulf* this device is carried to excess, each mention of the object being followed by a whole string of descriptive terms.

Beowulf gets a mixed reception nowadays. It was defended in memorable terms by J. R. R.

Tolkien, author of *The Lord of the Rings*: 'profound feeling, and poignant vision, filled with the beauty and mortality of the world, are aroused by brief phrases, light touches, short words resounding like harp-strings sharply plucked'. On the other hand, the late Brigid Brophy put it top of her list of 'works of literature we could do without'.

The author of *Beowulf* is unknown, and although a number of Old English poems have been preserved, the names of only two poets have come down to us. In the case of Caedmon (late 7th century), a monk of humble origins, who is said to have translated parts of the Bible into English verse, it is little more than a name, since only one poem can definitely be ascribed to him. Cynewulf, who lived later, about the early 9th century, has had many poems on religious subjects ascribed to him, but modern scholars accept only four, to which his name was attached in runic characters, as definite.

BEDE

Caedmon's poem was preserved in a manuscript by Bede, or Baeda, (A.D. 673–735), the great figure of the early Anglo-Saxon period, who spent most of his life in a monastery at Jarrow and was known to later generations as the Venerable Bede. As a monk and a scholar, he wrote in Latin, and his most famous work, among many on various subjects, is his *History of the English Church and People*, which he completed in about A.D. 731. It describes the history of Britain from the invasion of Julius Caesar (55 B.C.) up to his own day and, although displaying understandable bias in favour of the Church and of his native Northumbrian kingdom – and against the marauding Vikings, destroyers of monasteries – it is generally both reliable and perceptive.

KING ALFRED

Bede's *History* was translated into Old English as part of the literary revival associated with Alfred the Great, King of Wessex (A.D. 871–899). The King himself even translated some works from Latin for the furtherance of education, and he encouraged an important venture already in existence, the *Anglo-Saxon Chronicle*. The most important historical source for the period, the *Chronicle* was in fact several, produced in different versions in different towns: the *Peterborough Chronicle* is the most famous survivor. It eventually covered the period from the beginning of Christianity to the mid-12th century. The records for the early years are merely a brief register, but from the 5th century the entries become more detailed, especially for certain events, such as Alfred's wars against the Danes, and poems are included, notably one about the Battle of Brunanburh (A.D. 937), best known in a translation by Tennyson.

Left: **The Northumbrian saint, Cuthbert, abbot of Lindisfarne, on his travels. From a 12th-century manuscript.**

Below: **A page from the 7th-century Lindisfarne Gospels. Northumbria was the cultural heartland of early Anglo-Saxon England.**

Middle English, the language of Chaucer, is easier than Old English for the modern reader. The transition took place gradually, but is conveniently dated from the Norman Conquest (1066). Thereafter the ruling class spoke French and, inevitably, English absorbed many French words. A more fundamental change was the loss of most of the inflections that, in Old English, indicated the function of a word within a sentence. Thus, in Old English it was possible to have a sentence in which, for example, the object preceded the verb, as in *Urne dæghwamlican hlaf sele us todæ*, or 'Give us today our daily bread'. The suffix -ne (in *urne*) indicates the object of the verb *sele* ('give'). In Middle (or modern) English, it was necessary for the verb to precede the object.

MYTH AND MYSTERY

LEGENDARY HEROES

While the aristocracy spoke and wrote in French, the monkish chroniclers, such as William of Malmesbury and Geoffrey of Monmouth, wrote in Latin, the language of the Church. Geoffrey's *History of the Kings of Britain* (*c*.1148) helped to popularize the legends of King Arthur, and the first English version of Arthurian legend appeared near the end of the 12th century in a poetic history, the *Brut*, by Layamon, a Worcestershire cleric. It also contained the first English accounts of Lear and Cymbeline.

Arthurian legend, the standard medieval version of which was Sir Thomas Malory's *Le Morte d'Arthur* (1470), was not confined to England, and the story was developed by Chrétien de Troyes (late 12th century) and other French writers. Epic was characteristic of other European peoples. In France, the *Chansons de Geste*, dating from the 12th century, recounted heroic episodes in the time of Charlemagne. They were similarly infused with a spirit of patriotism and Christian idealism, dealing in particular with the contest with Islam.

THE SAGAS

The great Icelandic Sagas, mostly written down in the 13th century, also recorded the heroic pioneers of earlier times, such as Erik the Red who colonized Greenland in about A.D. 1000. They are prose narratives, however, in general less high-flown than French epic and more reliable historically. *The Volsunga Saga*, a retelling of the earlier, poetic *Edda*, the chief source for Norse mythology, provided the material for Wagner's operatic *Ring cycle* (1848–74).

Above: Medieval legend had a powerful appeal for Victorian writers and artists such as G. F. Watts, whose Sir Galahad captures the romantic mood.

Opposite: The deeds of the Vikings were commemorated in the Icelandic sagas, written down several centuries later.

MYSTERY PLAYS

Most medieval writing was religious, and miracle plays, as they were called, were dramatizations of miraculous episodes from the lives of the Christian saints. Later they included stories from the Bible (first translated in full into English in the 14th century) and were called mystery plays ('mystery' referred to a craft or trade). They were commonly performed in the market-place by local craftsmen, often with much humour, sometimes macabre, and (as in modern pantomime) with contemporary allusions. Each craftsmen's guild had responsibility for a particular piece, frequently linked with the craft concerned. In York, for example, the Shipwrights performed the story of Noah's Ark.

A later development was the 'morality play', in which the characters are personified virtues and vices (Beauty, Truth, Greed, etc.). The 15th-century *Everyman*, originally Dutch, is the best known. Mystery plays were first recorded in the 13th century; possibly they began as religious pageants associated with the feast day of Corpus Christi. ('Pageant' originally meant the stage on wheels on which the plays were performed.)

Complete cycles of mystery plays have survived from Chester, Wakefield and York, but many other towns had them. Some show considerable literary merit. They were popular in most of Europe, but in England they were finished off by a combination of the Reformation (opposed to religious pageantry), realist drama and professional theatre. They have been revived in the 20th century and *The Passion Play of Oberammergau*, Bavaria, dating from 1633, is still produced.

POETRY

The two poetic gems of medieval England, Chaucer apart, are *The Vision of Piers Plowman* and *Sir Gawain and the Green Knight*. Although William Langland, author of *Piers Plowman*, and the unknown author of *Sir Gawain* were contemporaries of Chaucer, they seem to have belonged to an earlier age, partly because they used the old technique of alliteration rather than the syllabic rhyming verse

introduced from France. *Piers Plowman*, often described as the greatest religious poem in English, opens with the narrator falling asleep on the Malvern Hills and dreaming that he sees 'a fair field full of folk', where he can observe the whole of society engaged in their tasks. The poem contains episodes of great imaginative power, unequalled by any other medieval writer.

The subject of *Sir Gawain* is an episode in Arthurian legend, in which Sir Gawain overcomes a supernatural opponent, the fearful Green Knight. Though an impeccable epic hero, Sir Gawain remains human and fallible, and the poem, about 2,500 lines long, is written in gorgeous and complex language. It survives in only a single manuscript, which also contains three other alliterative poems of high quality, 'The Pearl', 'Patience' and 'Purity' which, though of a completely different type, are probably by the same poet.

'After sharpe shoures,' quod Pees • 'moste shene [bright] is the sonne; Is no weder warmer • than after watery cloudes. Ne [nor] no love levere [dearer] • ne lever frendes, Than after werre [war] and wo • whan Love and Pees be maistres. Was nevere werre in this world • ne wykkednesse so kene, That ne Love, and [if] hym luste • to laughynge ne broughte, And Pees thorw pacience • alle perilles stopped.' 'Truce,' quod Treuth • thow telles us soth, bi Iesus! Clippe [embrace] we in covenaunt • and each of us cusse other!' 'And lete no peple,' quod Pees • perceyve that we chydde! For inpossible is no thyng • to him that is almyghty.'
Piers Plowman, (B-text) 17, (ed. Alastair Fowler).

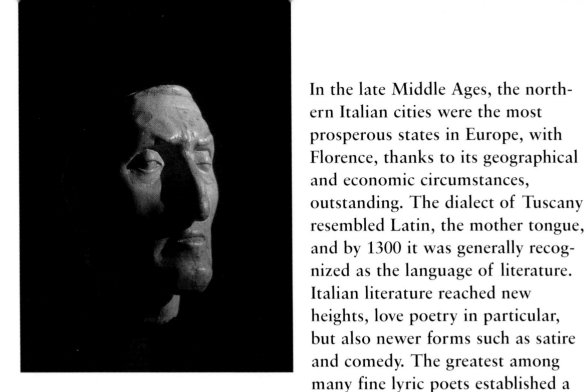

In the late Middle Ages, the northern Italian cities were the most prosperous states in Europe, with Florence, thanks to its geographical and economic circumstances, outstanding. The dialect of Tuscany resembled Latin, the mother tongue, and by 1300 it was generally recognized as the language of literature. Italian literature reached new heights, love poetry in particular, but also newer forms such as satire and comedy. The greatest among many fine lyric poets established a unique position in the Western literary tradition.

MEDIEVAL FLORENCE

DANTE

Dante Alighieri (1265–1321) was a prominent citizen of Florence, closely involved in the fractious politics of the time, but his personal circumstances were far more important than his public career. In his twenties he fell in love with the young woman whom in his poetry he calls Beatrice. When she died young, in 1290, Dante was inconsolable. She was the subject of most of the poems in his *Vita nuova*, probably written in the years immediately following her death, and she plays a prominent part in his later, most famous work, *Divina Commedia* (the *Divine Comedy*).

The *Divine Comedy* has been described as a summary of the civilization of the Middle Ages and heralded the Renaissance. The work, a magnificent structure in 100 cantos, is divided into three sections, 'Hell', 'Purgatory' and 'Paradise', around which the poet takes a guided tour, firstly with Virgil around Hell and Purgatory. In Paradise, a world of joy and beauty, his guide is Beatrice. The poem is based on Dante's considerable knowledge of philosophy and other learned subjects and is undeniably a challenge to the modern reader. However, no one could fail to find certain passages extremely moving, others charming and delightful, yet others horrifying.

It seems to have been written mainly in the last decade of Dante's life. A political revolution in Florence in 1300 had barred him permanently from his native city, and he spent his later years wandering, finally settling at Ravenna, where he completed the *Divine Comedy* just before his death. He was mentioned by Chaucer and was widely admired in 17th-century England. Out of fashion in the 18th century, he was enthusiastically

Above: **Dante's death mask. The** *Divine Comedy* **has figured so large in English literary history that a hefty two-volume work has been written simply on its numerous English translators.**

Opposite, inset: **An early printing shop.**

revived by the Romantics. In the 20th century his greatest advocate was T. S. Eliot.

PETRARCH

Petrarch (Francesco Petrarca, 1304–74) represented a milestone – his devotion to the Classics and his criticism of Aristotle suggest a Renaissance man, and he is regarded as the founder of Italian humanism. Although Petrarch considered them relatively unimportant, he is remembered especially for his lyrics, known as 'rime sparse', including the long series about Laura, Petrarch's Beatrice, whose identity is similarly obscure. He met her in 1327 in Provence, his home as a young man. Though his family had been exiled from Florence, Petrarch was often in Italy, and in 1341 was crowned Poet Laureate in Rome. He remained a great traveller, employed on diplomatic missions by various Italian courts, and was known and admired throughout Europe. He was the favourite Italian poet of the English Renaissance and his love sonnets had immense influence on 16th-century English poets from Wyatt to Sidney.

BOCCACCIO

Giovanni Boccaccio (1313–75), a close contemporary and friend of Petrarch, shared his admiration for Classical civilization, his love of the new Italian poetry and his wide-ranging interests. He was a great enthusiast for Dante, writing his biography and giving public lectures on the *Divine Comedy*. As a lyric poet, he was in neither Dante's nor Petrarch's class, his strong suit being narrative; like Petrarch, he became famous chiefly for what he would have considered a lesser work, *The Decameron*.

It is a collection of a hundred stories told by a party of young men and women sheltering in a house outside Florence to avoid the Black Death – the plague that carried off perhaps one-third of the population of Europe in the late 1340s. Most of the stories were written, or compiled, very soon after the epidemic. They were drawn from many sources and, provided rich material for other writers, notably Chaucer in *The Canterbury Tales* – although it is possible that Chaucer obtained them indirectly since he never mentions Boccaccio by name. (As there was no law, or even conception, of copyright, writers felt no need to disguise their sources.)

PRINTING

TODAY WE ARE LIVING THROUGH A REVOLUTION IN COMMUNICATION. IT REMAINS TO BE SEEN WHETHER IT WILL PROVE AS SIGNIFICANT AS AN EARLIER REVOLUTION – THE INVENTION OF PRINTING WITH MOVABLE METAL TYPE. THE EXPERIMENTS OF JOHANN GUTENBERG OF MAINZ CULMINATED IN THE FIRST BOOK PRINTED IN THIS WAY IN 1453, AND PRINTING PRESSES SPREAD RAPIDLY. BY THE END OF THE CENTURY MOST TOWNS AND UNIVERSITIES OF WESTERN EUROPE HAD ONE. PREVIOUSLY, ALL BOOKS WERE MANUSCRIPTS, INDIVIDUALLY COPIED. NOW THEY WERE ISSUED IN EDITIONS OF UP TO 1,000. BOOKS, WHICH HAD BEEN EXPENSIVE, DIFFICULT TO OBTAIN, AND OFTEN ERROR-STREWN, WERE NOW SWIFTLY AND COMPARATIVELY CHEAPLY AVAILABLE. NEW IDEAS TRAVELLED FASTER. A SCHOLAR IN LONDON KNEW WHAT HIS COLLEAGUES WERE WRITING IN PARIS OR ROME WITHIN WEEKS. WITHOUT GUTENBERG'S INNOVATION, THE GREAT CULTURAL HARVEST OF THE RENAISSANCE IS HARDLY CONCEIVABLE.

The learned John Gower (*d.*1408) was a contemporary and friend of Chaucer who wrote in three languages, French, Latin and English. He was responsible for bringing much classical literature (especially Ovid) and medieval romance into the mainstream of English literature. His greatest work is *Confessio Amantis*, which contains a series of stories in verse, rather like *The Canterbury Tales*. In fact several of Gower's stories are echoed in Chaucer's great work.

THE CANTERBURY TALES

In *The Canterbury Tales*, the framework for the stories is a group of pilgrims who meet at an inn in Southwark on their way to the tomb

THE AGE OF CHAUCER

Geoffrey Chaucer (*d.*1400) is one of the handful of great figures like Shakespeare or Samuel Johnson whose name alone sums up a literary age. He was a member of the minor gentry, who fought in Edward III's army as a young man, was captured in France and ransomed. He enjoyed the patronage of John of Gaunt, to whom he was related by marriage, he held several minor offices at court, and he undertook diplomatic missions abroad. One of these took him to Florence in 1373 and he could, conceivably, have met Boccaccio and Petrarch. His early writings show French and Italian influence, and culminate in *Troilus and Criseyde,* his most important work before *The Canterbury Tales,* which was written in 'rhyme royal' (seven-line units rhyming ababbcc).

of Thomas Becket in Canterbury and, for the prize of a free supper, agree to tell stories to pass the time. Some of the stories are fables, some are moral, some romantic, and some comical and coarse (schoolteachers used to avoid 'The Miller's Tale'). Several are based on Petrarch and Boccaccio. There are about 30 pilgrims but only 24 stories: the work was unfinished, but it runs to about 17,000 lines, most in rhymed couplets, some in prose. Although he could write lovely lines, Chaucer was not a great lyric poet. He was a great story-teller, a master of comedy, the first illustrious name in the great tradition of English comedy – and he had an understanding of human nature that rivaled Shakespeare.

The form of *The Canterbury Tales* is a familiar one. What is new is the intense realism of the characters. Chaucer not only had a profound and sympathetic understanding of human nature, he also seems to have had comprehensive knowledge of all levels of English society. His characters are the first in English literature who leap off the page, alive and kicking and totally believable, their virtues and still more their vices are all too easily linked with contemporary equivalents.

AFTER CHAUCER

Chaucer was widely admired in his own time. Thomas Hoccleve, a younger contemporary who is sometimes unjustly dismissed as a mere imitator of Chaucer (and there were many of those), called him his 'master dear, flower of eloquence'. The manuscript of Hoccleve's *De Regimine Principum* (*The Regiment of Princes*) has a portrait of Chaucer in the margin. The poet appears as an elderly, white-haired man: this is clearly intended to be a likeness, another example of the dawn of realism.

The flowering of English literature about the time of Richard II (1377–99) was followed by a comparatively barren period. In Scotland, however, the flowering came later, during the reigns of the cultured Stewart monarchs James III and James IV. The outstanding poets were Robert Henryson (*d.?*1506), William Dunbar (*d.?*1513) and Gavin Douglas (*d.*1522), who translated the *Aeneid* and was one of the first to emphasize the distinction between 'Scottis' and 'Inglis'. Henryson's *Testament of Cresseid* follows on from Chaucer's poem about the same lady. Chaucer is not always an easy read, even with modernized spelling, but the dialect of Henryson's poem, although written roughly a century later, is harder, which, together with his powerful, though humane, morality, may explain why it is not better known. Dunbar, a sharp satirist with a ribald sense of humour, is for most moderns a more attractive figure, although he is best known for a decidedly doleful work, his elegy on the transitory nature of life, 'Lament for the Makaris', with its haunting Latin refrain, *Timor mortis conturbat me* ('The fear of death convulses me'). Circumstantial evidence suggests that death came to Dunbar on the terrible battle-field of Flodden.

An equally well-known and evocative verse refrain is *Mais où sont les neiges d'antan?* (But where are the snows of yesteryear?). It comes from a poem *Ballade des dames du temps jadis* ('Ballad of the women of olden times') by François Villon, who lived in the mid-15th century and seems to have spent most of his life dodging the gallows. He was little known outside his own country until the 19th century, but is now widely regarded as the greatest poet of medieval France.

'Ful weel she soong the service dyvyne,
Entuned in hir nose ful semely,
And Frenssh she spak full faire and fetisly,
After the scole of Stratford attee Bowe,
For Frenssh of Parys was to hire unknowe.'
Chaucer, *The Canterbury Tales*, 'Prologue', l.122.

Left: **Several portraits of Chaucer appeared in manuscripts after his death. This one was commissioned by his friend Thomas Hoccleve.**

S. PAULES CHURCH

THAMESIS

The Eell Schipes

Three Cranes

The Gally fuste

The Bear Gardne

The Globe

The Stilliarde

Cheapse Crosse

THE RENAISSANCE
AND EARLY MODERN PERIOD

History gets more eventful, and change happens faster and more dramatically, the nearer you approach the present – or so it seems to us, at the leading edge. In the Middle Ages, change was so slow that people were hardly aware of it, there was a sharp quickening in the Renaissance and a tremendous spurt with the Industrial Revolution, since when the pace has become ever more frantic. Whatever the truth, this does not hold for literature.

It could be argued that, for European literature, the two centuries preceding the Industrial Revolution were more eventful than the two centuries following, though the reasons were not all literary. In the Renaissance, there was a hugely important development – the invention of printing with movable type, which made books as we know them possible. The establishment of nation states, especially in England and France, coincided with the establishment of the vernacular, a national language, which proved especially productive in England and France before the bones, so to speak, had set hard. By the 18th century, every form of literature was established in, or near to, its modern form, including the all-important genre of the novel, the one form of literature of which practically everyone today has some experience.

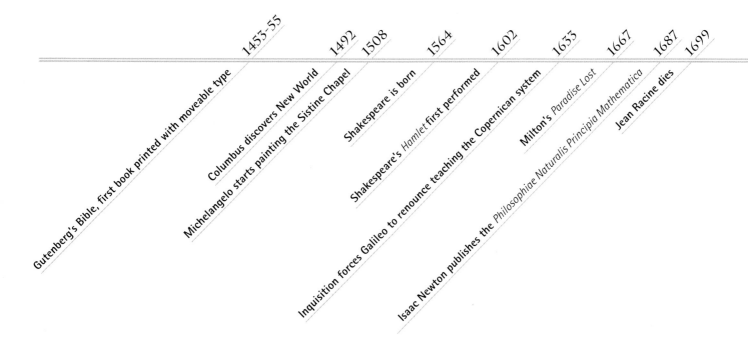

1453-55 Gutenberg's Bible, first book printed with moveable type

1492 Columbus discovers New World

1508 Michelangelo starts painting the Sistine Chapel

1564 Shakespeare is born

1602 Shakespeare's *Hamlet* first performed

1633 Inquisition forces Galileo to renounce teaching the Copernican system

1667 Milton's *Paradise Lost*

1687 Isaac Newton publishes the *Philosophiae Naturalis Principia Mathematica*

1699 Jean Racine dies

The Renaissance is the name given to the flowering of the arts, literature and politics that marked the transition from the European Middle Ages to the Modern Era. It began in the 14th century in Italy, where it reached its height in the early 16th century, and spread throughout Europe. The impulse for the Renaissance was the revival of interest in Classical (Greek and Roman) culture, and its predominant characteristic was humanism – an interest in human beings and in the potential of human nature, apart from religious values. Humanism was not anti-religion; on the contrary, the 16th century was an intensely religious age, but it did imply a reduction in the overwhelming authority that the Church had exercised in the Middle Ages. There was a new spirit of freedom, summed up by the young humanist philosopher Pico della Mirandola (1463–94): 'Constrained by no limits [Man] shall ordain for himself the limits of his nature'.

THE RENAISSANCE

ITALY

To us, the most remarkable characteristic of the great figures of the Renaissance was their versatility. Leo Battista Alberti (1404–72), best known as an architect, was also a painter, a poet, a philosopher, a musician and, by all accounts, a remarkable athlete. In literature, however, the writers of the High Renaissance never quite measured up to their great predecessors, Dante, Petrarch and Boccaccio. There was Ariosto's romantic epic *Orlando Furioso*, Castiglione's humanist dialogues in *The Courtier*, and Aretino's witty and scandalous satires. The most famous literary figure of Renaissance Florence is Nicolo Machiavelli (1469–1527). He is best known as a political philosopher, author of *The Prince*, a candid guide to statesmanship which admitted the necessity of using unpleasant means to gain desirable ends. It shocked Elizabethan England, where the adjective 'machiavellian' came to mean downright villainous. Machiavelli wrote many other works, including an excellent comedy, *La Mandragola*.

FRANCE

In the early 16th century, French was becoming established as a literary language. Poetry,

Above: Erasmus's less formal writings provided vivid descriptions of contemporary life that were exploited by novelists like Walter Scott.

Above right: Machiavelli brought realism into politics. As Francis Bacon said, 'We are much beholden to Machiavel and others, that write what men do, and not what they ought to do'.

especially lyric poetry, flourished; no more productive period for French poetry (excluding drama) would occur until the 19th century. However, the two greatest French writers of the century, especially in terms of their influence on literature in general, both wrote prose, though of totally different kinds. Rabelais (*d*.?1533) is now not often read, partly because of the difficulty of translating this exuberant genius. He was at one time a monk, then a wandering scholar, then a physician, who wrote learned works on medicine in Latin. But he is remembered for his humorous, ribald, life-affirming tales of the popular giants Gargantua and Pantagruel, a vast, bubbling collection of stories and learning, condemned by some as obscene. Like Machiavelli, he bequeathed us the adjectives 'rabelaisian', and 'gargantuan'.

The difference between Rabelais and Montaigne (1533–92) has been likened to the

'There is scarcely any less bother in the running of a family than in that of an entire state. And domestic business is no less importunate for being less important.'
Montaigne, *Essais*(1958 ed.), ch. 39.

difference between a pub at closing time and a quiet public library in mid-afternoon. A scholarly country gentleman, Montaigne is regarded as the inventor of the essay. His first volume of essays was published in 1580 and reissued several times with extensive additions. They reflect the author's changing philosophy and were increasingly based on his searching analysis of himself. Amused, tolerant, sceptical, Montaigne was the first great master of French prose, a model to later generations and a pervasive influence on other writers, including Shakespeare: one of his essays was a source for *The Tempest*.

ENGLAND

Little memorable poetry was written in England in the century after Chaucer's death, perhaps because everyone was trying to imitate Chaucer. As in so many other respects, English poetry of the early 16th century took its example from Italy. Thomas Wyatt, who visited Italy in 1527, wrote the first English sonnets as well as translating Petrarch, from whom he learned the art.

Henry Howard, Earl of Surrey, also wrote sonnets after Petrarch, but he adopted a different rhyming system, which became standard for Shakespeare and other English sonneteers. He was also the first to use blank verse – in his translation of the *Aeneid*. He was executed on an improbable charge of treason in 1547.

The same lamentable fate befell the admirable Sir Thomas More in 1535 when, as Lord Chancellor, he could not bring himself to accept Henry VIII's reformation of the English Church. Literature was More's great recreation, and he wrote (in Latin) *Utopia*, an early attempt to describe an ideal civilization, while he was on diplomatic business abroad. Prominent literary figures were often to be found at his house, and some were painted there by Holbein, who was introduced by another visitor, the Dutch-born Erasmus (*d*.1536), the greatest humanist scholar of the age whose output was prodigious. It was More who suggested the ideas behind Erasmus's most famous work, *The Praise of Folly*, a satire aimed chiefly at the leaders of the Church. His scholarly work on Classical and early Christian writers, and his translations of the Bible, had an immeasurable effect on contemporary European culture and encouraged the Reformation, though Erasmus himself remained loyal to, though critical of, the Roman Catholic Church.

Difpofed into twelue books.
Fafhioning
XII. Morall vertues.

LONDON
Printed for William Ponfonbie.
1590.

ELIZABETHAN ENGLAND

The Renaissance in England reached its peak late in the reign of Elizabeth I (1558–1603) which, in spite of the work of revisionist historians, still seems a golden age. Almost all forms of literature flourished. Poetry in the tradition established by Wyatt and Surrey was carried on by the prolific Michael Drayton. Some of the finest lyric poets were courtiers, like Sir Philip Sidney, hugely admired by contemporaries for his personal qualities as well as his poetry, and Sir Walter Raleigh, who also wrote a history of the world while imprisoned in the Tower of London. Drama rose in little more than one generation from modest beginnings to the supreme achievement of Shakespeare.

SPENSER

Edmund Spenser (*d*.1599) is the herald of the Elizabethan Renaissance, a poet who first attracted attention as a student with his Petrarchian sonnets. He joined a noble household and became friendly with Sidney, to whom he dedicated his long pastoral poem, *The Shepheard's Calendar*, in 1579. Soon afterwards he started to write *The Faerie Queen*, of which he completed only six of the planned twelve books. Its complex allegories make it difficult for the modern reader, and its greatest virtue is atmosphere: beautiful, musical language, a suggestion of magic in the air. It was written in a new metre, the 'Spenserian stanza', nine lines to a verse rhyming abab-bcbcc, the last line having six, rather than five, iambic feet. It was to be often copied. Spenser is a poet's poet, generally admired by his successors and an inspiration to Milton, Keats and others.

ELIZABETHAN PROSE

The sudden literary creativeness of the late Elizabethan period can be partly ascribed to the development of the language, which in the early 16th century was still relatively inflexible and dominated by foreign forms. The new confidence, spurred by national pride and increasing wealth, was no less evident in prose than in poetic drama. Sir Thomas North's fine translation of Plutarch's *Lives of the Noble Grecians and Romans* proved a treasure trove for Shakespeare, while Richard Hakluyt wrote an invaluable history of the Renaissance voyages of exploration. *The Chronicles* (1577) of Holinshed (and others), the first full account of English history in English, provided the raw material for the history plays of Shakespeare and others. Bishop Richard Hooker defended the Church of England in classic English prose, and the philosopher Francis Bacon, who rose to be Lord Chancellor and Viscount St Albans, explored almost every area of human knowledge in his Essays and other works. He was regarded by 17th-century thinkers as the father of modern science and by some 19th-century critics as the real author of Shakespeare's plays, a notion still not entirely dead.

There was prose fiction – hardly novels – at first influenced by the tales of Boccaccio (Rabelais was as yet untranslated and known to only a few). John Lyly's *Euphues* was written in the elaborate style called (after his book) 'euphuistic', in which verbal dexterity takes precedence over sense. The style was fashionable for a while, and was affected in conversation by ladies of the court, where Lyly, who was also a talented playwright, was an influential figure, but it is often excruciating to read. Robert Greene wrote a sequel to *Euphues*, among his many disparate publications. One of his stories gave Shakespeare, whom he famously attacked as an 'upstart Crow, beautified with our feathers', the plot for *The Winter's Tale*.

THE THEATRE

By the accession of Elizabeth, medieval religious drama was in decline, but for some time European kings and great nobles had supported their own companies of actors. The earliest surviving plays were also probably performed privately. The first known English tragedy is *Gorboduc*, by Thomas Norton and Thomas Sackville, a dull and static drama in inferior blank verse. Early tragedies are in general unsatisfactory, though a step forward was taken with Thomas Kyd's lurid 'revenge' drama, *The Spanish Tragedy* (1592), which continued to hold the stage throughout Shakespeare's time. Among comedies, *Ralph Roister Doister* (c.1553) was written by Nicholas Udall, headmaster of Westminster School, and was probably designed for his boys. It is a rustic comedy in rough verse.

Similarly, Gammer Gurton's *Needle*, another knockabout comedy, was performed at Cambridge University in 1563. Companies of boy actors performed at the royal court. Boys playing women, as they still did in Shakespeare's time, were probably more believable than boys playing the great heroes of antiquity, in plays by Lyly and others. Companies of professional actors, organized on the lines of a craft guild and supported by an aristocratic patron, at first performed in inn yards. That was to influence the design of Elizabethan theatres, the first of which, called simply The Theatre, was built in 1576.

'There wont faire Venus often to enjoy
Her deare Adonis joyous company,
And reape sweet pleasure of the wanton boy;
There yet, some say, in secret he does ly,
Lapped in flowres and pretious spycery,
By her hid from the world, and from the skill
Of Stygian Gods, which doe her loue envy;
But she her selfe, when ever that she will,
Possesseth him, and of his sweetnesse takes her fill.'
Spenser, *The Faerie Queene*, bk. 3, canto vi, st. 46.

Opposite: **Title page of Spenser's** *Faerie Queen.* **The title signifies both 'glory' in the abstract and 'Gloriana', i.e. Elizabeth I. The general scheme was to tell the stories of twelve of the Queen's knights, each of whom, as the title page implies, represents a particular moral virtue.**

Right: **The long gallery, a feature of Elizabethan houses, was handy for plays or for quiet reading.**

The work of the poet and playwright William Shakespeare (1564–1616), comprising about 36 plays (one or two are disputed), 154 sonnets and two long narrative poems, is more admired than that of any other writer in the history of Western civilization. Shakespeare's outstanding gifts are his ability to create vivid characters in profound psychological depth and his extraordinary command of language, both in blank verse and prose. His imagination is immensely rich, and the subtlety of his characterization allows almost unlimited scope for interpretation by actors and directors. Shakespeare studies have formed a major part of the Western cultural tradition for nearly 400 years and every generation finds something new and stimulating in him. He is universal.

Above: There's no life portrait of Shakespeare but this painting resembles the engraving that formed the frontispiece of the *First Folio* (1623).

SHAKESPEARE

THE MAN

In spite of diligent research by scholars, Shakespeare the man is elusive. The known facts are few, encouraging endless speculation on the basis of his writings. His understanding of so wide a range of human experience inclines soldiers to think he must have been in the army, lawyers that he had studied law, doctors that he must have had some medical experience, etc.

He was born in Stratford-upon-Avon, son of a successful merchant who fell on hard times. The son later restored the family fortunes. He probably attended the local grammar school, and in 1582 he married Anne Hathaway, eight years his senior and pregnant with a daughter, Susanna. Twins, Hamnet and Judith, were born in 1585, but ultimately the marriage seems to have been unsatisfactory. He may have taught in a local school, but by 1592 he was associated, as writer and actor, with a company of actors in London. The company, in which he held shares, built its own theatre,

the Globe, in 1599. In 1596 Shakespeare's application for a grant of arms was accepted, making him officially a gentleman. He bought a large house, New Place, in Stratford, and gradually cut down his business in London. He was buried in Holy Trinity, Stratford, and his last descendant, a granddaughter, died in 1670.

Most of his poetry seems to have been written in 1593–94, when the London theatres were closed by plague. His plays, on the other hand, were written for performance, and he apparently took no interest in their printing. *Othello* was not printed until 1622 and some scripts were supplied from memory by the actors; moreover, no manuscript of Shakespeare's has survived. Problems concerning accuracy and dating have exercised scholars since the 18th century.

THE PLAYS

Shakespeare began writing plays in the late 1580s, among the first being the three parts of *Henry VI* and their sequel, *Richard III*, which shows a growing grasp of his powers. In the early 1590s came the first of his Roman tragedies, *Titus Andronicus*, often dismissed as melodrama, but recently rising in reputation, and the early comedies, including *The Taming of the Shrew* and *Love's Labour's Lost*, another play that has proved more interesting in recent years. *Richard II* (probably 1595), is an enthralling dry run for the great tragedies, but in the following years, apart from *Romeo and Juliet*, Shakespeare concentrated mainly on comedy, including *A Midsummer Night's Dream*, *The Merchant of Venice*, *The Merry Wives of Windsor*, *Much Ado About Nothing*,

As You Like It and (in about 1600) the enchanting *Twelfth Night*. The best of his English history plays, *Henry IV*, Parts I and II, featuring Sir John Falstaff, and *Henry V*, were written about 1596–99, *Julius Caesar* about 1599. The first and probably the most famous of the great tragedies, *Hamlet*, came soon afterwards, to be followed within the next five years by *Othello*, *King Lear* and *Macbeth*. These are generally regarded as Shakespeare's greatest plays, though not necessarily the most popular. Some of his finest verse is to be found in *Antony and Cleopatra*, and the last of the Roman plays, *Coriolanus* (c.1607), is by some ranked close to the great tragedies.

Although only 43, Shakespeare now entered his 'late' period. *Cymbeline*, the enigmatic *The Winter's Tale* and *The Tempest* are neither tragedy nor comedy, but a romantic mixture of the two. *The Tempest*, first performed in 1611, is traditionally regarded as his last complete play, but he appears to have co-operated with other playwrights on several subsequent productions.

Within a few years of Shakespeare's death, two of his colleagues began to collect his plays. The collection, generally known as the *First Folio*, was published in 1623. It is a mark of his contemporary distinction, for no similar enterprise was launched for any other playwright. The work may be regarded as one of the most important publications in literary history. Not only does it provide texts which were as accurate as they could be in the circumstances, but it contains 16 plays of which no copy has survived in any other form. It also contains a poetic tribute by Ben Jonson, who describes his late colleague as 'not of an age, but for all time'.

'Our revels now are ended. These our actors,
As I foretold you, were all spirits and
Are melted into air, into thin air:
And, like the baseless fabric of this vision,
The cloud-capp'd towers, the gorgeous palaces,
The solemn temples, the great globe itself,
Yea, all which it inherit, shall dissolve
And, like this insubstantial pageant faded,
Leave not a rack behind. We are such stuff
As dreams are made on, and our little life
Is rounded with a sleep.'
The Tempest, IV, i.

Although solitary literary geniuses are far from unknown, they are more often to be found in a place or period where literary talent is flourishing. Shakespeare was not the only good Elizabethan playwright. Whether these writers have been overrated because they are associated with Shakespeare, or underrated because he outshone them, is a moot point. The latter view seems closer to the truth. There was plenty of work for them in London, as the theatre was immensely popular. But it did have its opponents. Some elements of the Church, especially the Puritans, were against it on moral grounds. More important, the mayor and aldermen were hostile, and it was for that reason that theatres were built in Southwark, across London Bridge and out of the City's jurisdiction. Hundreds of people, locals and visitors, flocked across the river daily to the Elizabethan equivalent of the present West End, where they could choose between a play and less edifying entertainment such as bear baiting.

SHAKESPEARE'S CONTEMPORARIES

MARLOWE

Christopher Marlowe (1564–93) was slightly ahead of Shakespeare in writing splendid dramatic blank verse, as his first tragedy, *Tamburlaine the Great*, was probably written before 1587. It is an extremely violent and savage play, and the dialogue has sometimes been seen as overripe. Shakespeare, despite being an admirer of Marlowe, poked fun at the scene in which Tamburlaine goads the conquered kings who are forced to pull his carriage: 'Holla, ye pampered Jades of Asia:/What! Can ye draw but twenty miles a day!'.

Marlowe's later plays were better, especially *The Jew of Malta*, *Edward II*, which

Shakespeare might have been proud of, and his last, *Dr Faustus*. He also translated Ovid and wrote a good deal of poetry, including the well-known song, 'Come live with me and be my love'. Marlowe was highly thought of in his time – a fellow playwright, George Peele, called him 'the Muses' darling' – but his private life was turbulent, even sinister. He was thrown out of the Netherlands for forgery, was involved in a street fight in which a man was killed, and was finally himself murdered in a tavern brawl, apparently in a quarrel over the bill, though there is a suspicion of a connection with Marlowe's (probable) activities as a spy.

JONSON

Ben (short for Benjamin) Jonson (1572–1637) was also no stranger to violence. As a young man he was a highly regarded soldier and later narrowly escaped execution after killing a fellow actor in a duel; but he is a more attractive character than Christopher Marlowe and, after Shakespeare, probably the finest playwright of the age. His first notable play, in which Shakespeare acted, was *Every Man in his Humour*, produced in 1598. *Every Man out of his Humour* was one of the first productions at the Globe. He also wrote tragedies and masques – courtly entertainments with music and dance designed by Inigo Jones, a celebrated English architect and stage designer – but comedy was his forte. He believed in Aristotle's unities of place, time and action, and was more learned, in a formal sense, than Shakespeare, but lacked his gift for character. Full of self-confidence, even for an Elizabethan, he could be scathing about his contemporaries, but had no doubts of Shakespeare's genius.

He wrote at least twenty plays, the finest of them in the decade 1605–14. *Volpone* is a brilliant satire on greed set in Venice, in which the names of the characters reflect their natures: Volpone (fox), Mosca (fly), Corbaccio (crow), Corvino (raven), Voltore (vulture). *The Alchemist* mocks human gullibility and lets fly at types of whom Jonson disapproved, such as fanatical Puritans, as represented by Ananias and Tribulation Wholesome. *Bartholomew Fair* is a vigorous, pungent pageant of London life at the great annual fair held at Smithfield on St Bartholomew's Day.

COLLABORATORS

The London playwrights inhabited a small, incestuous world. Their plays contain many comments on each other, sometimes good-natured, sometimes not, and they frequently collaborated. A prime example is Thomas Dekker (*d.*1632), the majority of whose works are collaborations, though the best, the lively London comedy *A Shoemaker's Holiday*, is his own. Francis Beaumont (1584–1616) and John Fletcher (1579–1625) were a well-established

Above: Work in progress on the reconstructed Globe Theatre, London, in 1996. It is a replica – as close as contemporary knowledge permits – of the original Globe of 1599, in which Shakespeare had a share.

Opposite: Sir Lawrence Olivier as the King in his film of Shakespeare's Henry V (1944), made during the Blitz, which, besides being considered one of the finest British films of all time, was a tremendous wartime morale-booster.

and immensely popular partnership who wrote over a dozen plays together. *The Knight of the Burning Pestle*, a sort of English *Don Quixote*, and the tragi-comedy *Phylaster* are among their best, though the former is now thought to be exclusively Beaumont's work. Fletcher also collaborated with many others, including Shakespeare and Ben Jonson. George Chapman wrote a number of somewhat slapdash comedies, among other works, and sometimes collaborated with John Marston, whose finest play was *The Malcontent*, a tragicomedy set in Italy (Marston's mother was Italian). Thomas Middleton (1580–1627), remarkably versatile even by Elizabethan standards and a frequent partner of Dekker, is remembered especially for *The Changeling*, a tragedy written with another frequent collaborator, William Rowley (*d.*1626).

Literary periods do not necessarily coincide with political ones. The extraordinary flowering of Elizabethan drama did not coincide with the reign of Elizabeth: many of the plays of Shakespeare and his contemporaries were actually written in the reign of James I (1603–25). As with so many other periods of artistic innovation, the golden age of Elizabethan poetry and drama began uncertainly, as writers found their way gradually and experimentally to a new conception of literature; it flourished for a generation and, again gradually, having surmounted the creative peak declined into mannerism, even (some critics would say) into decadence.

In prose, the glories of Shakespearean English shone most brilliantly in the King James Version of the Bible, a project completed between 1603 and 1611 (faster than any such project would be today). Numerous attempts have been made to produce a more accurate version and one more appropriate to modern times. None has replaced what is called the Authorized Version in the affections of the English people.

THE 17TH CENTURY

JACOBEAN DRAMA

Jacobean drama was more exotic and more obsessive, less vigorous, less direct in its appeal, and less popular. Puritan influence was growing, and theatre depended more upon Court patronage. Nevertheless, it was far from worthless and encompassed at least one playwright of near genius, John Webster (d.?1632). A coachmaker by trade, he wrote many plays in collaboration with Dekker and others, and his reputation today rests almost entirely on two plays, *The White Devil* and *The Duchess of Malfi*, both written in about 1612. Critics have pointed out Webster's technical deficiencies, and others have objected to the gruesome and shocking events – the fifth act of *The Duchess of Malfi* is a kind of literary chamber of horrors – but Webster has passages of sublime poetry and can be seen as a powerful moralist. Shakespeare apart, these two plays have been revived in the 20th century more often than those of any other playwright of the period. (One advantage is that both have challenging female leading roles). Another notable Jacobean dramatist is Cyril Tourneur (d.1626), a proponent of the 'revenge' tragedy, a famous example of which is Shakespeare's *Hamlet*.

Above: Busola, one of the theatre's most interesting villains, disposes of honest Antonio in the Act V of Webster's *The Duchess of Malfi.*

Opposite: The savage violence of Jacobean drama was part of public life: the executioner's axe, block and mask at the Tower of London.

SPAIN

The period was also a fruitful one for drama in the golden age of Spain. As in England, all parts in Spanish plays in the 16th century were played by males, and actors were organized into companies run by a manager. Public theatres were owned by local authorities or religious organizations and were set up in large open yards between buildings. The actual theatres were similar to those in England, with a platform stage backed by a building on two storeys, the spectators on balconies in the houses surrounding the yard or benches in the 'pit'. In the 17th century, the patronage of the Court became increasingly important, and stage design fell increasingly under Italian influence.

The greatest Spanish playwright was Lope de Vega (1562–1635), 'the Spanish Shakespeare', a passionate man, author of many love poems (to a variety of lovers), and of a ferocious attack on the depredations of the English, in particular Sir Francis Drake (Lope took part in the Armada). He had an inexhaustible imagination and is said to have written nearly 1,500 plays. About 500 survive, in every possible style, sacred and secular, pastoral and heroic, romance, tragedy and low-life comedy. He is remembered above all for the Spanish *comedia*, criticized at the time for its rejection of Aristotelian principles but very popular with less learned audiences. His influence spread well beyond Spain.

Lope's follower and nearest rival was Calderón de la Barca (1600–81), a royal chaplain and author of over 100 plays, similarly diverse in type, though later in life Calderón concentrated on highly regarded religious allegories.

ITALY

In matters of style, Italy was still the European leader. During the Renaissance, earnest efforts were made to reproduce the theatres of Classical times, which eventually led to the adoption of the proscenium arch and the proliferation of scenery and 'special effects', features that were adopted throughout Europe in the course of the 17th century.

The first professional actors were those of the *commedia dell'arte*, popular comedies based on a traditional plot with the actors wearing masks and employing much improvisation, also deriving ultimately from Classical theatre. The traditional characters, Harlequin, Pulcinella, Pantaloon, etc., developed only gradually into fixed stereotypes. These companies seem to have included female performers from an early date. Because they travelled widely outside Italy, they influenced other countries and were probably responsible for the admission of women to the acting profession much earlier in France and Spain than in England, where the *commedia dell'arte* did not venture, (see also page 49).

'To every thing there is a season, and a time to every purpose under the heaven:
A time to be born, and a time to die; a time to plant, and a time to pluck up that which is planted;
A time to kill, and a time to heal; a time to break down, and a time to build up;
A time to weep, and a time to laugh; a time to mourn, and a time to dance . . .
A time to get, and a time to lose; a time to keep, and a time to cast away;
A time to rend, and a time to sew; a time to keep silence, and a time to speak;
A time to love, and a time to hate; a time of war, and a time of peace.'
Ecclesiastes 3 (*Authorized Version of the Bible*).

The metaphysical poets were a recognizable group, sharing common characteristics, but they were not a close-knit school and the term was not applied to them until later. Broadly, they can be seen as having reacted against the honeyed smoothness of Spencer and the earlier Elizabethans. They approached the world in a rational manner, while simultaneously exhibiting strong feelings; they employed striking, sometimes unlikely, images and sophisticated stylistic devices. Results are sometimes beautiful, sometimes rather odd.

THE METAPHYSICAL POETS

JOHN DONNE

The greatest of the metaphysical poets was Donne (?1572–1631), a Londoner by birth, son of a prosperous tradesman and grandson of the playwright John Heywood. Gifted and handsome, he was brought up a Roman Catholic and had a varied career as a soldier and an M.P. before ruining his prospects by marrying a minor in 1601. After some difficult years, both materially and mentally (severe depressions, religious doubts), he was ordained in the Church of England, a sound move professionally, although there is no doubt of his increasingly profound religious spirituality. An outstanding preacher, he became Dean of St Paul's in 1621.

Donne's poetry, mostly published after his death, strongly influenced Sir John Suckling (1609–41) and the lyric poets loosely grouped as the 'Cavalier poets'. Donne's work falls into two: the earlier secular poems, especially on the subject of love (he was one of the first and greatest erotic poets), and the later religious works. The former, especially *Songs and Sonnets*, are more popular and easier to follow. Donne knew his ground, none better, on love, but his religious poems reflected his own uncertainties. Donne's ingenious rhetorical devices, puns, paradoxes and intellectual tricks, can have a dizzying effect, though at other times they are exhilarating. He was a poet of flashes: he wrote a good deal of indifferent verse, and good and bad are often found in the same poem. But Donne is one of those writers a few of whose poems are familiar to almost everyone.

GEORGE HERBERT

There are parallels between Donne and Herbert (1593–1633), a gifted young man, ambitious for advancement at court and briefly an M.P. In about 1625, his life changed, perhaps initially due to changing political circumstances, but also to the powerful strivings of his

Above: **Donne, a portrait painted when he was in his mid-twenties.**

Opposite: **Statues rescued from Old St Paul's, that was destroyed in the Great Fire (1666). The tall figure is St Paul's most famous dean, John Donne. He is flanked by two ministers, Christopher Hatton (left) and Nicholas Bacon (right), father of Francis.**

'Come live with me and be my love,
And we will some new pleasures prove
Of golden sands, and crystal brooks,
With silken lines, and silver hooks.'
Donne, 'The Bait'.

and diplomat, who has been called the 'father' of English Deism as a result of the principles of natural religion he described in *De Veritate*.

ANDREW MARVELL

Overall, the work of Marvell (1621–78) is a good illustration of the variety of verse forms in the 17th century, but in his own time Marvell was known almost exclusively as a political and religious satirist. His pastoral poetry ('The Garden', 'The Nymph Complaining for the Death of Her Fawn'), for which he is chiefly remembered today, was little considered until the 19th century. Marvell's political sympathies lay with Parliament and Cromwell, but he survived the restoration of the monarchy (1660), retaining his seat as M.P. for his native Hull and becoming a ferocious critic of the government of Charles II. His closely observed lyric poetry is clearly influenced by Donne, though his style is smoother. The erotic 'To His Coy Mistress' is probably his most famous poem.

Of the lesser metaphysical poets, the best were Henry Vaughan (1621–95) and Thomas Traherne (1637–74). Vaughan is remembered chiefly for the contemplative verse, written in rural Wales, of *Silex Scintillans*. He was deeply influenced by Herbert, though more visionary in style. Traherne held a living in Herefordshire. He was hardly known until the present century, when his delight in the natural world, combined with his deep religious sensitivity, established him as one of the finest minor poets of his time.

Abraham Cowley (1618–67), a qualified physician and possibly a Royalist spy under the Commonwealth, is also usually classed as a metaphysical poet, though not all of his work is in that vein. His love poems in *The Mistress*, in the style of Donne, and odes following Pindar are scholarly and rather difficult. At one time he was honoured most for his essays, notably 'On Myself', in the manner of Montaigne.

soul against his diminishing ambition for worldly success. He spent the last three years of his life as rector of a Wiltshire parish, earning a remarkable reputation for his humble devotion to pastoral duties. Before his death he sent his poems to a friend, Nicholas Ferrar, suggesting he either burn them or publish them. Ferrar chose to publish.

Herbert's reputation rests on the collection *The Temple*, reflecting 'the many spiritual conflicts that have passed between God and my soul'. Their simple piety, enhanced by clear, forceful expression and arresting imagery, had a strong appeal to Puritans especially. He was out of favour in the worldly 18th century but revived by Coleridge and the Romantics.

Herbert's elder brother was Lord Herbert of Cherbury (1583–1648), poet, philosopher

MILTON

The career of John Milton (1608–74) falls into three periods. As a young man, financially independent, he was something of a dilettante, pursuing his own, extensive, studies (he failed to take his degree at Cambridge), visiting Italy, and writing some superb poems. The finest of them were 'L'Allegro' and 'Il Penseroso', the volume-length *Lycidas*, the masque *Comus*, and several sonnets. The second period began with the onset of the Civil Wars when he became a propagandist, attacking the established Church in a series of pamphlets. His unfortunate marriage prompted him to argue for easier divorce, his experience as a teacher led to *Of Education*, which recommends a decidedly rigorous regime, but his most notable work in prose was *Areopagitica* (1644), a sterling defence of the freedom of the press. Otherwise, his pamphleteering in favour of Parliament and Cromwell tended to be unattractively strident, though it earned him a job in government (Andrew Marvell was one of his assistants). By 1651 he was blind – his sonnet on this subject ('When I consider how my light is spent . . .') is one of his finest short poems – though he continued his indefatigable defence of Cromwell and the Commonwealth.

PARADISE LOST

After the Restoration (1660), Milton was blind, ageing and in disgrace. His greatest work now

VIEWS OF PARADISE

Milton is the greatest English poet after Shakespeare and similarly dominates his era, the mid-17th century. It was a turbulent period of strong passions and internecine violence, yet it encompassed some of the finest lyric poets: Richard Lovelace, author of the famous couplet 'I could not love thee, Dear, so much,/Loved I not honour more' (from 'To Lucasta'); Robert Herrick, considered by many contemporaries a finer poet than Milton himself; and Edmund Waller, a pioneer of the heroic couplet. The religious and political divisions of the time naturally coloured most contemporary literature, not least the work of Milton himself.

Above: Milton as a young man. In spite of his great stature, few poets have inspired more diverse judgments (he wrote English 'like a dead language' said T. S. Eliot). Blake, an admirer, made the perceptive comment on *Paradise Lost* that Milton was 'of the Devil's party without knowing it'.

Opposite: Gustave Doré's engraving (1866) of Satan's cohorts heading for 'bottomless perdition'.

began. *Paradise Lost* was the result of Milton's long-cherished ambition to write a great epic. The twelve books (originally ten) of blank verse were probably written in 1658–63 and published in 1667, Milton receiving an advance of £5. The aim of *Paradise Lost*, as the poet explains, is 'to justify the ways of God to men'. It opens with the expulsion of Satan from Heaven and ends with the Fall of Man and the promise of future redemption through Jesus. The hero is Adam, the 'villain' Satan, though as many readers have remarked, Satan is almost too interesting as a character. Immensely long, it is a work of continually sustained intellectual imagination backed by prodigious learning, of glorious, inimitable verse and an unrivalled ear for language. As a work of Christian art, it stands with Michelangelo's Sistine Chapel vault.

Paradise Regained (published 1671) is a kind of sequel, shorter (six books), the language rich, but less exalted. The theme is again temptation – of Jesus by Satan. *Samson Agonistes* is a tragedy on the Greek model relating the last days of Samson, 'eyeless in Gaza'. It was not meant to be performed, but sometimes has been, and it provided the subject of one of Handel's finest oratorios.

PROSE

John Bunyan (1628–88) was a Puritan of a different stamp: son of a tinker and largely self-educated, he fought for Parliament in the Civil War and became a Nonconformist preacher, as a result of which he spent several years in prison. His religious allegory *The Pilgrim's Progress*, the simple man's search for truth, has a universal appeal resulting from its folklore quality, and the names of places and people encountered by the pilgrim (Vanity Fair, Doubting Castle, Giant Despair) have entered the language.

Two interesting figures on the other side of the political/religious divide were Sir Thomas Browne (1605–82) and Izaak Walton (1593–1683). Browne was a Norwich physician, best known for a religious work *Religio Medici*, though his *Vulgar Errors*, an attempt to correct quaint misconceptions (e.g. that

elephants have no knees) is more amusing reading. So is his correspondence with other literary figures, such as the great 17th-century gossip and connoisseur of trivia, John Aubrey (author of *Brief Lives*). The avuncular Izaak Walton was a friend and biographer of Donne and also wrote the life of George Herbert, as well as assorted bishops, but he is best remembered for *The Compleat Angler*, first published in 1653 and never out of print since. Written in the form of a dialogue, it is a loving invocation of the English countryside (a marked feature of much contemporary poetry), as seen from the river bank, and subtly seems to equate angling with Anglicanism. It was not the first book about fishing, and on technique Walton was not an outstanding expert (later additions included a section on fly fishing, which Walton knew very little about, by Charles Cotton), but it has a uniquely sympathetic flavour.

'Him the Almighty Power
Hurled headlong flaming from th' ethereal sky
With hideous ruin and combustion down
To bottomless perdition, there to dwell
In adamantine chains and penal fire
Who durst defy th' Omnipotent to arms.'
Milton, *Paradise Lost*, bk. 1, l. 44.

In France as in England, the language was being refined during the 16th century, notably in the poetry of Ronsard, du Bellay and the other poets of the Pléiade, who laid the foundations of modern French poetry. In the 17th century, as France emerged as the greatest power in Europe under Louis XIV, French literature entered its golden age. With monarchy supreme and Catholic influence predominant, the trend was towards Classicism – the virtues of reason, order, proportion, harmony as laid down by Nicolas Boileau-Despréaux in his seminal *Art of Poetry* (1674) and upheld by the Académie Française, founded by Cardinal Richelieu in 1635.

CLASSICAL DRAMA

CORNEILLE

Pierre Corneille (1606–84) came from Rouen and was a member of the *parlement* of Rouen for over 20 years. During that time he also wrote the best of his 32 plays. He is regarded as the founder of French tragedy, but his early plays were mostly comedies, though not without serious content and personal conflict. His major plays, starting with *Le Cid* (1637), are concerned with the conflict between the claims of society – honour, patriotism, politics, religion, etc. – and personal inclinations, notably love. The playwright transmits a powerful moral vision; his heroes, choosing public duty above private satisfaction at great personal cost, nevertheless experience moral growth. Corneille's later plays, like his early comedies, have traditionally been regarded as inferior, though modern criticism puts a higher value on his work as a whole and has reinterpreted some of his plays in a new light.

While Corneille's status as a master of the grand Classical style is undisputed, it must be admitted that his plays have a certain monotony. They have not often been performed in languages other than French.

RACINE

Jean Racine (1639–99), Corneille's contemporary and rival, infused the high Classical style with more passion and has been generally more popular. He was influenced by the Greek concept of fate – his plays are often set in Classical times – which he connected with the belief in human helplessness he derived from the Jansenists, to whom his grandmother (he was an orphan) entrusted his education (Corneille was educated by the Jesuits). Unlike

Above: Racine broke off his dramatic work suddenly, permanently and without regret, after thirteen years of brilliant achievement. He became an adroit courtier and a good husband – to a woman who, according to her son, 'did not know what a verse was'.

Opposite: An example of the marvellously rich baroque stage settings by Mansard and other notable architects at Louis XIV's Versailles.

Corneille, Racine's heroes and heroines generally fall victim to their own uncontrollable passions: it was said that Racine portrayed people as they are, Corneille as they ought to be. He was already a well-known literary figure when his first play, *La Thébaïde*, was produced by his friend Molière. His greatest plays were written between 1667 (*Andromaque*) and 1677 (*Phèdre*, his masterpiece), when he overhauled Corneille in public esteem, at least among the younger generation. Nevertheless, in his later years Racine came under fierce attack from rival playwrights, which was in part the cause for his abandonment of the theatre after *Phèdre*, except for a couple of religious plays written for female students.

MOLIÈRE

Far more influential internationally, especially on Restoration comedy in England, much of

IN FRANCE

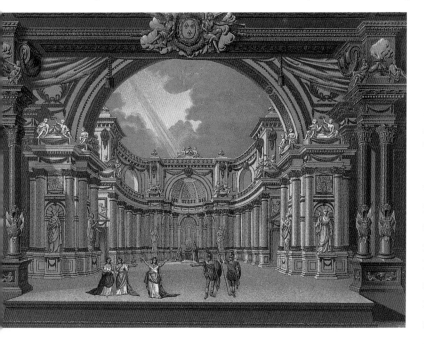

'M. Jourdain: "What? When I say, 'Nicole, bring me my slippers, and give me my night cap', is that prose?"
Master of Philosophy: "Yes, sir."
M. Jourdain: "Well I'm damned! I've been speaking prose for forty years without even knowing it.'"
Molière, *Le Bourgeois Gentilhomme*, II, iv.

which was a pastiche of his work, was the brilliant Jean-Baptiste Poquelin, who adopted the *nom de théâtre* Molière (1622–73). Actor, director and dramatist, he led a professional touring company for many years before attracting royal approval and a theatre in Paris. Soon hugely popular, not least with the King, he was also fiercely attacked by various vested interests.

In the 30 comedies that he wrote in Paris, Molière combined virtually all earlier comedic traditions from Plautus to the *commedia dell'arte*, and showed that comedy, without ceasing to be comic, could also deal with the oddities of human nature on a universal scale. His understanding of contemporary society, owing much to Montaigne (though Molière's outlook was more optimistic), and in particular his perception of human frailties, was Shakespearean in scope and depth, and his technical gifts – for the flavours of dialect and jargon for instance – were extraordinary. Plays such as *Le Tartuffe* (1664) and *Le Misanthrope* (1666) are ageless. Molière can still pack the house in the West End or even Broadway. Yet 17th-century France was no place for jokers, and Molière was a serious man, worried by his responsibilities and frail in health. Ill, he insisted on going to the theatre because so many people depended on him. He died on stage that same night, playing the leading role. The play was *Le Malade Imaginaire*.

Corneille and Racine established classical tragedy, Molière classical comedy, and the classical French novel, the novel of character, was also established by the end of the 17th century, in *La Princesse de Clèves* by the Comtesse de La Fayette (1634–93). Paris of the 17th century is deftly pictured in the letters of the Comtesse's friend, Mme de Sévigné (1626–96), and human nature and morality are crisply dissected in the *Maxims* ('Virtues are mainly vices in disguise') of another friend, the Duc de La Rochefoucauld (1613–80). The *Pensées* of Blaise Pascale (1623–62), also a remarkably creative scientist, were expressed in luminous prose and dealt with religious questions (among others) with a wit and intelligence far from common in that area during the 17th century.

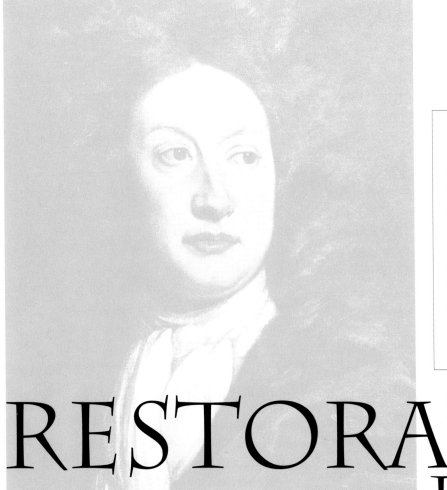

RESTORATION
DRAMA

The restoration of Charles II to the throne in 1660 was accomplished with remarkable political smoothness, but in cultural terms it introduced a strong reaction against the stern sobriety of the Puritan Commonwealth. The theatres reopened and – a sensation – with real actresses. There was initially a shortage of modern plays, but that was soon rectified. One has the impression that half the gentlemen at Court were excellent playwrights. This was an accomplished age: Milton, Locke, Newton and Purcell were all alive in 1660. It considered itself a sophisticated, witty and enlightened age, but it was also coarse and cynical, characteristics typified by the Royal Court. It was also, to the delight of posterity, well reported, in particular by England's greatest diarists, John Evelyn and the incomparable Samuel Pepys.

DRYDEN

The outstanding literary figure of the reign, created Poet Laureate in 1668, was John Dryden (1631–1700), an instinctive moderate in the vicious controversies of the time, a supporter of the Establishment, who eventually converted to Roman Catholicism. Dryden wrote prolifically in many genres: one criticism of him is that he wrote too much and was insufficiently self-critical, though he was a highly perceptive critic of others' work. To modern tastes, his satirical verse (*Absalom and Achitophel*, *MacFlecknoe*) is most entertaining, and his plays, mostly in heroic couplets, are seldom performed. The best is probably *All For Love* in blank verse, a rewrite of *Antony and Cleopatra* which, though Dryden did not think so, suffers from the comparison.

THE COMEDY OF MANNERS

Contemporary heroic drama, except for, perhaps, Dryden and Thomas Otway's *Venice Preserv'd* (1682) was second-rate (and amusingly mocked in the Duke of Buckingham's

The Rehearsal, 1672). The new comedy, owing much to Molière who was well-known in translation, was introduced by George Etherege (*She Would If She Could*, 1668; *The Man of Mode*, 1676) and William Wycherley (*The Country Wife*, 1675; *The Plain Dealer*, 1676). Like other leading exponents of the 'comedy of manners', such as Sir John Vanbrugh (the architect of Blenheim Palace) and George Farquhar, they were fashionable gentlemen writing for a fashionable audience. Plots, and often-confusing subplots, are broadly concerned with conflicts over sex and money, and the machinations of fashionable gentlemen to acquire a rich wife or conceal their adultery. Characters have names like Sir Fopling Flutter, Pinchwife and Loveless. The victor is usually the greatest wit, and the repartee is slick, steely, amoral and often obscene.

The ablest of these playwrights was also more or less the last, William Congreve (1670–1729), another well-heeled gentleman and lover of the Duchess of Marlborough. His plays are beautifully constructed and the dialogue is genuinely witty, as well as elegant. *The Double Dealer* (1693) and *Love for Love* (1695) are still revived, though less often than his undisputed masterpiece, *The Way of the World* (1700). By that time, Restoration comedy was under attack. In Colley Cibber's *Love's Last Shift* (1696), the rakish hero is reformed: the play indicates a reaction against moral decadence and points the way to the 'sentimental comedy' of the 18th century. When Jeremy Collier published his *Short View of the Immorality and Profaneness of the English Stage* in 1698, Congreve was stung. He published a refutation of Collier, and *The Way of the World* came down on the side of morality. However, it was not well received and Congreve never wrote another play.

SHERIDAN

The 'sentimental comedy' of the 18th century was hardly an improvement, and can now be seen as a kind of dress rehearsal for Victorian melodrama. Richard Brinsley Sheridan (1751–1816), born into a theatrical family in Dublin, restored the edge to English comedy by reviving the 'comedy of manners', which in his hands

achieved new heights. His first play was *The Rivals* (1775), set in the fashionable spa town of Bath. It was a shambles on the first night but, after hasty rewriting, became very popular. The character Mrs Malaprop has given a new word to the language, malapropism. As she says, 'Sir, if I reprehend (comprehend) anything in this world, it is the use of my oracular (vernacular) tongue, and a nice derangement (arrangement) of epitaphs (epithets)'. Even better is *The School for Scandal* (1777), the best play of the century, ingeniously plotted, extremely funny and frequently revived. Like *The Critic*, Sheridan's third great comedy, it was written for the Drury Lane Theatre in which he had an interest.

GOLDONI

Italian theatre in the 17th century was still dominated by the stock characters and improvisation of the *commedia dell'arte* tradition. It was rescued by Carlo Goldoni (1707–93) who, influenced by Molière, wrote comedies about the idiosyncrasies of ordinary people. The best-known internationally are *The Respectable Girl* (1749), *The Coffee Shop* (1750) and *The Mistress of the Inn* (1753), but Goldoni was highly productive. He wrote over 130 comedies in Italian (some, said to be his best, in his native Venetian dialect), and at least 100 others in French for the Italian theatre in Paris, where he died – in wretched poverty.

CHAPTER FOUR

THE RISE OF THE NOVEL

Everyone knows, more or less, what a novel is, but it is a term that is not easily defined. The *Oxford Dictionary* says: 'A fictitious prose narrative of considerable length, in which characters and actions representative of real life are portrayed in a plot of more or less complexity', and dates the use of the word in that sense to the mid-17th century. The Latin *novella* or *novellae* ('news') was in use 200 years earlier to describe short stories such as those of Boccaccio. The *Oxford Companion to English Literature* admits it cannot improve on the definition of Sir Walter Scott in 1824: 'a fictitous narrative . . . accommodated to the ordinary train of human events'. Any concise definition must fail to be all-inclusive, but it is agreed, first, that the developments culminating in the novel as we know it took place in the 18th century and, second, that its origins are vastly older, older indeed than written literature.

1615 The final part of Cervante's *Don Quixote* is published

1666 The Great Fire of London

1711 The *Spectator* is founded

1726 Jonathon Swift's *Gulliver's Travels*

1740 Samuel Richardson's *Pamela*

1749 Henry Fielding's *Tom Jones*

It is assumed that human beings have told each other stories of some kind for as long as they have had the language and the leisure to do so, but it is less certain when they began to invent fictitious tales primarily for entertainment. The oldest form of extended narrative was the epic, which was discussed as an art form by Aristotle. Usually in verse, it contained a coherent story or theme, though often with additional material, and was typically composed in a 'heroic' style, dealing with great events and extraordinary characters. Homer was the first great composer of epic (the *Iliad* and the *Odyssey*), and Milton (*Paradise Lost*) perhaps the last in the traditional sense, although the word has been applied to later works of especially ambitious scope.

THE RISE OF THE NOVEL

'Eumolpus, who was so lecherous that he even looked on me as a potential catamite, wasted no time inviting the girl to receive instruction in certain vital matters. But he had made it known that he was physically frail and rheumaticky in the joints, and he had to maintain this façade if disaster was to be averted. So, to keep faith with this falsehood, he managed to persuade the girl to set herself on top of him and ordered Corax to stretch himself under the bed so that, with his hands pressed against the floor, he could move Eumolpus up and down.'

Petronius, Satyricon.

Above: This portrait by Velasquez (1599–1660) is one his character studies, which is named, presumably by the painter, 'Aesopus'.

Opposite: Aesop's Fables are the oldest surviving examples of what Dr Johnson described as 'narratives in which beings irrational, and sometimes inanimate, are, for the purpose of moral instruction, feigned to act and speak with human interests and passions'.

FABLE

The subject matter of the epics of Homer and Virgil was mythology and legend, but there were other kinds of narrative. The fables of Aesop, which are anecdotes of human idiosyncrasies disguised as amusing animal tales, date from approximately the 6th century B.C., though written down much later. They are traditional folk tales, although the very existence of Aesop is doubtful; there is a legend that he was a Thracian who was for some time a slave on the island of Samos. Aesop's fables, and later ones such as 'Reynard the Fox', were widely used by Chaucer, Henryson and Jean de La Fontaine, the great 17th-century fabulist (see page 56). Fable is often closely allied with allegory. *The Insect Play* (1921) by the brothers Capek and Orwell's *Animal Farm* (1945) might be regarded as modern fables of this type.

CLASSICAL TALES

One of the earliest surviving – though in fragments only – fictional narratives in prose is *Milesiaka*, 'Milesian Tales', written in the late

2nd century B.C. by Aristides, consisting of stories, largely erotic, of life in his home town of Miletus. More like a novel in form is *The Golden Ass*, the best-known work of Apuleius, written in Latin in the 2nd century A.D. It is really a series of stories strung together by a tenuous narrative thread and can be regarded as an early precursor of the picaresque. The central story is 'Cupid and Psyche', a reworking of an old tale of Greek origin in which a mortal princess, Psyche, is loved by Cupid, the god of love, who remains invisible and forbids her to try to see him. She disobeys, and the angry Cupid deserts her. Several of Apuleius's stories were adopted by Boccaccio, and the Cupid and Psyche story has inspired numerous writers since the Renaissance. Another Classical work that can reasonably described as a prototype of the picaresque novel is Petronius's unbuttoned satire, *Satyricon*.

Greek romances typically involve two lovers who are separated and undergo various trials, during which chastity is nobly preserved, but they include more realistic, incidental stories depicting ordinary, earthy life, which form a contrast with the high romance of the main story. Heliodorus of Emesa, a Syrian, was the author of a characteristic tale of this kind, *Aethiopica*, in the 3rd century A.D., translated into French and English in the 16th century. *Daphnis and Chloe* is probably the best of the Greek romances that have survived. The author, Longus, is known only by name, but he probably lived around A.D. 300. A charming, pastoral, love story, it is also very explicit and for centuries was regarded as obscene. Today it is most familiar as the ballet (1912) for which Ravel wrote the music.

LEGEND AND ROMANCE

The early Middle Ages were entertained by the great legend cycles, no doubt originally based on fact, of King Arthur or of Charlemagne – the *chansons de geste*, of which the most famous is the story of Roland – and other courtly heroes. French medieval romances also included stories of Classical heroes such as Alexander the Great, and they were often translated into English (the English translator of part of the famous allegorical *Roman de la Rose* may have been Chaucer). From the 15th century, English romances were usually written in prose.

The name 'romance', originally referring to the 'Roman' language, has the same root as roman, while 'novellae', or novel, was a word sometimes applied to the short stories of, for example, Boccaccio's *Decameron* or Marguerite of Navarre's *Heptameron* in the 15th century.

THE TALE OF GENJI

Nearly one thousand years ago, Murasaki Shikbu, a high-born Japanese lady, wrote for the amusement of the Emperor and his Court in Kyoto. The tale relates the adventures of a younger son of some ancient emperor, his love affairs in particular, in a style that mingles oriental romanticism with down-to-earth candour. It is greatly admired, and has a certain penetrating simplicity that seems allied to traditional Japanese painting. Extremely long yet apparently unfinished, it had no influence on the development of the novel in Europe because it was not translated into English until the 1920s by the poet and Japanese scholar Arthur Waley.

The adjective picaresque comes from the Spanish *picaro*, a rogue, and is applied to a story in which the roguish hero undergoes a series of loosely-linked adventures, often encountered on a journey, as in the English novels of Fielding or Smollett. Usually cited as the first picaresque novel is the anonymous *Lazarillo de Tormes* (1533). Cervantes's famous story of Don Quixote and Sancho Panza is the greatest example of the genre, but it is much more than that, and is now often regarded as the first 'modern' novel. Moreover, many would argue it is the greatest novel ever written, which influenced not only the early English novelists but also writers of many cultures over the centuries.

PICARESQUE

CERVANTES

Miguel de Cervantes Saavedra (1547–1616) was a slightly younger contemporary – and rival – of Lope de Vega. He had an adventurous career as a soldier for Philip II of Spain and in 1571 fought in the great sea battle of Lepanto, where he lost the use of his left hand. He was captured by Barbary pirates in 1575 and spent nearly five years as a slave, making several unsuccessful attempts to escape before he was ransomed. Back in Spain, he became a lowly, underpaid official in the government while writing rather unsuccessful plays, a pastoral romance, and a lament in verse for the defeat of the Armada (1588). He was several times imprisoned for debt, and began writing *The History of the Valorous and Witty Knight Errant Don Quixote* while in prison. It was published in 1605 and was an immediate success not only in Spain but across Europe. Cashing in on the success, someone brought out a spurious sequel, provoking Cervantes into writing a second part himself. It appeared in 1615, not long before Cervantes died, which was apparently on the same day as Shakespeare (23 April 1616).

DON QUIXOTE

The hero of Cervantes's masterpiece, from whom we gain the word 'quixotic', is an elderly, stick-thin and destitute nobleman of La Mancha, labouring under delusions induced by reading too many chivalric romances. He embarks on a one-man knightly crusade through Andalucia, riding his emaciated 'charger', Rosinante, and accompanied by his weary, cynical but loyal 'squire', the tubby Sancho Panza, seeking adventures through which he may gain honour and fame. He treats everyone he meets as if they are characters from pastoral or chivalric romance, including Dulcinea, a humble peasant girl whom he sees as the exquisite high-born maiden that every chivalrous knight required to spur him on his quest. In perhaps the most famous episode, the gallant hero attacks windmills that he takes for giants (hence our phrase, 'tilting at windmills'); in another, he rides to assist a great Christian host fighting a Muslim army, heedless of Sancho Panza's advice that they are in fact a flock of sheep. His exploits generally end in bruises and embarrassment.

Don Quixote is one of the funniest books ever written, but as in all good humour there are deeper resonances. Cervantes himself declared that his purpose was to put an end to the popularity of Spanish chivalric romances. The book is certainly fine satire: the Don is the very antithesis of a knightly hero, being old, ugly and barmy. Yet he is also sympathetic. He represents romantic imagination and idealism as against the earthy realism of the picaresque Sancho Panza. By combining these two traditions, broadly 'medieval' and 'modern', Cervantes creates a rich tapestry, incorporating a picture of contemporary life and culture, with vivid, comic characters equalled on this scale perhaps only by Chaucer and Dickens.

SPAIN AND DON QUIXOTE

In the end Don Quixote, having been tricked by friends, returns sadly home, rid of his delusions, renouncing the knightly enterprise. The curtain is coming down, just as the curtain was coming down on the 'golden age' of Spain, an age built largely on illusions – such as the belief that importing American treasure by the ton would make the country rich. But while Spain, the greatest Christian power, entered its decline, Spanish literature, with Castilian now established as the language of Spanish culture, flourished. Besides the world-renowned figures of Cervantes and Lope de Vega, Mateo Alemán's *Guzmán de Alfarache*, an orthodox picaresque novel, was also read all over Europe. Francisco de Quevedo, best known as a satirist, wrote a picaresque novel, *The Rogue*, in 1626, and many playwrights found an audience, despite Lope de Vega's prodigious output. Still, the enduring image of the country is the dusty plain of La Mancha, heroically if unsteadily traversed by a lean and lengthy Don, 'the Knight of the Doleful Countenance', followed by a short round squire on his donkey, with windmills slowly turning in the background. The image has fascinated the world, and it is as Spanish as dry sherry.

Right: **An illustration for Sir John Mandeville's** *Travels,* **from 14th century France. Despite being largely derivative it is surprisingly accurate. Early travel books like this were influential on the Picaresque style of the adventurous journey.**

Above: **Cervantes, a later sketch.**

'Blessings on him who invented sleep, the mantle that covers all human thoughts, the food that satisfies hunger, the drink that slakes thirst, the fire that warms cold, the cold that moderates heat, and lastly, the common currency that buys all things, the balance and weight that equalizes the shepherd and the king, the simpleton and the sage.' Cervantes, Don Quixote, ch. 68.

The modern novel had its roots in the verse romance, or *fabliau*, though it is a long line of development with many sideshoots. Chaucer is a key figure in the change to more modern modes of narrative, with his unusual interest in character for its own sake and his realistic observation of contemporary social life; the first novels in this, modern, sense are the picaresque stories associated with Spain and above all with Cervantes. Thereafter, the most important developments are, arguably, to be found in France and England and, just as the English romance was largely derived from (and inferior to) the French *fabliaux*, early French narratives had a marked influence on the English novel of the 18th century.

FORERUNNERS

The revocation of the Edict of Nantes (removing toleration of the Huguenots) in 1685 is often taken as a convenient marker for the changing literary era in France. Cervantes and other satirists notwithstanding, Romance was not yet dead. Madeleine de Scudéry was still alive, and though her improbable tales of love and war set in antiquity had mostly been written in the 1650s, they remained popular. However, the romance was transformed by the Comtesse de La Fayette, in particular by her *La Princesse de Clèves* (1678), with its sympathetic study of character. (It was a good time for women in literature, though as writers they still used synonyms, and the wonderful *Letters of Mme de Sévigné* were not published until 1725, nearly thirty years after her death.) Another important influence was Jean de La Fontaine, whose verse Fables ('The Grasshopper and the Ant' etc.), drawn from a wide variety of sources, were published between 1668 and 1694. Paul Scarron, first husband of the future Mme de Maintenon – Louis XIV's mistress and (secret) wife – was the author of the two-part *Le Roman Comique*, the Comic Novel (1651 and 1657), the story of a theatrical company in Le Mans which gives a lively account of provincial life. However, as far as the novel is concerned, the 17th-century heritage is not especially impressive, yet by the end of the century the novel was set to become a major genre.

GIL BLAS

Alain-René Lesage (1668–1747) was a prolific author, said to have been the first French writer to live exclusively by the pen who, often with others, wrote about 100 popular comedies for the fairground stages of Paris. Many were based on Spanish originals. His *Le Diable*

DEVELOPMENT OF THE NOVEL
IN FRANCE

Boiteux (1707) is an imaginative, picaresque-satirical tale, but of interest chiefly as a rehearsal for his masterpiece, *The Adventures of Gil Blas Santillana*, which was published in instalments between 1715 and 1735. One of the most successful novels in French literary history, it was, along with Rabelais, probably the single greatest French influence on the English comic novels of Fielding and Smollett (who translated it into English). Again, the Spanish influence is strong; in fact Lesage was accused of plagiarism. The form is broadly picaresque – the adventures of Gil Blas as he travels across Spain, with extraneous tales inserted here and there, written in a lively, earthy style, with a sharp but relatively benign eye for human idiosyncrasies and presenting a detailed panorama of contemporary life and manners.

MANON LESCAUT

Manon Lescaut (1731) represents a big step forward. It was the last of a series of novels by the Abbé (Antoine François) Prévost (1697–1763), whose work as a translator of Richardson did much to popularize English literature in France. The *Histoire du Chevalier des Grieux et de Manon Lescaut*, its original title, tells of the love of the young aristocrat, des Grieux, torn disastrously between his conscience and his – stronger – passion for the beautiful but treacherous courtesan, Manon Lescaut. It was enormously successful, and later inspired operas by Massenet and Puccini.

Manon Lescaut appeared in the same year as the first part of *Marianne*, a novel by Pierre Marivaux, best known as a playwright, who gave the French language the term *marivaudage*, light-hearted banter.

THE EPISTOLARY NOVEL

An important minor form of the early novel, written in the form of letters or a diary, dates from the 17th century, an early example being the French *Letters from a Portuguese Nun*. The chief proponent of the form in England was Samuel Richardson, whose work, translated by the Abbé Prévost, was an influence on Jean Jacques Rousseau's *Julie, ou La Nouvelle Héloise* (1761), in which the love story is

Above: Le Boudoir by Jean-Baptiste Joseph (1695–1736).

Opposite: A 19th-century view of Lesage's protagonist, Gil Blas, who, with Don Quixote and Rabelais, was a major influence on the English comic novel in the 18th century.

mingled with a survey of contemporary ideas and customs. It was so popular when first published that libraries used to charge readers by the hour. The novel as memoir, which also originated in 17th-century France, took the form of autobiography, though in fact fictional. Early examples are on the whole less interesting than genuine memoirs of the time, of which there were many, the *Mémoires of the Duc de Saint-Simon*, which cover the last years of the court of Louis XIV, being the best-known.

DEFOE
AND HIS TIMES

One reason for the comparatively late development of the novel as a literary genre was that relatively few people could read. Literature was written for a comparatively small elite, and everyday stories of country folk were not in great demand. In 18th-century England, however, most males (fewer females) of the middle and upper classes, together with perhaps half the male working classes, could read. Production, as usual, expanded to satisfy the market.

In spite of promising beginnings in the Elizabethan era, realistic English narrative fiction made slow progress in the 17th century, partly no doubt because political turmoil turned writers in other directions. Bunyan emerged as the first proletarian writer, though his literary method was practically medieval, and it was not until the turn of the century that the real beginnings of the English novel appeared.

DEFOE

Daniel Defoe (1660–1731) was himself something of a *picaro*, who served spells in prison, even the pillory, and was not noted for his high principles either in life or literature. He was a prodigious writer, and a complete bibliography of his works poses a formidable challenge to the most assiduous researcher armed with the heftiest computer. He took to fiction late (though there is a fair amount of it in his historical works), adopting a true-life incident for *Robinson Crusoe* (1719), his story of the experiences of a shipwrecked sailor which was calculated to appeal to a public fascinated by travel stories. It displayed Defoe's talent for organizing an effective narrative and his eye for telling and convincing detail. It was an enormous success (it still is) and he followed it with five more novels, the most famous of which today is *Moll Flanders* (1722), a picaresque novel of a female rogue. Defoe has little time for form and structure – his novels simply go on until they stop and are liberally sprinkled with inconsistencies – but *Moll Flanders* in particular is a novel of character, not just another 'romance'.

GULLIVER'S TRAVELS

Jonathan Swift (1667–1745) was a gifted but complex person and a writer of incandescent talents, variously described as a poet, pamphleteer and satirist, who devoted much of his energy to propaganda for the Tory cause. From 1714 he was a virtual exile from the London literary scene as dean of St Patrick's in Dublin, his birthplace. His *The Conduct of the Allies* (1711), against the further prosecution of the War of the Spanish Succession, is often cited as the greatest work of its kind in English, but the book that established his immortality in literature is *Gulliver's Travels*, published anonymously in 1726.

Gulliver makes four voyages of which the first two, to Lilliput, where the people are very small, and to Brobdingnag, where they are very large, are the best known. They are usually published in abbreviated versions that make them more suitable for children. For some critics, the last section, in the country ruled by the

THE SPECTATOR

Swift was a friend of the essayists Joseph Addison (1672–1719) and Richard Steele (1672–1729), leading figures in the London literary scene who contributed to *Tatler* and founded *The Spectator* (1711). They had none of Swift's satirical violence, but wrote on a variety of subjects in beautifully simple and coherent prose, achieving a standard of journalism seldom equalled, let alone excelled, thereafter. The journal contained the work of a fictional group of gentlemen, the Spectator Club, representing various walks of life (the Army, trade, etc.), in particular a country gentleman, Sir Roger de Coverley. Its amusing character sketches contributed to the development of the English novel.

Left: Gulliver captures the enemy fleet on behalf of Lilliput. That everything is so small in scale shows the absurdity of the human quarrels.

Opposite: Frontispiece of Defoe's romance, *Robinson Crusoe*. The original 'Crusoe' was a Scottish pirate named Alexander Selkirk, not the 17th-century buccaneer that we see here.

rational Houyhnhms, who are horses, and their subjects, the bestial Yahoos (one of many Swiftian inventions that has entered the language), are more or less humans, is the best. When Gulliver finally returns home, he prefers to live in a stable, where the company is more congenial.

Gulliver's Travels is, in the first place, a good story, which can be simply read as that and little more. However, it is also a seering political satire, guying contemporary politics and politicians, and, most powerfully, it is a savage indictment of human intolerance, meanness and small-mindedness, as relevant today as it was in the 18th century. Swift was no novelist and *Gulliver's Travels* has little structural coherence or characterization. Nevertheless, it is one of the most popular, most often reprinted books ever written, and the main reason for its success is clearly its brilliantly imaginative narrative.

'I cannot but conclude the bulk of your natives to be the most pernicious race of little odious vermin that nature ever suffered to crawl upon the surface of the earth.'
(The King's response to Gulliver's proud account of the achievements of humanity.)
Swift, Gulliver's Travels, 'Voyage to Brobdingnag', ch. 6.

THE RISE OF THE NOVEL 59

THE NOVEL COMES OF AGE

Although Defoe had no obvious successor, Samuel Richardson's *Pamela* (1740), generally regarded as the first true English novel, was in some ways a reaction against the kind of risqué, incident-driven, narrative tradition that Defoe represented. Its heroine is a virtuous servant, who resists the advances of a young gentleman and gains the reward for her virtue in the form of marriage. A priggish tale perhaps, but Richardson knew the human heart, and had an instinctive understanding of the feelings of ordinary folk.

RICHARDSON AND FIELDING

Samuel Richardson (1689–1761), known as 'Serious' as a boy, was a printer by trade, who discovered an aptitude for writing model letters for the illiterate, and when he turned late in life to novel writing (*Pamela* was followed by *Clarissa*, 1747, perhaps his best, and *Sir Charles Grandison*, 1753), he adopted the epistolary form. The limitations of that form and Richardson's image of rigid, middle-class respectability provoked the antagonism of Henry Fielding (1707–54), who mocked him in *Shamela* and set out to do so in *Joseph Andrews* (1742), until plot and characters took him over and his satirical purpose was largely forgotten.

Richardson's reputation has undergone severe ups and downs. Immensely popular in his day, especially with female readers, he was denigrated in the 19th century, especially in comparison with Fielding, but has since risen again in critical esteem. Still, few people would read *Clarissa* rather than *Tom Jones* (1749), Fielding's masterpiece.

Tom Jones is a foundling, brought up by the benevolent Allworthy along with his own nephew and heir, the devious Blifil, who is destined to marry Sophia, Squire Western's daughter, with whom Tom falls mutually in

'His designs were strictly honourable, as the phrase is; that is, to rob a lady of her fortune by way of marriage.'
Fielding, Tom Jones, bk. xi, ch. 4.

love. As a result of indiscretions with a game-keeper's daughter, Tom leaves Allworthy's household and embarks on a series of adventures, which are enhanced by Fielding's brilliantly drawn minor characters. The construction of the novel is masterly – Fielding planned it with great care – and the story carries real suspense up to the highly satisfactory conclusion. Tom Jones is no Richardsonian hero, being impulsive and even foolish, but a generous, open-hearted soul. Sophia, the heroine, is a thoroughly convincing character, not a personification of feminine virtues. With Fielding's *Tom Jones*, the English novel came of age.

Fielding, a gentleman by birth, wrote many plays and other works – skillful, inventive, often amusing. He was a man of large human sympathies who from 1748 was a highly committed magistrate in Westminster. His powerful, deeply felt opposition to social injustice and judicial corruption is manifest in a series of essays.

SMOLLETT

Tobias Smollett (1721–71), a Scot by birth, was a ship's surgeon, and made excellent use of his seafaring experience in his first and best-known novel, the picaresque *Roderick Random* (1748). His stories are violent and boisterous, and the comedy is sometimes spoilt by crudeness. But Smollett is still enjoyably readable, although he lacks the vision of Fielding and his major characters, especially his heroines, are hard to believe in. Of his later novels, perhaps the best is the last, *Humphrey Clinker* (1771), written in a modified epistolary form in which the same events are seen through the eyes of different characters. It contains some fierce, sometimes unconvincing satire on English fashionable society, but in general the humour is less coarse.

STERNE

Even by the standards of Church of England clergymen, Lawrence Sterne (1713–68), a parish priest in Yorkshire, was very odd. An admirer of Rabelais and Cervantes, he wrote one great novel, *The Life and Opinions of Tristram Shandy*, published in instalments from 1760. At first sight it is total anarchy. The hero is not even born until the third book, and the narrative is an apparently incoherent succession of episodes, conversations, strange digressions, bawdy humour, mini-lectures and sentiment, with unfinished sentences and even blank pages. All this, however, is by design, since Sterne wishes to convey that life and the human mind are not orderly. For all his sympathy with the miseries that human beings endure (Sterne's wife was a manic depressive), he sees them as essentially comic, even in appearance. Sterne had some formidable opponents and *Tristram Shandy*, though it sold well, was not really appreciated until after his death.

Richardson, Fielding, Smollett and Sterne are the giants of the first great period of the English novel, but they were not alone. Samuel Johnson's *Rasselas* (1759) is largely a tract in the form of a novel, but Oliver Goldsmith's *The Vicar of Wakefield* (1766), another 'novel of sentiment', has proved to be of long-lasting popularity.

DANGEROUS LIAISONS

The late 18th century produced two master-pieces in France. *Les Liaisons Dangereuses* by Pierre Choderlos de Laclos was published in 1782. The form was influenced by Richardson, but it is a very different kind of novel, a cynical treatise on the art of seduction. The second was *Paul et Virginie* (1787) by Bernardin de Saint-Pierre, friend of Rousseau. The story is of two children raised in a Rousseauesque state of nature, brought to destruction by the dire influence of modern society.

Above: **An incident on the road in** *Tom Jones.* **Fielding's great novel is too carefully structured to be called picaresque, and the characters are realistic individuals.**

Opposite: **The virtuous heroine, a servant fancied by her employer's son, holds sensuality at bay, one of 12 illustrations for Richardson's hugely successful** *Pamela* **by Joseph Highmore.**

CHAPTER FIVE

THE ENLIGHTENMENT

'The Enlightenment' is the term that describes the philosophical movement in the 18th century in which great emphasis was placed on the power of human reason, and traditional religion and politics were critically reviewed. Its roots ran deep and spread themselves widely, but major branches can be traced to the 'scientific revolution' of the late 17th century, to the classical writers of Louis XIV's France, to the thought of Blaise Pascal and to the philosopher René Descartes (1596–1650), who placed the reasoning human being firmly at the centre of the universe: 'I think therefore I am'. The Enlightenment encouraged innovation and experiment (even *Tristram Shandy* is its product), and politically it laid the ideological basis for the American and French Revolutions.

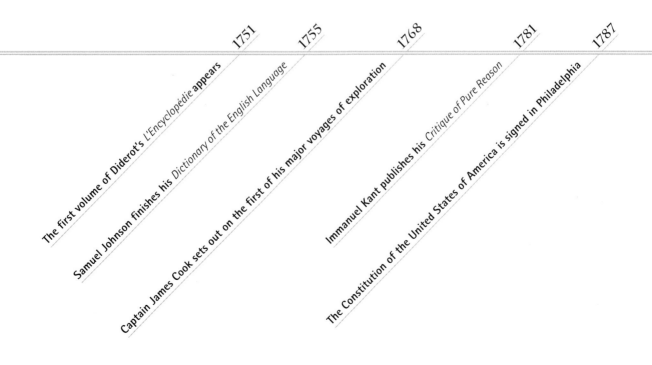

1751 — The first volume of Diderot's *L'Encyclopédie* appears

1755 — Samuel Johnson finishes his *Dictionary of the English Language*

Captain James Cook sets out on the first of his major voyages of exploration

1768 — Immanuel Kant publishes his *Critique of Pure Reason*

1781 — The Constitution of the United States of America is signed in Philadelphia

1787

THE PHILOSOPHES

The term enlightenment originally came from the German *Aufklärung*, and the 'age of reason' was not, of course, an exclusively French phenomenon, but an international movement. Some of the leading thinkers were German (Kant), or Scottish (Hume), for example, and the French *philosophes* saw themselves as the heirs of Bacon, Galileo, Leibnitz, Newton and Locke, as well as of fellow Frenchmen such as, pre-eminently, Descartes.

MONTESQUIEU

The Baron de Montesquieu (1689–1775) published his *Persian Letters* in 1721, a highly satirical view of the autocratic French state as seen by Persian visitors, but his greatest work was the *Spirit of the Laws* (1748). It compared the French Constitution unfavourably with the English, where power was more broadly spread, and was an important influence on the framers of the U.S. Constitution. The oldest of the leading *philosophes*, Montesquieu was a kind of forerunner for the three leading figures, Rousseau, Voltaire and Diderot.

ROUSSEAU

An orphan of Swiss Protestant background, Jean-Jacques Rousseau (1712–78) was the Enlightenment's wild card. A wanderer, erratic (he quarrelled with almost everybody) and unstable (he died insane), his intellectual brilliance was breathtaking. Best known for the political theories, notably the doctrine of the general will, expressed in the *Social Contract* (1762), in the same year he published *Émile*, a treatise on education in narrative form.

It would be hard to exaggerate the influence of these works on later generations. Rousseau believed that natural man – the 'noble savage' – had been perverted by society; he emphasized individual liberty and the inward life. Unlike the other *philosophes*, he did not believe that art and science, or material progress, contributed to the improvement of human beings, rather that they had corrupted them. He did not share the common faith in the power of reason, and in many ways he had more in common with the later Romantics than with the thinking of the Englightenment. Of Rousseau's other writings, most memorable are his *Confessions*, a uniquely candid autobiography published after his death, in which Rousseau in his last years struggled to come to terms with his own extraordinary self.

Above: Voltaire, the very essence of the Enlightenment. Lean, positively skeletal in his later years, he was, someone said, 'all brain'.

Opposite: A characteristically comprehensive and well-drawn illustration of sandals from *L'Encyclopédie*, one of the greatest achievements in the history of European publishing.

VOLTAIRE

It is hard to imagine two people more dissimilar than Rousseau and François Marie Arouet, known as Voltaire (1694–1778). A gentleman of great wit and polish, rational, well-balanced – in another age he would have been the perfect courtier. But as a free-thinker and a devastating critic of the *ancien régime*, his ideas earned him the hostility of Church and State, resulting in a prison term, a period of exile in England and long-term exclusion from Paris. From 1750 until they quarrelled in 1753, he was closely associated as adviser and friend with Frederick the Great, the 'enlightened despot' of Prussia. He spent his later years, for safety, at Ferney just inside the border from Switzerland.

The great universal genius of the Enlightenment, Voltaire was a staggeringly productive writer, who earned contemporary fame primarily as a playwright, though he is best known for his philosophical and satirical works, in various forms, and as a historian. His *Philosophical Letters* (1734) celebrated his belief in political and religious liberty, and he summed up his ideas with characteristic wit and clarity in his *Philosophical Dictionary* (1764). His greatest work in modern eyes, however, is *Candide* (1759), a philosophical tale (a genre that Voltaire invented), whose hero puts up with a series of misfortunes on the basis of the ironic motto that 'All is for the best in the best of all possible worlds', but eventually becomes disillusioned, concluding that the world is beyond hope and the only solution is to stay at home and 'cultivate our garden'.

DIDEROT

Denis Diderot (1713–84) was another polymath, whose early work was translations from English (Diderot was perfectly fluent in several languages), essays on various subjects (an attack on religion landed him in prison) and plays for the new, bourgeois theatre. He originated and, against the opposition of the government and other obstacles, brought to a conclusion over more than twenty years the single greatest product of the Enlightenment, the famous *Encyclopedia*, published in 35 volumes from 1751. A genial man as well as a determined and industrious one, Diderot secured contributions from his fellow *philosophes*, including Voltaire and Rousseau, who wrote on music as well as other subjects. The work began as a translation of the *Cyclopedia* of Ephraim Chambers (no relation to the modern firm), but developed into something far greater, aiming to cover all human knowledge and coming very close to achieving such an ambitious aim. Diderot was a rationalist and a materialist, and also the son of a tradesman – one of the most remarkable features of the *Encyclopedia* is its coverage of contemporary technology, with detailed engravings. Diderot's numerous other writings included *Rameau's Nephew* (first published much later in a German translation by Goethe), a witty and satirical novel or dialogue now generally considered his masterpiece, and *Jacques le Fataliste* (not published until 1796) which was influenced by Sterne.

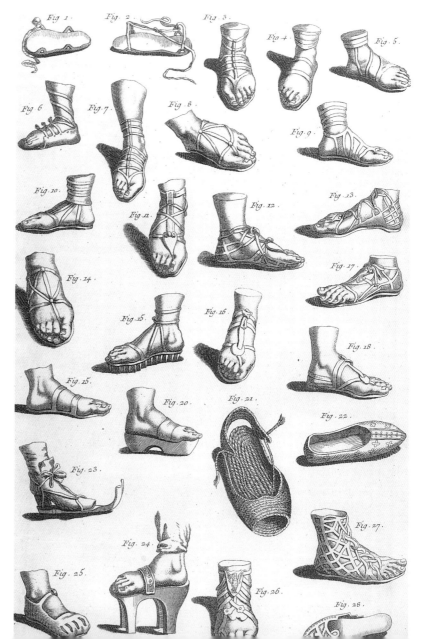

'True ease in writing comes from art, not chance,
As those move easiest who have learn'd to dance.'
The heroic couplet, effectively exploited by Dryden and made famous by Pope, proved to be an appropriate verse form for the age of reason, being clear, simple and ordered. It was not, however, the only kind of poetry being written, nor – in spite of Pope's famous statement that 'The proper study of mankind is man' – were 18th-century poets exclusively concerned with human society and institutions. The countryside was coming into vogue, long before the Romantics, and there was a common preoccupation with death and graveyards.

POPE
AND HIS CONTEMPORARIES

POPE

Technically, Alexander Pope (1688–1744) was one of the greatest of English poets (and one of the most quotable). His sensitive and elegant *Pastorals* were written at the age of 16, and he was only 31 when the publication of his collected works established him firmly as the greatest contemporary figure in English literature. Though he did not have the vision of a Milton or the passion of a Wordsworth, he had a penetrating moral sense and a commitment to the pursuit of perfection, evident in his 'Essay on Man' (1733). He was at his best as a satirist, and 'The Rape of the Lock' (1712) is his most sparkling work in the comic vein. The title refers to an incident in society in which a young gentleman cut off a lock of hair from a lady he admired. The incident caused an absurd, but serious, quarrel. Pope treated it in hilarious, mock-heroic style, which only made matters worse! Apart from his uncompleted *magnum opus* of which the 'Essay on Man' formed the first part, Pope's greatest work was his translation of Homer which, though more Pope than Homer, was still a huge achievement and made Pope perhaps the first English writer other than

Right: While Pope and his successors mocked society, the coarseness beneath the elegance of Georgian England was effectively satirized by the great English painter and patriot, William Hogarth.

Opposite: A scene by Hogarth from *The Beggar's Opera*. It was first produced soon after the execution of the notorious thieftaker and gangster, Jonathan Wild, and Gay's character, Peachum, was apparently based on Wild. The play had the unexpected effect of glamorizing the criminal underworld.

dramatists able to live – and in some style – on the profits from his pen.

Pope's health was fragile from childhood, he was almost a dwarf (4ft 6in), wore a corset to support his spine and needed help dressing. These circumstances may help to explain his reputation for antagonizing friends and perhaps his capacity for writing some of the most vitriolic invective in literature. In the Romantic period, Pope fell from favour, and he has only been again appreciated at his true worth in the 20th century.

RURAL SCENES

The heroic couplet was also employed by Samuel Johnson, by John Gay and by Goldsmith. Gay (1685–1732), however, is best known for his evergreen musical play *The Beggar's Opera*, which followed up Swift's suggestion for a 'Newgate [prison] pastoral', Gay writing the lyrics which were set to the tunes of popular contemporary ballads. First

'All nature is but art unknown to thee;
All chance, direction which thou canst not see;
All discord, harmony not understood;
All partial evil, universal good;
And, spite of pride, in erring reason's spite,
One truth is clear, "Whatever IS, is RIGHT."'
Pope, *An Essay on Man*, Epistle i, 289.

performed in 1728, it is said to have been the most successful play ever presented in London up to that time. Since 1928 it has taken on new life in the form of the Brecht-Weill adaptation, *The Threepenny Opera*.

The Anglo-Irish Oliver Goldsmith (died 1774) was blessed with immense natural talents that were never quite fulfilled, perhaps because, in spite of a large and varied output, there was a certain indolence about him. Apart from the two poems, 'The Traveller' and 'The Deserted Village', based on childhood memories of Ireland, he was the author of a famous comedy, *She Stoops to Conquer*, frequently revived, and a memorable novel, still read, *The Vicar of Wakefield*.

James Thomson (1700–48) preferred blank verse for his four-part *The Seasons*, which exemplified the theme of Nature, always present in English literature and now becoming more evident, though Thomson himself has never been quite as popular as he was in his own time. Nature was generally preferred in orderly garb. People were becoming interested in landscapes and views, and the improvement in roads and carriages meant that it was possible for the well-off to view and admire their parklands in comfort. Others, however, found the countryside encouraged more melancholy thoughts.

Of the so-called 'churchyard school' of poets, outstanding was Thomas Gray (1716–71), whose 'Elegy Written in a Country Churchyard' is one of the most familiar poems in the language. Gloom, depression and thoughts of death represent the dark side of the Age of Reason. The funniest poem of the era, the rollicking 'John Gilpin' was written by William Cowper (1731–1800) while he was suffering intense mental torment. But Cowper's masterpiece is *The Task* (1785), which was written when that struggle was largely won, thanks partly to Cowper's intense interest in quotidian detail overpowering metaphysical gloom. His description of rural scenes is in simple, unpretentious language, signifying the change from the formal, classical style of Pope and his contemporaries to the more intimate style of the Romantics.

The period from the late 17th to mid-18th century, roughly from Dryden to Johnson, is sometimes called the Augustan Age, in complimentary reference to the reign of the Emperor Augustus, the golden age of Classical Roman art and literature. It is characterized by elegance of style, precision, orderliness, good sense and a dislike of extremes, a classic example being Edward Gibbon's *Decline and Fall of the Roman Empire* (1776–88). The term was occasionally used by contemporaries: Goldsmith wrote an essay on 'The Augustan Age in England', but the presiding genius of English literature in the 18th century was Samuel Johnson (1709–84).

AUGUSTAN PROSE

APPRENTICESHIP

By popular convention, Johnson is called 'Dr Johnson' though his doctorate was honorary, awarded by his old university, Oxford, in 1775. Modern critics would like to stop this habit, but it is probably too late. Anyway, it suits him.

He was born in Lichfield, son of a bookseller who died in 1731 leaving his family penniless. Johnson worked as a school teacher in the Midlands and in 1735 married a widow nearly twice his age. It proved a successful marriage. After an attempt to found their own school in Lichfield, they moved to London in 1737, bringing with them a former pupil, David Garrick, soon to become the greatest actor of the age. Johnson, who had already done some provincial journalism, found a useful patron in Edward Cave, proprietor of *The Gentleman's Magazine*, for which he wrote a profusion of verses, essays and political pieces. From 1747 he worked sporadically on his *Dictionary of the English Language* (see page 72). His poem, 'The Vanity of Human Wishes', his longest and best, was

Above: **Dr Johnson reading, the famous portrait by Johnson's great friend, and founder of the Royal Academy, Joshua Reynolds.**

published in 1749 and his tragedy *Irene*, written years earlier, was staged by the loyal Garrick in the same year (it has rarely been staged since).

MAN OF LETTERS

Backed by Cave, in 1752 Johnson started a twice-weekly periodical, *The Rambler*. It ran for two years and was almost entirely written, anonymously, by Johnson himself, an extraordinary workload. But writers were ill-paid, and Johnson barely scraped a living, in spite of his industry. The *Dictionary* was published in 1755, but Johnson was fully occupied writing articles, essays and reviews for a variety of journals, as well as biographies. In 1759, his *Prince of Abyssinia*, later known as *Rasselas* and usually categorized as a 'philosophical romance', was published. It demonstrated, with kindly wisdom, that no human occupation is a recipe for happiness. He wrote it in the evenings, allegedly in a week, to pay for his mother's funeral and pay off his debts. A government pension of £300 a year, awarded in 1762, eased his circumstances somewhat. In 1765 he published his edition of Shakespeare's plays, with its long and intelligent preface.

Johnson had many friends and in 1764 he and the painter Joshua Reynolds (first president of the Royal Academy) founded their literary club, which met in a London tavern. Among those who attended were Garrick, the politicians Charles James Fox and Edmund Burke, Goldsmith, Sheridan and a young Scottish lawyer, James Boswell. Johnson was a humane and affectionate man and he was also a writer who talked as well as (perhaps better than) he wrote. He was the dominant figure on the literary scene, and his opinions – always intelligent, often dogmatic – were eagerly sought on every subject. At Boswell's suggestion, they undertook a journey together to the Western Isles of Scotland in 1773, only a generation after the terrible destruction of Culloden. Johnson was then sixty-four and they both wrote fascinating accounts of their travels in the Highlands. Johnson's last major work was his *Lives of the Poets* (1781), 52 biographies displaying great learning, sympathy and characteristically provocative opinions.

'There are two things which I am confident I can do very well: one is an introduction to any literary work, stating what it is to contain, and how it should be executed in the most perfect manner; the other is a conclusion, shewing from various causes why the execution has not been equal to what the author promised to himself and to the public.' Boswell *Life of Samuel Johnson*, vol i, p. 292.

THE BIOGRAPHY

Johnson was a great literary scholar, a fine writer and an excellent critic, as well as a fascinating and likable man. However, the great reputation he enjoys to this day is due in no small part to the famous biography by his friend and admirer, James Boswell, probably the greatest biography in English literature, and published seven years after Johnson's death. Boswell collected data for years, having gained Johnson's approval for the project after the great man had read (in manuscript) Boswell's account of their journey to the Hebrides. Boswell's methods were in fact those recommended by Johnson in a piece on the subject in *The Rambler*; his legal training encouraged accuracy (few errors have been found in the account of Johnson's life before Boswell knew him) and, most important, he had a remarkable ability to get the best out of his subject in conversation. Johnson, who expressed lively opinions on everything, is one of the most quoted figures in literature – thanks largely to Boswell's work.

During the 17th century, Scottish writers tended to write more in English than in Scots, a tendency encouraged by the Act of Union (1707). On the one hand, the extraordinarily vivid language of, for example, Sir Thomas Urquhart (died *c.*1660), the translator of Rabelais into Scots, was lost. On the other hand, some of the finest English prose of the 18th century was written by Scots (this was the period when Edinburgh gained its reputation as the 'Athens of the North'). These writers included the philosopher David Hume; Adam Smith, the author of the seminal work on political economy, *The Wealth of Nations* (1776); James Boswell, the biographer of Johnson; and the novelist Tobias Smollet. 'Is it not strange', asked Hume, 'that, at a time when we have lost our . . . independent Government, . . . speak a very corrupt Dialect of the Tongue in which we make use of . . . that . . . we shou'd really be the People most distinguish'd for Literature in Europe?' Two writers in particular were to spread the fame of Scottish literature far and wide and at the same time restore national pride and self-confidence: Robert Burns and Walter Scott.

ROBERT BURNS

BURNS

Scotland's national poet, Robert Burns (1759–96) has become a cult figure. Communist leaders invariably cite him as their favourite British poet. His early verse was written in the early 1780s whilst working a farm at Mossgiel, Ayrshire, with his brother (and finding time for a vigorous love life). The best poems, including the famous 'To a Mouse', were published in the first 1786 edition of *Poems Chiefly in the Scottish Dialect*. It made him instantly famous, and he went to Edinburgh where he was lionized by the literati as a rustic genius, the 'Heaven-taught ploughman'. Although it encouraged his taste for material enjoyments and provoked a few experiments in a more 'Augustan' style, this literary acclaim left him unmoved. His stature was enhanced by his genial, gregarious good nature and handsome appearance, but more importantly by his reworking of hundreds of traditional songs, including 'Auld Lang Syne', 'Ye Banks and Braes', 'Scots Wha Hae', and dozens of others equally familiar. In 1788, Burns was able to buy a farm at Ellisland with his former paramour, now wife, Jean Armour. Life was still hard, and Burns joined the Excise Service to raise his income. His support for the

early stages of the French Revolution disconcerted some admirers, and in 1792 he gave up the farm and moved to Dumfries. The major work of his last years was his narrative masterpiece, 'Tam O'Shanter'. Rheumatic fever weakened his heart and he died at 37.

THE WORK

In spite of poverty, Burns had a sound if basic education. He was also a voracious reader who knew English and French poetry intimately, but he acknowledged the influence of Scottish predecessors, notably the poets Allan Ramsay and Robert Fergusson. He wrote with equal ease in formal English and in his native Scots, sometimes shifting from one to the other in the same poem (e.g. 'The Cotter's Saturday Night'), though some critics feel that the racy vigour of Scots lends something extra to his poems – songs, satires, animal poems, letters in verse – in the vernacular. His poems in both are notable for broad-minded tolerance and a strong emphasis on human nature, good and ill. He gave Scotsmen an attractive image: 'more human than most, warm-hearted and open-handed to a fault, great drinkers and lovers and sturdy fighters for freedom and the rights of man' (Sir Fitzroy Maclean). For Scots everywhere, Burns Night (25 January, his birthday) is a great festival, where haggis, neaps and tatties are consumed along with a patriotic quantity of the national beverage.

OSSIAN

A 'bosom favourite' of Burns was Henry Mackenzie's *The Man of Feeling* (1771), a

Opposite: Portrait of Burns framed by characters and incidents from his poems. Burns has been hijacked by posterity for political and other causes, with the result that both the man and the nature of his achievement have been obscured.

Left: A view of Edinburgh from the west in the 18th century by T. H. Shepherd.

'sentimental' novel in both the 18th-century sense and the more critical modern sense. Mackenzie was later the chairman of the group set up to investigate the origins of *Fingal, An Ancient Epic Poem, in Six Books*, published by James Macpherson in 1762. It purported to be a translation of a work by an ancient Scottish-Irish bard, Ossian. Macpherson had hinted at the existence of such an epic in an earlier collection of *Fragments of Ancient Poetry . . .* collected by him and translated from the Gaelic. Ossian had a huge impact, not only on Scots delighted at this unknown national treasure, but also throughout Europe, and especially in Germany. But there were doubts, two formidable sceptics being David Hume and Samuel Johnson. Mackenzie's panel confirmed (after Macpherson's death) that the work consisted of freely edited Gaelic fragments, plus Macpherson's own compositions. Nevertheless, it is a truly remarkable work; the fact that it was proved to be largely a fake hardly diminished its popularity, and perhaps Macpherson's fame – and large profits – were after all deserved.

Dictionaries of a sort, for instance glossaries of obscure words in Homer, were compiled in ancient Greece. They had few of the features we associate with dictionaries now and were not alphabetically arranged. Glossaries were also compiled in the Middle Ages, often as a feature of a general work of reference, and what appears to be the first use of the word 'dictionary' occurs in the title of a Latin work by a 14th-century Frenchman. There were also a large number of foreign-language dictionaries (or vocabularies) for the benefit of merchants and other travellers. A French-English vocabulary was one of the works printed by Caxton in about 1480 at his Westminster press. In the 16th–17th centuries, the new academies in Italy and France took the lead in publishing dictionaries, although an alphabetical arrangement was not generally adopted until the second edition of the French dictionary produced by the Académie Française in 1694.

THE DICTIONARY

JOHNSON'S DICTIONARY

In late 16th-century England, the distinction between 'literary' and 'popular' English encouraged the publication of glossaries of terms in two versions, in the same manner as foreign-language vocabularies. Robert Cawdrey's *A Table Alphabetical . . . of Hard Usual Words* (1604) is regarded as the first English dictionary. It contained about 3,000 words. A substantial dictionary was compiled by Nathan Bailey in 1721. The 1730 version, *Dictionarium Britanni-cum*, was exploited by Samuel Johnson.

Johnson's *Dictionary*, the best and most famous dictionary before the *Oxford*, occupied him from 1746 until its publication in 1755. Though he had assistants, it was fundamentally a one-man production, and was carried through at the same time as much other work, including *The Rambler*. Johnson's declared purpose was to produce a dictionary by which 'the pronunciation of our language may be fixed . . .; by which its purity may be preserved, its use ascertained, and its duration lengthened.' It defined about 40,000 words and, to illustrate their use and justify his definitions, he included about 115,000 quotations from every field of literature. This prodigious feat was an entirely new aspect. Novel, also, was the attention given to pronunciation and Johnson's inclusion of many ordinary

Above: Noah Webster (1758–1843). The famous lexicographer wished to separate American culture from English influence. His two-volume dictionary of 1828 was based on a series of earlier, lesser dictionaries and on his 'blue-backed speller', which sold literally millions of copies.

Opposite: Title page of Johnson's *Dictionary*. He allowed himself a few, often-quoted jokes, but it was a thoroughly scholarly work.

words, as well as what Cawdrey called 'hard' ones. Johnson's *Dictionary of the English Language*, which went through five editions in his own lifetime, is sometimes regarded as a subjective work that manifests the compiler's own wit and prejudices. In fact, the number of definitions in which Johnson allowed his sense of humour (or resentment) to emerge is very small. This was a work of solid scholarship and great common sense, produced at a time when knowledge of etymology was slight.

THE OED

Johnson's *Dictionary* remained supreme until the *Oxford* (originally *New*) *English Dictionary* was published between 1884 and 1928, largely under the editorship of James Murray, in 125 parts. This is widely regarded as not only the greatest English dictionary, but also perhaps the greatest dictionary of any modern language. Famously compiled 'on historical principles', and combing the language back to the 13th century, it was largely designed as an aid to reading and has proved an inexhaustible source of information for literary scholars.

Noah Webster's *American Dictionary of the English Language* was published in 1828. It was the first modern 'encyclopedic' dictionary and was quickly established as a sound guide to spelling and pronunciation in America. Other languages also acquired authoritative dictionaries during the 19th century. In France, Larousse issued a series of dictionaries, and Emile Littré's dictionary of 1873–78 was especially admired for its etymologies and literary illustrations. The brothers Grimm began work on the *Deutsches Wörterbuch* in the 1850s, though it was not completed for over a century.

MODERN DICTIONARIES

The third edition of *Webster's* (1961) provoked controversy by including categories previously classed as 'inferior' – slang etc. – on an equal footing with orthodox usage. It established a trend towards the classification of language as it is spoken rather than as it 'should' be spoken, according to generally accepted, though hard to define, conventions. No serious scholar, including Johnson, supposed that correct

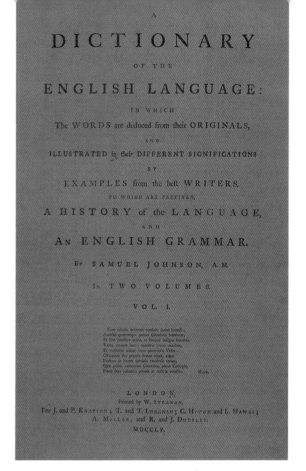

'Lexicographer: A writer of dictionaries, a harmless drudge. Oats: A grain, which in England is generally given to horses, but in Scotland supports the people. Patron: Commonly a wretch who supports with insolence, and is paid with flattery.'
Johnson's *Dictionary of the English Language*.

English was set in stone, or that a dictionary, in Johnson's words, could safeguard the language against 'corruption and decay' or, to put it less conservatively, against change. The argument was rather that a dictionary that accepted any current usage was inviting linguistic anarchy.

Current cultural trends appear to support *Webster's* editors. Perhaps a more significant development occurred in the 1980s, when computer technology produced changes amounting to a lexicographic revolution. The second edition of the *OED* (1989) was completed in a mere seven years, thanks to an electronic database of over 50 million words. The CD-ROM version, which you could put in your pocket, compared with the printed version that required 5 ft of shelf space, offered mind-boggling additional information: for example, it was possible within a few seconds to discover how many times Shakespeare was quoted in the course of the dictionary (33,150 times).

CHAPTER SIX

ROMANTICISM

The preoccupations of any age tend to produce contrary reactions in a succeeding one, and the Romantic movement was an especially fierce reaction to the Enlightenment. As a literary movement, it embodied a dramatic change in prevailing habits of thinking and feeling. The Romantic poets looked inward, placing unprecedented importance on their own personal emotions, while at the same time finding exaltation in the beauties of Nature, especially in spectacular scenery. Broadly speaking, they were against the classical, the conservative and the moderate, and in favour of liberty, both political and individual, the imagination and the exotic.

1762 Rousseau publishes *Émile* and *The Social Contract*

1764 James Hargreaves' spinning jenny invented, revolutionizing the textile industry

1774 Goethe's *The Sorrows of Young Werther* is published

1789 The beginning of the French Revolution

1798 Coleridge and Wordsworth's *Lyrical Ballads* are published

1812 The first two cantos of Byron's *Childe Harold's Pilgrimage* appear

1822 Shelley drowns off the coast of Italy

THE ROMANTIC MOVEMENT

Like all literary movements, the Romantic movement encompassed many different tendencies and cannot easily be tied down by time or by place. It extended roughly from the last third of the 18th century to the middle of the 19th, and aspects of it are evident in every region of Western civilization. However, Rousseau, such an important influence on Romanticism, belongs to the previous generation; earlier poets such as Gray and Cowper show some Romantic elements, as do some who were active after 1850. Many writers who were at work within the Romantic period – Jane Austen for example – cannot be called Romantics, and some who do fall into that category acquired their 'Romantic' image as much from their lives and personal circumstances as from their published writings.

GOETHE

An early example of the Romantic revival was the *Sturm und Drang* (Storm and Stress) movement of the 1770s, a time of great literary excitement in Germany. It was inspired by the idealism of Rousseau and its leading influence was Johann Gottfried von Herder (1744–1803), philosopher and critic, whose followers included the young Goethe and Schiller. They rebelled against literary conventions, demanded poetry of strong passions, and exalted the original genius, notably Shakespeare.

The most famous work of this movement was *The Sorrows of Young Werther*, by Johann Wolfgang von Goethe (1749–1832), the greatest figure in German literature and a 'universal man', whose work ranged over philosophy, science, music and art. This early work, in the form of an epistolary novel, and partly autobiographical, tells of a sensitive young artist, hopelessly in love with an unat-

tainable girl, who ultimately commits suicide. It had an electric effect on Europe, becoming something of a cult (Wertherism). Goethe was later much embarrassed by this work.

Goethe, who spent most of his life at the court of Weimar, Germany's leading centre of culture, soon outgrew the *Sturm und Drang* movement and, after visits to Italy, turned towards Classicism. He collaborated closely with Friedrich von Schiller (1759–1854), the great dramatist and lyric poet, in a 'golden age' of German literature (roughly 1790–1830), which integrated German Romanticism with the ancient classical tradition. Through the advocacy of Carlyle, who portrayed him as 'the Wisest of Our Time', Goethe had an important influence on many Victorian writers. He is probably best known for his novels, and especially for his two-part drama *Faust*, which he began about 1770 and did not finish until shortly before his death. In the meantime, he had made great contributions to practically every field of human experience.

THE TRANSCENDENTALISTS

Both German philosophy and the English Romantics had a powerful effect on a group of American intellectuals who, in the late 1830s, gathered at the house of Ralph Waldo Emerson (1803–82) in Concord, Massachusetts. Emerson's essay *Nature* (1836) explained the basis of Transcendentalism, a mystical, semi-religious concept that encompassed social and economic ideas, as well as religion and philosophy. Along with self-reliance and self-knowledge, reverence for Nature was fundamental: 'Nature is the incarnation of

> 'I wanted to live deep and suck out all the marrow of life . . . to drive life into a corner, and reduce it to its lowest terms, and, if it proved to be mean, why then to get the whole and genuine meanness of it, and publish its meanness to the world; or if it were sublime, to know it by experience, and be able to give a true account of it in my next excursion.'
> Thoreau, 'Where I lived, and what I lived for'.

Above: Part II of Goethe's *Faust*, Euphorion, son of Faust and Helen of Troy, symbolize the union of the Romantic and the Classical.

Opposite: Rousseau, whose formidable intellectual gifts were balanced by a difficult, emotional temperament.

thought', said Emerson, who became a national sage in America like Goethe or Emerson's friend, Carlyle.

Some of the Transcendentalists attempted to put their ideas into practice at the Brook Farm Institute, where philosophical discussion alternated with manual labour. European influences notwithstanding, Emerson advocated the independence of American culture: 'We have listened too long to the courtly muses of Europe', he proclaimed in a lecture at Harvard. His essays and poems were published in *The Dial*, the organ of the Transcendental Club, which he edited.

THOREAU

Besides Emerson himself, the most interesting and popular of the Transcendentalists was Henry David Thoreau (1817–62). Though some of his poems appeared in *The Dial*, he published only two books during his lifetime and depended for income on various jobs, ranging from teacher to pencil-maker. It took him, he said, six weeks to earn enough for a year's existence. His first book was *A Week on the Concord and Merrimack River* (1849). His masterpiece, though little noticed at the time, was *Walden, or Life in the Woods* (1854), the result of two years spent living in a hut he built himself on Walden Pond. Describing his experiments in self-sufficient living, the local wild life and his visitors, it also expresses his sensitivity to the pre-colonial past and, with forceful clarity, his antagonism to the materialism of the modern age.

In his, often neglected, essay 'Civil Disobedience' (1849), Thoreau claims the right of individuals to refuse to pay taxes on grounds of conscience. This belief, like his enactment of an Emersonian life-style at Walden, was also put into practice – his objections to the Mexican-American War and to slavery having earned him a spell in prison. Thoreau was not recognized as a literary genius, philosopher and expert naturalist until British admirers publicized his ideas towards the end of the century. His views on civil disobedience were later adopted by Gandhi, and he is now seen as a forerunner of the Green movement.

WILLIAM BLAKE

Romantic English poets, who were not of course so called in their own time, fall largely into two distinct generations. Although there was no 'school' of poets in either generation, there was often close co-operation and friendship, for instance between Wordsworth and Coleridge in the first generation and, in a rather different way, Byron and Shelley in the second. But one image of the typical Romantic, as posterity saw him, was the solitary dreamer, the eccentric – and egocentric – artist, vitally concerned with his own mind and his own soul, sturdily resistant to authority and social convention, and oblivious to tradition, who stands apart from his fellows and from the world. Someone, in short, like William Blake.

THE VISIONARY

As a poet, a painter and an engraver, William Blake (1757–1827), was a highly individual genius, so strange and so uncompromising that some people thought him insane, though Wordsworth is said to have remarked that Blake's madness was more interesting than the sanity of other poets. Later generations have seen him as a prophet, inspired by a hatred of the materialism of the 18th century; as a liberator who, for all his loathing of social injustice and oppression, saw farther, something even beyond Good and Evil; as a mystic at odds with contemporary religion, who aspired to build a new Jerusalem 'in England's green and pleasant land'.

Son of a well-to-do London tradesman, Blake had no formal education but was taught by his mother and himself, learning Greek and Hebrew among other languages, and acquiring a special fascination with legend and the Middle Ages. He became an engraver and, as a student at the Royal Academy, he met painters and intellectuals, some of whom financed the publication of his *Poetical Sketches* in 1783. His radical sympathies later brought him into friendly contact with revolutionary sympathisers such as William Godwin and Tom Paine, who influenced his antipathy to conventional Christianity and authority. He was poor all his life, though not quite as isolated from the world, nor as deliberately perverse, as legend suggests. When he died he was buried in a pauper's grave – but he left no debts.

SONGS OF INNOCENCE AND EXPERIENCE

The collection *Songs of Innocence* was published, together with the poet's own illustrations, in 1789. Here Blake is at his simplest and gentlest, and, for most readers, probably his most approachable. The poems are largely about childhood, some written in a deliberately child-like manner, although the declamations of the prophet can already be heard. Blake's early mysticism and love of emblems are apparent in *The Book of Tirel* of the same year, again with his illustrations. The *Songs of Innocence* were reissued in 1794, together with the grimmer *Songs of Experience* which balance the adult world of corruption and oppression against that of the innocent child, expressing with extraordinary economy Blake's highly original ideas about the connection between good and evil and his doctrine of 'contraries' – angels as devils, energy against reason.

These ideas are also active in Blake's chief work in prose, *The Marriage of Heaven and Hell*, which consists of a series of aphorisms that overturned conventional ideas of morality. In *The Visions of the Daughters of Albion* (1793), *America: A Prophecy* (1793), and several subsequent works, Blake introduced his own mythology: Urizen, the repressive moral authority, and Orc, the archetypal rebel (like the poet himself), and other personifications, of 'body', 'passion', 'spirit', etc. These 'prophetic books' are extremely obscure and inaccessible to ordinary readers without scholarly commentary. Blake employs what amounts to a secret language, the symbolism of which has only recently been fully worked out by devoted scholars.

IMAGINATION AND REALISM

Blake was born within two years of Robert Burns and three years of the Suffolk poet George Crabbe (1754–1832). In spite of some common themes, a more disparate trio would be hard to imagine. Crabbe, Jane Austen's favourite poet, was a realist. He used the heroic couplet of Pope and he wrote of the ordinary experiences of rural life, without romance. His strong points in *The Village* (1783) and *The Parish Register* (1807) are his sincerity and his grimly observant eye. In spite of a very 'Romantic' addiction to opium (acquired through unwise medical advice), he knew little or nothing of the forces that manipulated the imagination of Blake, yet he is a rewarding poet who in his own day was considerably the more popular. One of his tales in *The Borough* (1810) concerns the tormented fisherman Peter Grimes, the subject of Benjamin Britten's well-known opera (1945).

'For nature then
(The coarser pleasures of my boyish days,
And their glad animal movements all gone by)
To me was all in all. – I cannot paint
What then I was. The sounding cataract
Haunted me like a passion: the tall rock,
The mountain, and the deep and gloomy wood,
Their colours and their forms, were then to me
An appetite; a feeling and a love,
That had no need of a remoter charm,
By thought supplied, nor any interest
Unborrowed from the eye.'
Wordsworth, 'Lines composed a few miles above
Tintern Abbey'.

THE LYRICAL BALLADS

The most important event in English Romantic literature was the publication of *Lyrical Ballads, With a Few Other Poems* in 1798. It marked the beginning of a new age. It was the result of the co-operation of two poets, Wordsworth and Coleridge, briefly neighbours in Somerset where most of the poems were written. They felt stifled by the rigid conventions of 18th-century poetry and wished to release feeling from the rule of intellect, or as Coleridge put it, to concentrate on 'the two cardinal points of poetry: the power of exciting the sympathy of the reader by a faithful adherence to the truth of nature, and the power of giving the interest of novelty by the modifying colours of the imagination . . .'

THE POEMS

Wordsworth, whose combative preface attacked the 'gaudy and inane phraseology of many modern writers', concentrated on the 'truth of nature' and Coleridge on the 'colours of the imagination'. Wordsworth's poems were the most personal, including 'Lines composed . . . above Tintern Abbey'. Coleridge contributed only four poems to the original edition, among them 'The Rime of the Ancient Mariner', one of the best-known poems in the English language. It was singled out for attack by the critics, who gave the *Lyrical Ballads* a mostly hostile reception. Nevertheless, a second edition, with more poems and a new preface by Wordsworth which amounted to a Romantic manifesto, appeared at the beginning of 1801, and a third edition in 1802.

WORDSWORTH

A lawyer's son born in Cumbria, William Wordsworth (1770–1850) is one of England's greatest lyric poets. Despite his fairly prosaic descriptions of nature, Wordsworth had an almost mystical outlook – 'we are part of all that we behold' – and the history of his mental development is to be found in *The Prelude*, probably his greatest work, which he began in 1798. It was published in 1805, but he revised it continually for the rest of his life. As well as a spell at St John's College, Cambridge, he spent a year (1791–92) in France – like most English Romantics, he enthusiastically supported the French Revolution, but became disillusioned later – where he had a love affair resulting in the birth of a daughter. Otherwise, Wordsworth spent most of his life in the Lake District, his presence attracting others, notably Coleridge and Southey (the 'Lake Poets'). He lived with his sister Dorothy, to whom he was devoted from childhood and on whom he was emotionally dependent. From 1799, they lived at Dove Cottage, Grasmere, now a place of literary pilgrimage, notwithstanding the poet's marriage in 1802 to a childhood friend.

Although he lived a long and productive life, Wordsworth wrote most of his great poetry in a single decade, 1797–1807, after he had recovered from a period of severe mental and professional doubts, the latter ameliorated by a friend's substantial legacy. It included 'Michael', 'Resolution and Independence', his 'Ode [on] Immortality', and the 'Lucy' poems, written mostly during travel in Germany with his sister (who may have been the original Lucy), and included in the second edition of *Lyrical Ballads*. In his later years Wordsworth, who was Poet Laureate from 1843, politically moved steadily Right, and although he continued to write fine poetry, it lacked the fire of inspiration.

COLERIDGE

It has been remarked that no one can write a satisfactory study of Samuel Taylor Coleridge (1772–1834) because no one has a brain large enough to encompass the vast range of his intellectual and artistic interests. Coleridge was Wordsworth's chief intellectual stimulus, as Dorothy was his emotional prop. Son of a Devon vicar, like Wordsworth he did not stay long enough at Cambridge to take a degree. His first poems appeared in a newspaper in 1794, when he settled in Bristol, lodging with his friend, the poet Robert Southey, lecturing on politics, religion and education, and marrying the sister of Southey's fiancée. He produced a radical weekly publication, started a family and began his study of German literature, also acquiring the habit of taking opium against depression.

Moving to Somerset, he met the Wordsworths in 1797, the start of a literary partnership that produced the foundation of English Romanticism, the *Lyrical Ballads*. An annuity from a rich pottery family, the Wedgwoods, alleviated his financial problems, and he produced a succession of poems, including the strange, magical, fragmentary, opium-induced 'Kubla Khan'. In 1798 he visited Germany with the Wordsworths, confirming Coleridge as the spokesman on German Romanticism. He moved to the Lake District in 1799 to be near the Wordsworths, and fell in love with Mrs Wordsworth's sister, a cause of profound personal anguish, manifested in a series of poems in 1800–02 and in virtual addiction to opium. In 1808 he began lecturing at the Royal Institute, notably on Shakespeare.

Top: Wordsworth and his wife in 1839. Traditionally, Romantic poets are supposed, to die young, but Wordsworth lived to a good age.

Above: Grasmere. Wordsworth settled there in 1799, beginning of the association of the Lake District with the Romantic poets.

Crisis came in 1810, caused by a breach with Wordsworth (later healed, though never completely), and feelings of desperation induced chiefly by his relationship with Wordsworth's sister-in-law. As a poet, his career was closing, but as a philosopher and critic he still had fruitful years ahead.

YOUNG HEROES

The idea of the Romantic hero as a beautiful young man of turbulent emotions, passionate, devoted to liberty, widely travelled, and destined for a premature death was personified in the leading members of the second generation of English Romantic poets, Byron, Keats and Shelley. All of them, but Byron especially, have become almost as famous for their lives, loves and letters as for their poetry.

BYRON

George Gordon, 6th Lord Byron (1788–1824) inherited Newstead Abbey, but little money, and gained a reputation as a wild young man at Cambridge. His earliest poems were highly sensual, and he destroyed most copies. He responded to early criticism with sharp satire, attacking Scott and the Lake poets, though he later recanted. After a long tour of the Mediterranean, vividly described in letters, he wrote the first two cantos of *Childe Harold's Pilgrimage* (1812), the wanderings of a young man in various settings, partly autobiographical, which made him famous. As a handsome young aristocrat, he was also fashionable, until the break-up of his unsuitable marriage (1815) turned public opinion against him.

He left England for ever in 1816, stayed in Switzerland with the Shelleys while writing the third canto of *Childe Harold* and had a daughter by Mary Shelley's sister. In the next two years he produced some of his best work, including *Manfred* and the first cantos of *Don Juan*. He was now a famous figure throughout Europe: a character in Goethe's *Faust* is based on him. He was closely involved with the Italian nationalist movement until 1821, when he threw himself into the cause of Greek independence. He died in Greece, his heart being buried in Athens.

In his public quarrel with Southey, Byron gave Romanticism a new and more combative image. Literary critics now rank him just below the great poets, and regard *Don Juan*, an 'epic satire' (16 cantos, but unfinished, in *ottava rima*) as his masterpiece.

SHELLEY

More radical than Byron, Percy Bysshe Shelley (1792–1822) regarded poetry and politics as one. Called 'Mad Shelley' at Eton, he was expelled from Oxford for his public espousal of atheism. Eloping with 16-year-old Harriet Westbrook lost him his family inheritance, and his ultra-democratic views attracted the attention of the secret service. William Godwin, the anarchistic philosopher, was for a time his mentor and in 1814 he eloped with Mary, Godwin's daughter by the feminist pioneer Mary Wollstonecraft. He married her after Harriet's suicide in 1816.

Always a wanderer, Shelley spent the summer of 1816 at Lake Geneva with Byron and from 1818 lived in Italy. There he entered his poetically most creative period: the dramas *Prometheus Unbound* and *The Cenci*; the great political poem 'The Mask of Anarchy', inspired by the Peterloo Massacre; and some of his most famous short poems, such as the 'Ode to the West Wind' (written in a few hours), 'To a Skylark', 'The Cloud' and *Adonais* an elegy for Keats (1821). In 1822 Shelley was drowned in a boating accident at La Spezia.

Shelley is regarded as one of the finest lyric poets in the language, though for a time he was comparatively little read. His high reputation among critics today arises largely from his revolutionary thoughts and ideas, which studies have shown to be wider-ranging, more profound, also more ambiguous, than Shelley's contemporaries realized.

KEATS

The popular image of John Keats (1795–1821) as the ultra-sensitive, tormented, young Romantic artist 'half in love with easeful until after his death. At Hampstead in 1817 he wrote his most ambitious work so far, *Endymion*, in friendly rivalry with Shelley, currently working on a comparable work (*The Revolt of Islam*). Despite mutual admiration, Keats kept his distance from Shelley's more powerful personality.

Hyperion (begun in 1818) reflected Keats's travels in the north and west, although mainly written in Hampstead, where he had fallen in love with Fanny Brawne. There followed 'The Eve of St Agnes', a wonderful montage of Romantic medievalism; his finest odes; the

Death', applies, if at all, to his last, death-threatened years. At school he was remembered for his love of sports before his appetite for reading. Keats is, with Wordsworth, the most popular of the English Romantics, and one or two of his odes ('To Autumn', 'On a Grecian Urn', 'To Psyche', 'To a Nightingale') are as famous as any English poetry outside Shakespeare. He came from a poor, devoted family that was riven by tuberculosis, and trained, but never practised, as a surgeon.

His early work, including the sonnet 'On First Looking into Chapman's Homer' (1816), received little attention, while his letters, now a major reason for his fame, were not published

Above: Shelley's funeral. Byron wrote of the 'extraordinary effect such a funeral pile has, on a desolate shore, with mountains in the background and the sea before... All of Shelley was consumed, except his heart, which... is now preserved in spirits of wine'.

Opposite: The manuscript of Keats's 'Ode to [a] Nightingale'.

sonnet on 'Fame'; and the ballad 'La Belle Dame Sans Merci'. By early 1820 he was seriously ill with tuberculosis. He went to Italy, avoiding Shelley's circle at Pisa, in a bid for recovery, but died in Rome. His reputation rose steadily after his death and has never declined.

As a literary movement, Romanticism was essentially poetic, but it was also a period in which a new kind of prose developed. One aspect of the movement was an intense interest in the inner or private life of the individual, which found expression in the popularity of letters, memoirs and biographies. Autobiography, partly through the inspiration of the Romantic poets, became a literary genre for the first time. Criticism gained psychological depth; essayists discussed the fantastic, the process of creativity and the inadequacy of Reason and Classicism. They embraced new subject matter, including science and technology, or treated familiar subjects in a novel way.

CRITICS AND COMMENTATORS

COLERIDGE

Perhaps the most original and capacious mind of the Romantic era, Coleridge brought a subtler, more philosophical interpretation to literary criticism, both in his lectures and in works such as *Biographia Literaria* (1817), a massive if ill-organized work on 'literary life and opinions'. It contained practical advice to potential writers, but was fundamentally concerned with the meaning of 'imagination', and included studies of then little-known German writers, memorable reconsiderations of Shakespeare, and essays on the psychology of the creative process.

THE ESSAYISTS

Though a precocious youth, William Hazlitt (1778–1830) was nearly 30 before he concluded that he was intended for a life of letters, having spent much of his early years painting. The freshness of his style owed something to the early Romantics, though he later quarrelled with them on political and literary grounds. His vigour sprang from the intensity of his radical but idiosyncratic opinions, whether on great events such as the French Revolution, or on humbler matters such as mail-coach travel. Hazlitt's early works dealt with philosophical questions, but his true *métier* was as a critic and essayist, and he is almost unique in English literature in establishing so high a reputation entirely on such writings. Of his many volumes of essays, perhaps the best are *Characters in Shakespeare*, dedicated to Charles Lamb and much admired by Keats, *Lectures on the English Comic Writers*, and especially *The Spirit of the Age* (1825), containing critical portraits of many contemporaries.

Thomas de Quincey (1785–1859) is chiefly remembered for *Confessions of an English Opium Eater* (1821), which first appeared in the *London Magazine*. He was devoted to the Wordsworths and took over Dove Cottage from them in 1834, but they were alienated by his opium addiction and his *Recollections of the . . . Lake Poets* (1834–39). From 1826, with a family to support, he wrote extensively for Blackwood's, including 'On Murder Considered as One of the Fine Arts' (1827, 1839), a minor masterpiece of black humour. As a stylist, he lacked Hazlitt's sparkle, adopting an original, if rather laboured, 'poetical' style to describe his opium-induced dreams.

COBBETT

A breezy contrast with the Romantics is presented by Thomas Cobbett (1763–1835), a democrat, patriot and powerful advocate of parliamentary reform. The kind of 'sublime' scenery that inspired the Romantics would have been roundly condemned by Cobbett for its barrenness – he liked to see a good field of turnips. A voluminous writer, with the knack of engaging the reader's sympathy with his strongly expressed views, he is remembered chiefly for his classic *Rural Rides* (1830, 1853), a collection of accounts of his exploration of the English counties on horseback.

THE WITS

The Essays of Elia (1823, 1833) are responsible for the affection in which Charles Lamb (1775–1834) has been held. They are largely 'blithe trivialities' (e.g. 'A Dissertation upon Roast Pig'), and the smiling, sentimental face that Elia presents reflects the kindly character of Lamb, who had a large circle of literary friends, maintaining lifelong friendships with Coleridge and Hazlitt. There is more to Lamb than that, however. He was a fine critic, even of writers who dealt with subjects that he was temperamentally unable to approach, such as Shakespeare (*Lamb's Tales from Shakespeare*

'I believe Shakespeare was not a whit more intelligible in his own day than he is now to an educated man, except for a few local allusions of no consequence. He is of no age – nor of any religion, or party or profession. The body and substance of his work came out of the unfathomable depths of his own oceanic mind; his observation and reading, which was considerable, supplied him with the drapery of his figures.
Coleridge, *Table Talk*, 15 March 1834.

Above: 'There was little cautious sparring... none of the *petit-maîtreship* of the art – they were almost all knock-down blows...' Hazlitt, 'The Fight' (1822). Etching by Rowlandson.

Opposite: Thomas de Quincey, an admirer of Wordsworth, took over Dove Cottage and edited the *Westmoreland Gazette*.

for children was hugely popular for generations). An edge to Lamb's poetry and essays is lent by knowledge of his private life: he devoted himself to caring for his insane sister, who had murdered their mother, and as a young man he himself suffered brief insanity. He also stuttered, a disability he sometimes exploited. (A lady at a dinner party: 'And how do you like babies, Mr Lamb?' 'B-b-b-boiled, Madam.')

A sharper, though genial, wit was the Revd Sydney Smith (1771–1845), a born satirist whose articles published in *The Edinburgh Review*, one of the first and weightiest of the political-literary journals founded in the early 19th century, were often devoted to mocking the Romantics.

Lamb's circle did not include the notoriously short-tempered Walter Savage Landor (1775–1864), who spent most of his adult life abroad. A man of great learning and fine critical perceptions, Landor's prose is distinctive, sometimes beautiful, and outside the mainstream, though his poetry is largely forgotten. He was much admired in the 19th century, not least by Browning, who looked after the angry old man in his last years in Florence.

THE GOTHIC NOVEL

An offshoot of Romanticism was the Gothic novel, inhabiting a literary underworld that has remained significant ever since and is currently manifest in innumerable science-fiction fantasies and tales of horror set in American suburbs. In fact it precedes the Romantic movement, dating from the mid-18th century. The word Gothic in the later 18th century came to mean wild and undisciplined, even crude – the antithesis of Classicism. Gothic novels were frequently set in the Middle Ages (a taste not confined to literature), in castles, monasteries and dungeons, and the plot depended on suspense and fantasy, frequently with a supernatural element.

WALPOLE

Horace Walpole (1717–97), son of the so-called 'First Prime Minister', was in many respects a quintessential 18th-century man of letters. He had a brilliant mind, no need to earn a living, no strong convictions, and much of his time was taken up with social matters: he had a large acquaintance and was a prolific correspondent. He also had a distaste, ahead of the Romantics, for commercialism and the rule of Reason and, prior to the Pre-Raphaelites, a love of medieval culture, or at least his notion of that culture. The tangible memorial of this predilection is his jewel-like 'medieval' villa, Strawberry Hill, near Twickenham, where the bookcases were modelled on the altar screen at Chartres. Walpole's *The Castle of Otranto* (1765) is generally cited as the first 'Gothic' novel. It is a medieval daydream, set in Italy, full of mysterious terrors and supernatural menace. It was a great popular success, which perhaps misled the cultured Walpole into supposing he had composed a work of art.

William Beckford (1759–1844), a millionaire, built himself a larger, though less attractive, Gothic residence, Fonthill Abbey, and wrote *Vathek* (1786), set in the mysterious and fantastic Orient, full of strange and cruel passions, the sort of book whose author would now be suspected of harbouring deviant and anti-social desires, as indeed Beckford seems to have done.

TERROR TALES

The best-known later exponents of the *fin-de-siècle* 'terror tale' were Mrs Ann Radcliffe (1764–1823) and Matthew Gregory Lewis (1775–1818), generally known as 'Monk' Lewis after his most famous book *The Monk*, a debased version of Faust. The most popular of Mrs Radcliffe's five novels is *The Mysteries of Udolpho* (1794), a fairly typical example of the genre: the innocent young heroine falls into the hands of Montoni, the cruel and all-powerful proprietor of a grim, remote and haunted castle. Eventually the supernatural elements turn out to have a rational explanation. Novels such as these were extremely popular among readers at the circulating libraries, where books could be borrowed for a small fee, a major stimulus to fiction writing in the late 18th and 19th centuries.

The Gothic novel had some effect on better writers, including Byron and Shelley. In *Northanger Abbey*, probably written about 1798–1800, Jane Austen mocked the genre by contrasting it with real life. Shelley's friend Thomas Love Peacock (1785–1866) exploited aspects of the genre in his satires of Romantic excesses. The Brontës, on their Yorkshire moor, certainly read Gothic novels: Charlotte Brontë's Rochester (in *Jane Eyre*) has been called a middle-class Montoni, and Emily's *Wuthering Heights* provides further evidence.

FRANKENSTEIN

The supernatural and macabre tales of the Romantic era are today almost completely unread, with one most notable exception: *Frankenstein, or the Modern Prometheus* (1818) by Mary Shelley (1797–1851). It certainly transcends the genre, though whether it can bear all the critical weight that has been loaded on it is another question. Mary Shelley said that the idea came to her in a half-dreaming state, arising from a light-hearted agreement with Shelley and Byron in Switzerland in 1816 that each should write a story of the supernatural. The others never completed theirs. She adopted the epistolary form, technically perhaps something of an advantage with this type of subject matter.

Frankenstein, a well-meaning philosopher-scientist, discovers how to create life artificially in a creature he assembles from spare parts of corpses. The result is a monster, hideous in appearance and superhuman in strength, who horrifies all normal human beings, and having acquired human emotions through its reading of Milton, Goethe and so on, turns murderous when Frankenstein breaks his promise to provide him with a mate. Frankenstein pursues it to the Arctic, meeting the British explorer whose letters tell the story, and dies. The monster disappears into the frozen wastes, seeking its own death.

Besides being a pioneer work of science fiction, *Frankenstein* is also a variation on the theme of the Rousseauesque 'Noble Savage', a good creature ruined by 'civilized' society. It has inspired a legion of films, most of them failing, or not attempting, to capture the resonances of the story.

After Shelley's death, Mary settled in England and later wrote a number of other novels, one (*The Last Man*, 1826) set in the future, but none has the power and vision of *Frankenstein*.

SIR WALTER SCOTT

The historical novel, meaning one dealing with a time before the author's birth, was not invented by Sir Walter Scott. An early example was the Comtesse de La Fayette's *La Princesse de Clèves* and many 18th century Gothic novels were set in earlier times. *Castle Rackrent* (1800) by the Irish writer Maria Edgeworth, a pioneer of both the historical and the regional novel, was acknowledged as an influence by Scott, always a man to pay his debts. Still, *Waverley* (1814) first made the historical novel widely popular and established it permanently, not only in Britain, but throughout Europe.

LAIRD OF ABBOTSFORD

So far, the revisionists have hardly dented Scott's reputation as one of the most attractive and honourable people ever to publish a work of fiction. In his day he was hugely popular, but now he is little read. He trained at Edinburgh University as a lawyer, and acquired a profound knowledge of country folk and legends, travelling on horseback around Scotland on legal business. He was a poet first, and became famous after *The Lay of the Last Minstrel* (1805), the first of several verse romances. The most notable are *The Lady of the Lake* and *Marmion* (1808), about the Battle of Flodden.

Scott's industry and output amazed even his contemporaries, for he was also involved with a vast range of other literary work and public duties. One of his idiosyncrasies, only puritans would call it a fault, was a tendency to spend lavishly and live well, and in 1811 he bought the magnificent Borders estate of Abbotsford. Later, the failure of publishing companies with which he was involved brought him to the edge of bankruptcy. His *Journal*, covering this fraught period, makes moving reading. (One result, benefitting all writers, was that Scott's need for cash, backed by his ability to command huge sales, induced larger payments from publishers.)

Yet visitors to Abbotsford gained an impression of a lairdly if not leisurely existence, as if novel writing was a pastime undertaken on idle evenings. Such was Scott's output that it was suggested he must have written many of his novels much earlier, and merely produced them from a drawer on demand. Except for *Waverley*, started and abandoned several years before it was published, this was true only in the sense that much of Scott's material had long been stored away in his mind. Overwork was responsible for serious physical ailments in 1817–19,

Opposite: The march of the Highlanders through Edinburgh in 1745, an illustration from Waverley.

Left: The hall at Abbotsford, Scott's splendid – but expensive – residence above the Tweed, with a glimpse of the debt-laden author at work; after a watercolour by David Roberts, 1834.

and the frenetic activity of his last years, when he might have taken refuge in bankruptcy, but honourably insisted on working to pay his debts, led to his final illness and death. All creditors were paid in full.

THE NOVELIST

The success of *Waverley*, which sold out four editions in its first year, turned Scott permanently from poetry to fiction. It was published anonymously: all Scott's later novels bore the phrase, 'by the author of *Waverley*', and he did not publicly admit authorship until 1827. It concerns a young, romantic army officer at the time of the rebellion of 1745 who is attracted to the Jacobite cause. The novels thereafter came thick (literally, for they are immensely long) and fast. The majority, and on the whole the best (*Old Mortality*, *The Heart of Midlothian*, *Rob Roy*, *Red Gauntlet*), were also set in the Scotland of the recent past. Those set in the Middle Ages (*Ivanhoe*, *The Talisman*) lack some of the vigour and conviction of the Scottish novels, although *Kenilworth*, set in 16th–17th century England, and *Quentin Durward*, set in 15th-century France, albeit with many Scottish characters, have been especially popular.

Scott's most obvious contribution to the development of the novel was the addition of background. Fielding and Jane Austen created characters within a restricted environment, but Scott presents a great social panorama, with picturesque details drawn from his unrivalled knowledge and fertile imagination as well as fine descriptions of landscape and nature (ironically, a factor that probably alienates the impatient modern reader). In his rich array of characters, Scott surpasses Dickens, though, like Dickens, it may be said against him that psychologically, his characters are relatively superficial, their feelings and motives simple.

Scott was by nature perhaps too easy-going to deal with real tragedy, or with spiritual agony, and religion meant little to him. It has often been pointed out that his picture of the Middle Ages virtually omits the period's most powerful social institution, the Church. Modern historians can also criticize Scott on facts, but for good or ill, the popular – not to say romantic and superficial – image of Scottish history, perhaps even in Scotland, derives more from Scott than from the output of the historians. That mantle has, it seems, been inherited by Hollywood, which in turn colours our idea of Scott. He was certainly a great story teller, but he was also a serious writer with a deep concern for history and society.

O Caldeonia! stern and wild,
Meet nurse for a poetic child!
Land of brown heath and shaggy wood,
Land of the mountain and the flood,
Land of my sires! what mortal hand
Can e'er untie the filial band
That knits me to thy rugged strand!
Scott, *The Lady of the Lake* (1810), Canto VI.

GOBLIN MARKET
and other poems
by Christina Rossetti

"Golden head by golden head"

London and Cambridge
Macmillan and Co. 1862

CHAPTER SEVEN
THE 19THCENTURY: POETRY AND DRAMA

If this book had been written a century ago, Jane Austen might not have been mentioned. Posterity tends to linger before it picks and chooses, and partly for that reason – but also because of the sheer growth of literacy and reading – in the recent past more and more names clamour for inclusion, so that the task of selecting those who have contributed most to the development of literature becomes more difficult. At the same time, the variety of writing, the different schools and traditions, increases rapidly. There is a danger of being overwhelmed by '-isms'. However, in drama and, to a degree poetry also, the road is fairly well marked out until the last few decades of the 19th century, when the stirrings of modernism open paths leading in many new directions.

1845 Edgar Allan Poe's poem 'The Raven' is published in a New York paper

1848 The Pre-Raphaelite Brotherhood founded in England

1850 Tennyson is made Poet Laureate

1867 Charles Baudelaire dies

1879 Ibsen completes A Doll's House

1898 Chekhov's The Seagull is performed by the Moscow Art Theatre

The period corresponding roughly to the Romantic movement was also a period of dramatic social change, of transformation in the lives of many people and many parts of the country by the Industrial Revolution, and of struggle and social eruptions connected with the battle for reform. Naturally, these developments had profound effects on literature and the arts.

CLASSICISM AND NATURALISM

Above: **The well-to-do eased their consciences, and compensated for laissez-faire government, with charitable works to help ease the plight of the new, urban poor.**

REVOLUTION AND REFORM

Romanticism is sometimes pictured as a reaction to the Industrial Revolution, and, although that is too simple a view as in most countries Romanticism predated factories, the new industrial society certainly made an impression on the later Romantics and on other aspects of 19th-century literature. The social and economic changes produced a new, prosperous middle class of factory owners and merchants, self-made men often of little education – the Victorian burst of public-school building only benefitted their sons – and of even less taste. In so far as their aesthetic considerations went, they tended to favour the Classical rather than the Romantic tradition.

CLASSICISM

The stature of the great Romantic poets tends to conceal the fact that, during the Romantic period, not all artists and writers, not even all poets, were Romantics. George Crabbe, admired more than Wordsworth by Shelley and Byron, and Jane Austen's favourite poet, continued to write in the heroic couplets of the classical tradition. But what exactly was this tradition? The terms Classical, classic, and Neo-Classical tend to be interchange, which can cause confusion.

In a narrow sense, 'Classical' refers to the ideas and criteria of ancient Greece and Rome and, by extension, to the styles of later periods that largely follow from them. These aesthetic styles and ideas are generally regarded as embodying such qualities as simplicity, harmony, order and reason, and general obedience to accepted rules. In one sense or another, the Classical tradition has never been completely abandoned, but it has been more prominent in some periods than in others. The driving force of the European Renaissance was the rediscovery and revival of Classical (Greek and Roman) art and culture, with works such as Aristotle's *Poetics* and Horace's *Ars Poetica* being widely studied. Literature was governed by rules derived from them and defined in works such as Boileau's *Art of Poetry*(1674).

The revival of Classicism in the 18th century is often referred to as 'Neo-Classical'. It was

Lo! where the heath, with withering brake grown o'er,
Lends the light turf that warms the neighbouring poor;
From thence a length of burning sand appears,
Where the thin harvest waves its wither'd ears;
Rank weeds, that every art and care defy,
Reign o'er the land, and rob the blighted rye;
There thistles stretch their prickly arms afar,
And to the ragged infant threaten war...
George Crabbe, 'The Village' (1783).

Above: Every European country experienced revolutionary outbreaks in 1848, but in England it was confined to a large but peaceful demonstration for moderate reforms.

largely a revival of Renaissance Classicism rather than the genuinely Classical, although the name 'Augustan' applied to English literature in the late 17th–18th centuries signifies the impulse to formal perfection inspired by Roman literature of the early imperial period. The Enlightenment represented the peak of intellectual Classicism and (as further evidence of the misleading effects of creating categories) one of the greatest figures of the Enlightenment, Rousseau, was also the pioneer of Romanticism.

The two strains, Classical and Romantic, can be distinguished in a broad way in practically every generation. Shakespeare, it could be said, was a Romantic writer, but not a Classical one, whereas Racine and Corneille (who, unlike Shakespeare, followed the Aristotelian rules) were Classical. However, Shakespeare was a classic writer. The Latin word *classicus* meant a citizen of the highest rank, and 'classic' simply means, or should mean, first-rate, the best of its kind.

REALISM AND NATURALISM

The term Realism in literature also has more than one meaning. In general it means, simply, true to life, and can therefore be applied to at least some of the literature of practically any age or culture: the events narrated in an epic such as the *Iliad*, may not be realistic, but the details are. More narrowly, it is the name given to the movement, first evident in France before 1830, that represented a reaction against Romanticism. It was chiefly characteristic of the novel, where Realism is generally most readily achieved. Romanticism offered an idealized version of life, in which personal feelings figured prominently. Realism was down-to-earth, presenting a more accurate picture of life as it really is, with careful description of the world based on close observation.

In the general sense, the terms Realism and Naturalism are not clearly distinguishable. However, in the 19th century, Naturalism was the movement that followed from Realism – again, with France setting the pace. Realism was influenced by developments in the social sciences, some Realist novels resembling sociological tracts, and Naturalism was also largely a product of contemporary scientific developments, such as Charles Darwin's explanation of evolution. Accuracy of detail – truth to nature – was even more important, and greater emphasis was placed on the effects of environment on behaviour and the effects of heredity on the individual character. While also a characteristic of much fiction, Naturalism was of particular significance in drama too.

Partly as result of the upheavals of the French Revolution, and partly because Classicism was more strongly entrenched, the Romantic movement arrived later in France. It was influenced by England and Germany, although its father figure was François-René de Chateaubriand (1768–1848), whose *Genius of Christianity* (1802) was a major influence in the revival of religion in post-revolutionary France, and its most provocative leader was the novelist Victor Hugo (see page 116).

ROMANTIC POETS

The outstanding poets in France were less central to the Romantic movement than their equivalents in England. Alphonse de Lamartine (1790–1869) established his reputation with his lyrical and deeply personal *Méditations poétique* (1820). The most popular of the French Romantic poets, he not only wrote poetry, but also extensively on history, politics (he was a leading political figure), biography, travel and memoirs. Like Vigny, he had an English wife, wrote a poetic tribute to Byron,

FRENCH POETRY

and was widely translated into English from the 1820s.

The best poems of Alfred de Vigny (1797–1863) were published after his death. Vigny's Romanticism is pessimistic and stoical: he described his work as an 'epic of disillusionment', but retained his faith in the 'unconquerable' human mind. Unusually for a Romantic poet, he was a professional soldier for over a decade and his *Servitude et grandeur militaires* (1835) still finds a place in the knapsack of intellectually inclined soldiers (Vigny's reflections on the military life are wittily discussed in Anthony Powell's novel *The Valley of Bones*, 1964).

The lover of George Sand before her liaison with Chopin, Alfred de Musset (1810–57) made his mark with a translation of De Quincey's *Confessions*. His most famous poems, 'Les Nuits' (1835-37) and 'Le Souvenir' (1841) deal with the familiar Romantic theme of love denied. He is probably best known for his plays, in which humour and parody are more evident; in general, his work is suffused with that contemporary melancholy called *mal du siècle*.

BAUDELAIRE

One of the most significant influences on modern poetry, Charles Baudelaire (1821–67) was associated with the Parnassians, a group of poets in reaction against Romanticism, whose aims were formal perfection, restraint ('Classical' virtues), and objectivity. His great

Above: **Baudelaire's sensitivity was often offended, and his search for 'artificial paradises' via drugs accelerated his decline and early death.**

Right: **A cartoon of Rimbaud, the boy poet of the Symbolists, whose sonnet on the vowels in** *Les Illuminations* **gave each vowel a colour.**

work is *Les Fleurs du mal* (*The Flowers of Evil*, 1857), a collection of a hundred poems in various different metres, technically brilliant, in which the poet seeks to find beauty and order in a world that is often hideous, cruel – and boring. Baudelaire was arrested and six of the poems were banned as offensive to public morals, but the last edition, published just after his death, contains about fifty more poems, and the work is regarded as one of the greatest treasures of French literature. Today Baudelaire is rated highly as a critic, notably on art (painting and poetry were often closely linked in France). His prose includes commentary on De Quincey and descriptions of his own experiences with opium and hashish, and he was the French translator of Edgar Allan Poe.

RIMBAUD AND VERLAINE

Around the spectacularly intense revolutionary Arthur Rimbaud (1854–91), forerunner of Symbolism and Surrealism, legends cluster like flies around a carcass. From an early age he was in full revolt against every orthodox authority. His most famous poem, 'Le Bateau ivre' (The Drunken Boat), which exalts the quest for some unknown reality (the key to Rimbaud's alienated existence), was written aged 17 and he abandoned poetry altogether at 19. His finest works are the prose poems of *Illuminations* (1886) and *A Season in Hell* (1873), experimental products of his efforts to acquire the wisdom of a seer through 'disorientation of the senses'. For a troubled period in the early 1870s, he was the lover of Paul Verlaine (1844–96). He became a wanderer and spent his latter years as a trader deep in Africa.

Verlaine was a tormented, unstable character, one of the Parnassians and generally regarded as a Symbolist (though he rejected the label), who served a prison term (1873–74) for shooting and wounding Rimbaud in a quarrel. Reconverted to Catholicism, he wrote some of the finest religious poetry of any age, as well as some of the most musical and original lyrics of the century – especially in the early *Fêtes galantes* (1869) and *Romances sans paroles* (1874). He was a popular lecturer in England in 1875.

MALLARMÉ

Stéphane Mallarmé (1842-98), another of the founders of modern European poetry, was the outstanding master of Symbolism, the movement which, reacting against the objectivity of Realism and Naturalism, stressed the importance of suggestion and reverie and found subtle relations between sound, sense and colour. Mallarmé's 'L'Après-midi d'un faune' (1876) is a key Symbolist work. The preoccupations of the Symbolists led to obscurity, and Mallarmé's 'Un coup de dès jamais n'abolira le hasard' (1897), which employed ingenious typographical devices to suggest music, has been called the most difficult poem in the French language.

LONGFELLOW
AND HIS SUCCESSORS

After independence, there was a conscious attempt in the U.S.A. to forge a national literature, but in spite of the popularity of the tales of Washington Irvine and James Fenimore Cooper, there were few poets who achieved international stature, excepting William Cullen Bryant, whose *Thanatopsis* (1817) showed the influence of the Graveyard poets and early English Romanticism.

LONGFELLOW

Henry Wadsworth Longfellow (1807–82), however, became the most popular poet in the English-speaking world after Tennyson. A genius of narrative verse, Longfellow spent some years in England before taking up a professorship aged 29 at Harvard, where he remained the rest of his working life. His first major work was basically a prose romance, *Hyperion* (1839). *Ballads and Other Poems*, containing such sentimental favourites as 'The Wreck of the Hesperus' and 'The Village Blacksmith' appeared in 1841. He was already immensely popular long before publication of his best-known work, *The Song of Hiawatha* (1858), with its hypnotic, unrhymed metre, and in the same year, *The Courtship of Miles Standish*, based on a New England legend. *The Chaucerian Tales of a Wayside Inn* (1863)

contained the lively 'Paul Revere's Ride', commemorating a famous incident at the beginning of the American Revolution. The death of his second wife in a fire and advancing age lent a more sombre tone to Longfellow's later work.

POE

The enigmatic Edgar Allan Poe (1809–49) was a very different kind of poet, uninterested in 'national' literature and, as master of the macabre, representing the darker side of the Romantic movement. After a disastrous spell in the military (dishonourably discharged from West Point) he became a journalist and a fierce critic of what he considered second-rate American writing. His early poetry, technically complex and tinged with mysticism, was published at his own expense. His most famous poem, 'The Raven', appeared in a newspaper in 1845. Meanwhile, Poe's private life became increasingly disastrous, owing to illness, poverty, drink and mental instability, but he achieved some success, if not wealth, with his short stories, such as 'The Gold-Bug' and 'The Fall of the House of Usher', which appeared with other extraordinary Gothic horror stories in *Tales of the Grotesque and Arabesque* (1840). An early death prevented his enjoyment of international fame. Admirers included Baudelaire, Swinburne,

Wilde and Yeats, and psychologists, including Freud, have long been fascinated by the disquieting themes in Poe's work. He has been called the first detective-story writer and claimed as a pioneer by the existentialists, among others.

WHITMAN

Leaves of Grass (1855), the first collection of Walt Whitman (1819-92), was dedicated to Emerson and generally adhered to Transcendentalist doctrines, celebrating communion with nature. The sensual overtones provoked disapproval and lost him a good job in government, but more controversial was Whitman's style. In following Emerson's call for a genuinely American literature, Whitman adopted a loose, 'unbuttoned' style, employing colloquial language and specifically American idioms, which contemporary readers found coarse.

In general, apart from one favourable anonymous review (by himself), Whitman, previously known as a journalist and author of short stories, received little critical attention. This changed after the second (1860) edition of *Leaves of Grass*, containing many new poems, and still more after the Civil War, which cast some shadows over his vision of America. As a volunteer nurse, he experienced its horrors at first hand and led to some of his most famous poems, including his elegy for Abraham Lincoln, and 'O Captain! My Captain!'. After the war he worked in Washington D.C., and wrote, in prose, his vigorous defence of democracy, *Democratic Vistas* (1871). New editions of *Leaves of Grass* continued to appear, the last in the year of his death, when the original twelve poems had increased to over three hundred.

The image – rough, tough, old Walt, the prophet of American democracy and friend of the common man – was phoney, and some of Whitman's verse is as poor as people initially said it was. On the other hand, he was the first great American poet, a genuine original.

DICKINSON

In common with many poets of the time, Emily Dickinson (1830–86) came from New England. A lively and amusing young woman, she became a recluse in her mid-twenties, communicating only through letters. Her poetry was almost entirely unknown until after her death. Publication in 1890 created no immediate sensation, and her reputation as a major poet of arresting originality was only established recently. Her character, in spite of much research and speculation, remains mysterious.

Her poetry is peppered with allusions to violence, human and natural, and she is preoccupied with death, immortality and, above all, poetic vocation. She seems to have felt isolated, while simultaneously belonging to an exalted elite. She wrote in a unique style: 'sharp, staccato, often awkward, never far from thoughts of death, but when successful . . . wonderfully bold and concentrated . . . making the men of her time seem timid and long-winded.' [JBP]

'I think I could turn and live with animals,
they are so placid and self-contain'd,
I stand and look at them long and long.
They do not sweat and whine about their condition,
They do not lie awake in the dark and weep for their sins,
They do not make me sick discussing their duty to God,
Not one is dissatisfied, not one is demented with the mania of owning things,
Not one kneels to another, nor to his kind that lived thousands of years ago,
Not one is respectable or unhappy over the whole earth.'
Whitman, 'Song of Myself' (1855).

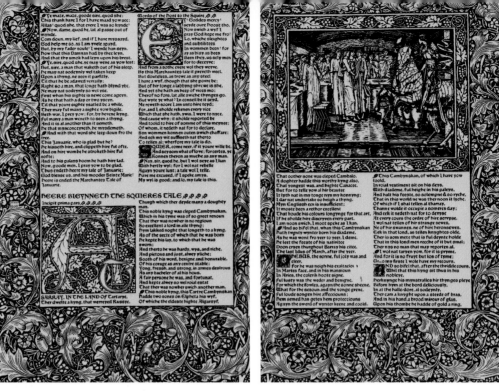

THE PRE-RAPHAELITES

The Pre-Raphaelite Brotherhood was founded in 1848 by Holman Hunt, John Everett Millais, the Rossetti brothers and others, a group of painters. They were in revolt against contemporary artistic standards as typified by the Royal Academy, and determined to revert to the principles prevailing before the High Renaissance, as represented by Raphael. Encouraged by Ruskin (see page 120), the Brotherhood existed as a close-knit group only for a few years. Broadly, Pre-Raphaelitism carried on the Romantic tradition. Its preoccupations included the study of nature in close detail, sound technique, and an inclination towards mystical (often medieval) subjects, influencing a number of later artists and writers.

ROSSETTI

The Rossettis' father was a political refugee from Naples, and Dante Gabriel Rossetti (1828–82), though born in London, grew up in an Italian household. Famous in his own day as a painter, he is the author of some of the most musical sonnets in English. As a student he knew Holman Hunt and Millais, and was one of the founders and leading representatives of the P.R.B. Like his painting, his early poetry was closely detailed, symbolic, concerned with remote subjects and often included archaic usage. Eroticism was another Pre-Raphaelite characteristic, and Rossetti married what the Pre-Raphaelites called a 'stunner', Elizabeth Siddal, in 1860. She died of an overdose of laudanum two years later, possibly encouraging the morbid strain in Rossetti's later work. His *Poems* of 1870 included works he had buried with Elizabeth, but later recovered. Some of his most attractive work, besides his translations of Dante and other Italian poets, appeared a year later in *Ballads and Sonnets*, but by that time he was in terminal decline due to drugs and incipient paranoia.

His younger brother William was another founder member of the PRB and editor of their journal, *The Gem*. He wrote profusely on literary subjects and worked for nearly fifty years for the Internal Revenue service.

Their sister Christina (1830–94) was a poet who is now widely regarded as being more gifted than her brothers. She was deeply religious and physically frail, an invalid in her later years. Probably her most famous work is *Goblin Market* (1862), a vigorous, enigmatically symbolic fairy tale, highly original in technique. A love of verbal and metrical experiment is characteristic of her work, which included many religious poems. Of these the most admired is the sonnet sequence 'Monna Innominata' (1881), which dwells on the superiority of divine love over human love, a conviction which seems to have influenced her private life.

MORRIS

Of all the people associated with the Pre-Raphaelites, William Morris (1834–96) was the greatest. However, he is remembered primarily in politics as a profound influence on British socialism, and in design as the leading light of the Arts and Crafts movement. His abilities were prodigious, his influence was – still is – enormous. His doctor explained his death as the result of being William Morris, having done more work than ten normal men. He was a copious writer, but his poetry, highly regarded in his day, is now seldom read. Probably his most famous literary work is his novel *News from Nowhere* (1890), a critique of contemporary society subsumed in a portrait of a communist, non-materialist utopia.

MINOR POETS

Among contributors to *The Gem* was the poet Coventry Patmore (1823–96), who became very popular through his series in praise of married life, *The Angel in the House* (1854–63), a sure winner in Victorian England (and a sure loser since). Arthur Henry Clough (1819–61) spent part of his life in America and was associated with Emerson and the Transcendentalists. He has only recently been recognized as having an unusual lyric gift (e.g. 'Say Not the Struggle Nought Availeth'), as well as a perceptive view of contemporary social and spiritual problems. Edward Fitzgerald (1809–93), a retiring country gentleman, was noted for one great poem, his translation (after having learned Persian in his forties) of the 11th century *Rubaiyat of Omar Khayyam* (1859).

SWINBURNE

When D. G. Rossetti was viciously attacked by Robert Buchanan in 'The Fleshly School of

Above: **A drawing of Christina Rossetti by her brother, the poet and painter Dante Gabriel Rossetti.**

Opposite: **Pages from the Kelmscott Press Chaucer. William Morris designed fonts and ornamental borders for the Press.**

Poetry', he was defended by Algernon Charles Swinburne (1837–1909), always ready for a literary fight. Swinburne was a prolific poet, immensely gifted, but often criticized for lack of depth – a safe judgment on someone who published so much. He first hit the headlines with his *Poems and Ballads* (1866), which, rebellious and perverse, might have been designed to irritate the bourgeoisie ('libidinous laureate of a pack of satyrs' fumed the critic John Morley). Swinburne, a 'Decadent' before his time, was certainly a shock after Tennyson. By 1879 he was a serious alcoholic, but was taken over by Theodore Watts-Dunton, who installed him in his house in Putney and reformed him. Surprisingly, Swinburne's muse survived this new regime, and he continued to publish his flamboyant poetry and criticism for another thirty years. He was a splendid scourge of prudes and pedants, and an invigorating influence on literature with his outspoken, if often wrong-headed, criticism.

The two giants of the later 19th century were Browning and, especially, Tennyson. In spite of periods of fierce critical antagonism, their reputation remains high today. The Romantics were either dead or poetically played out by the 1830s, and Browning and Tennyson represented a change, though not a particularly sudden or dramatic one. Romantics such as Byron were essentially popular poets, whose poetry was 'easy'. Although Tennyson, the only poet to become a peer, was hugely popular, both he and Browning moved on a somewhat higher plane. They nevertheless succeeded in maintaining a large audience for poetry in an age in which the novel had become the most popular form of literature.

THE BROWNINGS AND TENNYSON

THE BROWNINGS

Robert Browning (1812–89) is almost equally famous for his partnership with Elizabeth Barrett Browning (1806–61), who was initially the more popular poet. Although she had published previous collections, Elizabeth became famous with her *Poems* of 1844. At that time, illness, neurosis and a dominant father had reduced her to housebound hypochondria, but her work attracted Browning, who made contact. Romance followed and they eloped in 1846, settling in Italy. The 1850 edition of her *Poems* included 'Sonnets from the Portuguese', love poems written to her husband before their marriage. They have proved her most enduring work.

Although both were abundantly blessed with the gift of poetic imagination, the Brownings were otherwise dissimilar poets. Browning came to poetry very early, rejecting any other occupation, but his early work, some of it almost impenetrable, attracted little and

generally unfavourable notice. He only became famous after his wife's death with *The Ring and the Book* (1863), 21,000 lines of narrative blank verse about a terrible crime in 17th-century Rome. At a stroke, he became England's most celebrated poet after Tennyson, and his previously published work, notably *Men and Women* (1855), became immensely popular. In fact, nearly all Robert's best work was done during the course of his fifteen years of marriage, not the least of Elizabeth's contributions to English literature. Technical gifts apart, his greatest gift, in the opinion of many critics, was his intense curiosity. He enjoyed probing a problem, however complex, which largely explains a degree of obscurity in his work. He was also typically Victorian in the massive volume of his output, much of which seems today to be unduly verbose, but few writers excel him in capturing – often in dialogue – the atmosphere of an earlier age.

TENNYSON

What Gladstone was to Victorian politics, the tall and handsome, in later life shaggy-bearded Alfred Tennyson (1809–92) was to Victorian letters – the 'Grand Old Man', Poet Laureate for nearly half a century. He came from the large and doom-laden family of a Lincolnshire rector. It was something of a relief to escape to Cambridge University, where he became a devoted friend of an able contemporary, Arthur Hallam, and published two volumes of poetry that included 'The Lotos-Eaters' and 'The Lady of Shalott'. Hallam's death in 1833 was a terrible blow, which eventually produced *In Memoriam* (1850), perhaps the poet's most studied work and an extraordinary tribute which immortalized its subject.

Meanwhile, Tennyson's poems had made him famous, but not content. Twice during the 1840s he suffered near breakdowns, but his marriage to a devoted wife in 1850 brought him comparative peace and happiness. It also, coincidentally or not, marked the end of his period of creative genius. He was never to lose his almost unparalleled verbal artistry, and some of his most popular poems were written late in life, but his passion and originality faded after *Maud*, published in 1855, which he regarded as his greatest work, 'a little Hamlet, the history of a morbid, poetic soul, under the blighting influence of a recklessly speculative age'. In suiting the metre to the hero's mood, it is a fine example of Tennyson's extraordinary virtuosity, though it is not always readily comprehensible.

Poet Laureate from 1850, and one of the best in what tends to be a poetically uninspiring office, Tennyson, by nature extremely shy, became increasingly a public man. Popular fame accrued through poems such as his 'Ode on the Death of the Duke of Wellington', 'Charge of the Light Brigade' – one of the most famous in the language – and, more substantially, *The Idylls of the King* (1859–69), his most ambitious work, a retelling of Arthurian legend which he had started in 1833, returning to it in 1855. The first four (of twelve) books sold 10,000 copies within six weeks of publication in 1859.

It is Tennyson's earlier work, his more melancholy, pessimistic phase, that is most highly regarded by the majority of modern critics. 'His imagination responded most deeply to the doubtful and dismaying' (Christopher Ricks), but one of the great rewards of reading Tennyson is his visually perceptive descriptions of the world, especially the world of nature, which raise the question whether Tennyson was not a kind of Romantic after all.

Above: A contemporary caricature of the author of *The Idylls of the King*. Tennyson did not marry until 1850, perhaps fearing the 'black blood' of his family of depressives, epileptics and alcoholics.

Opposite: Browning in 1881. He was mainly self-educated, writing his first book of poetry at twelve.

With blackest moss the flower-pots
Were thickly crusted, one and all:
The rusted nails fell from the knots
That held the pear to the gable-wall.
The broken sheds look'd sad and strange;
Unlifted was the clinking latch;
Weeded and worn the ancient thatch
Upon the lonely moated grange . . .
Tennyson, 'Mariana' (1830).

As in England, so in Germany the 1830s represented a literary watershed. After the Romantic Golden Age, the Biedemeier poets retreated to domesticity. The careers of more progressive writers were hindered by the repressive censorship of conservative governments, led by Metternich's government in Vienna, and interrupted by the Revolution of 1848, when many (including Karl Marx) sought refuge abroad. Throughout the 19th century, the forms introduced by Goethe and Schiller, continued, such as the *Lied* in poetry derived from the folksong and the historical tragedy in drama from blank verse continued. In general, and in terms of their wider influence, the most significant literary figures in later 19th-century Germany were philosophers (Hegel, Nietzsche, Schopenhauer), historians (Ranke, Lamprecht) and dramatists, rather than poets. Though literary Romanticism was in decline, Romantic ideas were influential in other spheres, notably in politics, where they merged with the advance of German nationalism. The death of Goethe marked the end of the German classical tradition, yet among writers his influence was greater than that of the Romantics, though sometimes this was manifest as a rebellion against his predominance.

THE LEGACY OF GOETHE

Above: **The mausoleum of Schiller and Goethe at Weimar, where the partnership of the two giants of German literature is commemorated.**

Opposite: **Hamburg in the 1840s, about the time of Heine's visit there which inspired his epic,** *Deutschland: Ein Wintermärchen.*

HEINE

One of Germany's greatest poets, Heinrich Heine (1797–1856) preferred the more liberating atmosphere of Paris, where he lived from 1831, writing in both German and French. He called himself the last Romantic, but the Romanticism of his ever-*popular Book of Songs* (1827) is well laced with irony, and his critical works, which included ruthless attacks on Romanticism, are notable for savage and witty satire. Some of his best, and most sombre, poetry was written during his last eight years, when he was bedridden.

GRILLPARZER

The greatest Germanic playwright of the early 19th century was the Austrian Frans Grillparzer (1791–1872). His poetic tragedies were written in the Classical tradition, but lack its strength and confidence, his heroes and heroines generally coming to grief because of the feebleness of the individual will against the force of circumstances. Ambition, for Grillparzer's characters, is folly, or worse: the individual's only hope of happiness is to turn inwards, seeking spiritual peace through cultivating inner resources. In his earlier plays, there is a suggestion of the hostile Fates of Greek tragedy, but in his *Medea* (1822), a marriage leads to disaster when the two partners are so overburdened with guilt that they cannot take positive action: weakness of will, rather than the ineluctability of fate, is the fundamental cause of catastrophe. As his work suggests, Grillparzer was himself a gloomy character, beset by personal difficulties and self-doubt. In 1838, a particularly hostile reception for his latest play, surprisingly a comedy, caused him to withdraw permanently from the theatre, leaving several dramas unperformed (they were published after his death).

The sombre mood of Grillparzer's plays was characteristic of most contemporary German drama, even comedy. Neither Romanticism nor the Classical tradition appeared to have anything more to offer, but nothing had yet appeared to replace them. There were some signs of future developments, however, for example in the plays of Christian Friedrich Hebbel (1813–63), whose greatest work was the trilogy *Die Nibelungen*, based on the 12th-century epic which was exploited more famously later in the century by Wagner. Hebbel shared the common pessimistic outlook, but his work looked forward to realism and the psychological depth of the founders of modern drama.

BÜCHNER

A far more significant figure – to us though not to his contemporaries, who had never heard of him – is Georg Büchner (1813–37). Büchner was trained as a medical research scientist, and died, probably of typhoid, as he was about to take up a post at the University of Zurich. Although he was only 23, and never had a play performed in his lifetime, he was the author of an influential, prophetic and startling body of dramatic work. A revolutionary, he was forced to flee Germany as a result of his pamphlet, *The Hessian Courier* (1834), which anticipated Marx's *Communist Manifesto*, and wrote his first play, *Danton's Death* (1835) while in hiding. Though it celebrated the eponymous French Revolution hero, Büchner's pessimism later led him to conclude that

revolution was pointless and freedom a pipe dream. *Leonce and Lena* (1836) satirizes the Romantic tradition, and *Dantons Tod* (1835) is a tragedy of hopeless heroism. But it is Büchner's last play, the stark drama *Wozzeck*, or *Woyzeck* (1837), about an ill-used barber who stands for the insignificance and vulnerability of individuals in a hostile and vicious universe, which, far ahead of its time, chiefly accounts for his reputation as the forerunner of many movements in modern drama – Expressionism, Naturalism, Absurdism, etc. The play was the basis for Alban Berg's scarcely manageable – and therefore seldom staged – but powerful opera, *Wozzeck* (1925).

'Dieses merkt Euch, Ihr stolzer Männer der Tat. Ihr seid nichts als unbewusste Handlanger der Gedankenmänner . . . Maximilien Robespierre war nichts als die Hand von Jean Jacques Rousseau, die blutige Hand, die aus dem Schosse der Zeit den Leib hervorzog, dessen Seele Rousseau geschaffen.'

'Note this, you proud men of action. You are nothing but the unconscious hodmen of the men of ideas . . . Maximilien Robespierre was nothing but the hand of Jean Jacques Rousseau, the bloody hand that drew from the womb of Time the body whose soul Rousseau had created.'
Heine, *Neue Gedichte* (1844), trans. Untermeyer.

In general, 19th-century European drama was undistinguished. It was artificial and out of touch with changing times. Theatre-going was increasingly popular, but more for the Italian opera, for the crude melodrama that represented a hangover from Romanticism, and for early forms of 'variety'. The productive Anglo-Irishman Dion Boucicault was responsible for about 200 plays, including adaptations, but is chiefly remembered for establishing playwrights' copyright in America. In France, Eugene Scribe pioneered the genre of the 'well-made play', well-constructed, but not much else. The most popular playwright in the later 19th century was probably Victorien Sardou, with his intense, but phoney, emotionalism lavishly staged. The theatre awaited a genius, and he arrived, like Father Christmas, from the north.

IBSEN AND STRINDBERG

No one disputes the status of the Norwegian Henrik Ibsen (1828–1906) as the founder of modern dramatic realism. He was the first to find the material of great tragedy in the lives of ordinary people. His literary career began in the 1840s, but it was the poetical plays, *Brand* (1866), originally a poem, and *Peer Gynt* (1867) that established his reputation in Norway. His genius was not widely recognized abroad until later – in Britain through partisans such as the critic William Archer and, subsequently, George Bernard Shaw. A single London performance of *Ghosts* (1881), which concerns adultery and mentions syphilis, caused an outcry and made him famous, if controversial.

Ibsen learned stagecraft as a theatre director in Bergen and Christiana, later Oslo, in 1851–62, and he was influenced by the dramatic theories of Hermann Hettner, who emphasized the importance of psychological truth in tragedy, and the middle-class tragedies of Hebbel. Cramped in Norway, from 1864 to 1891 he and his wife lived abroad. His literary career, which lasted half a century and produced twenty-five plays as well as some poetry, can be roughly divided between a Romantic phase, up to 1875,

THE BIRTH OF MODERN DRAMA

when he wrote mainly dramatic verse, and the remaining period when he employed everyday language in the interests of greater realism.

In plays up to *An Enemy of the People* (1882), he was chiefly concerned with moral, social and political themes, but in his last plays, including *Rosmersholm* (1886) and *The Master Builder* (1896), he sought to penetrate the unconscious (earning the approval of Freud). Besides those mentioned, the plays most often performed today are *A Doll's House* (1879), *The Wild Duck* (1884) and *Hedda Gabler* (1890).

The neurotic Swedish writer August Strindberg (1849–1912) was almost as influential in modern drama as Ibsen. He was constantly at

CHEKHOV

The subtle, humane, and perceptive Russian writer Anton Chekhov (1860–1904) was possibly more influential in Britain than either Ibsen or Strindberg. Equally admired for his short stories, Chekhov wrote, late in his career, four great plays: *The Seagull* (1895), *Uncle Vanya* (1900), *Three Sisters* (1901) and *The Cherry Orchard* (1904). In conjunction with Stanislavsky's productions, the plays made the reputation of the Moscow Art Theatre, though Stanislavsky's Naturalism was probably not the best style for Chekhov (opinions on what that best style is are still in question), in whom Naturalism is blended with Symbolism.

SHAW

George Bernard Shaw (1856–1850) remarked that seeing Chekov made him want to tear up his own plays. Not the least of Shaw's virtues was his powerful advocacy on behalf of the great European originals, Ibsen, Strindberg and Chekhov. Enormously intelligent, wonderfully witty (there is something in the criticism that what he said was less original than the way he said it), a propagandist for every good cause from vegetarianism to women's rights, Shaw bestrode his age in an almost Johnsonian fashion, and the dip in his reputation since his death is no doubt temporary. That he was not a truly great playwright is due to the fact that he was primarily interested in ideas, not in people. Nevertheless, his plays have a unique and enjoyable Shavian flavour. Comedies such as *Arms and the Man* (1894) and *Pygmalion* (1913) still sparkle, *Saint Joan* (1923) is a fine historical drama, *Heartbreak House* (1919) a lesson in how to construct a play out of a debate.

odds with convention – social, moral and sexual. He was once tried (but acquitted) for blasphemy and was three times married and divorced, though the charge of misogyny often made against him seems rather simplistic. *Inferno* (1898), written in French, is an extraordinary account of his mental crisis in Paris in which he came near to madness. Sexual conflict and psychological anguish are frequent themes, notably in *Miss Julie* (1888), his most often performed play today, which is also concerned with another of Strindberg's obsessions, social class. Besides *Miss Julie*, his best plays in his aggressive and unusual brand of Naturalism, are *Master Olof* (1881), *The Father* (1887) and *Creditors* (1889). Later plays – intense, symbolic, psychological dramas, notably the trilogy *To Damascus* (1898–1901), and *The Dance of Death* (1901) – are suffused with religious longing.

'The Archbishop: . . . If I were a simple monk, and had not to rule men, I should seek peace for my spirit with Aristotle and Pythagoras rather than with the saints and their miracles.
Le Trémouille: And who the deuce was Pythagoras?
The Archbishop: A sage who held that the earth is round, and that it moves round the sun.
Le Trémouille: What an utter fool! Couldn't he use his eyes?'
Shaw, *Saint Joan*, sc. ii.

The last decade of the 19th century, when the great Victorian poets had passed from the scene, was a period not of great literature but of great literary interest. In English poetry, the dominant influences were French – Rimbaud and Verlaine – and there was a prevailing preoccupation with the notion of end-of-the-century decadence, with the poet as a doomed figure ('decadent' poets and artists certainly tended to die young: Ernest Dowson at 33, Lionel Johnson at 35, the illustrator Aubrey Beardsley at 26, Oscar Wilde at 46).

OSCAR WILDE
AND THE AESTHETIC MOVEMENT

THE AESTHETIC MOVEMENT

The aesthetic movement derived largely from the Pre-Raphaelites, and aroused some mockery in less refined circles for its exaggerated preference for antique ideals of beauty and affectations of speech and dress, which were motivated to some extent by the now customary desire to shake up the bourgeoisie. On a more serious level, as explained by one of its progenitors, the much-renowned critic Walter Pater (1839–94), it was concerned with 'not the fruit of experience, but experience itself . . . for ever curiously testing new opinions and courting impressions, and never acquiescing in a facile orthodoxy'. Among artists, the current phrase, again originating with Pater though current earlier in France, was 'art for art's sake' (l'art pour l'art), the idea that art was not and should not be in any way 'useful' and, as Wilde put it, 'never expresses anything but itself'. As with the Pre-Raphaelities, there were strong bonds between artists and writers, who co-operated in the

pages of *The Yellow Book* and the Savoy magazine, while Wilde and Whistler famously exchanged quips in the Café Royal.

WILDE

A few years before his death Oscar Wilde (1854–1900) told the young André Gide that he had put his talent into his works and his genius into his life. No one would question his genius, and his literary reputation is now higher than it was once, but the impression remains that his cherished memory is due more to his persona than his writing. Born in Dublin (like Shaw), he was the son of a prominent physician and an egotistical poet who called herself Speranza. After Trinity College, he went to Oxford, where he won the Newdigate Prize for English verse. His journalism and his flamboyant espousal of the aesthetic movement and 'art for art's sake' made him a public figure. He shocked the Americans too, on a lecture tour, with his velvet breeches and silk stockings, not to mention his statement to the New York Customs, that he had 'nothing to declare except my genius'. He was satisfyingly guyed by Gilbert and Sullivan in *Patience*, and got married in 1884 to a pretty and tolerant young woman who gave him two sons. Their London home became a social centre of the avant-garde.

In 1892, none too soon, Wilde finally achieved popular fame with his play *Lady Windermere's Fan*, a witty and edgy social comedy. He followed it with *A Woman of No Importance* (1893), *An Ideal Husband* (1895) and *The Importance of Being Earnest* (1895). Wilde's reputation depends largely on his last play, one of the most brilliant comedies in the British theatre, a cornucopia of briskly witty dialogue enhanced by brilliant characterization, especially of the minor characters – Lady Bracknell, Miss Prism, Canon Chasuble – and a deft if superficial plot. At the height of his success, Wilde became involved in a sexual scandal as a result of his association with Lord Alfred Douglas, son of the crude and reactionary Marquess of Queensberry. Convicted of homosexual practices, he was sentenced to two years in prison. Afterwards, ruined in every sense, he went to Paris, wrote 'The Ballad of Reading Gaol' (1898) and died two years later. 'Neither in literature nor in life was tragedy his natural element', wrote Peter Quennell. 'His role was not to plumb the depths of feeling, but to flicker delicately across the surface.' Besides *Salomé*, the basis of Richard Strauss's opera, and other plays, his writings included a novel, *The Picture of Dorian Gray* (1890), *The Happy Prince* (1888), fairy stories for his children, and *The Soul of Man Under Socialism*, a plea for artistic and individual freedom, provoked by a lecture by G. B. Shaw.

FARCE

The 1890s was also the decade in which French farce reached its peak, in the concoctions of Georges Feydeau (1862–1921). Unlike the stock characters and improvisation of the *commedia dell'arte* tradition, the type of farce of which Feydeau was the supreme exponent (in *Hotel*

Above: **Covers from early editions of** *The Yellow Book*, **designed by its art editor, Aubrey Beardsley, who died of tuberculosis aged 26.**

Opposite: **The Prince of Decadence: Oscar Wilde, a cartoon from** *Punch* **after he had achieved fame with** *Lady Windermere's Fan.*

Paradiso, *The Lady From Maxim's* and others) depended on careful plotting and elaborate, precise staging, with minimal characterization (since it would hold up the breakneck action). The subject matter was invariably domestic life and extramarital escapades, with misunderstandings, mistaken identities, etc., all resolved with remarkable ingenuity.

Duchess of Berwick: Do you know, Mr Hopper, dear Agatha and I are so much interested in Australia. It must be so pretty with all the dear little kangaroos flying about.

Wilde, *Lady Windermere's Fan*, Acts II, III.

CHAPTER EIGHT
THE 19TH CENTURY:
PROSE

In the 19th century the Romantic movement, the Industrial Revolution and the – largely hostile – interaction between them, combined to create a culture markedly different from the assured and orderly world of the 18th century. The attempt made by European statesmen in 1815 to bottle up the effects of the French Revolution and the reforms of the Napoleonic era looked to be in constant danger of disintegration, especially in the first half of the century. After 1848, growing material prosperity reduced the likelihood of bloody revolution and class war, especially in Britain, but that is only evident in hindsight. Large social problems remained: they occupied the attention of many practitioners of what became the major literary form – the novel.

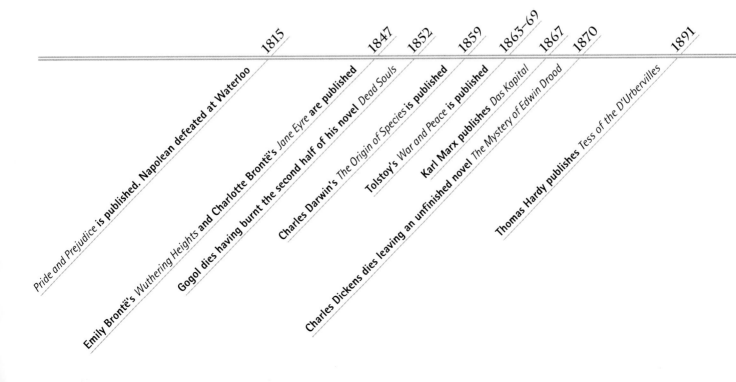

1815
Pride and Prejudice is published. Napolean defeated at Waterloo

1847
Emily Brontë's Wuthering Heights and Charlotte Brontë's Jane Eyre are published

1852
Gogol dies having burnt the second half of his novel Dead Souls

1859
Charles Darwin's The Origin of Species is published

1863–69
Tolstoy's War and Peace is published

1867
Karl Marx publishes Das Kapital

1870
Charles Dickens dies leaving an unfinished novel The Mystery of Edwin Drood

1891
Thomas Hardy publishes Tess of the D'Urbervilles

THE SPREAD OF
LITERACY

In Europe during the 19th century there was an enormous increase in the number of books published and read. The sheer volume of literary – and, increasingly, sub-literary – production makes it increasingly difficult to generalize about styles, movements and taste, or to keep track of significant writers. There is, too, an increasingly sharp divide between the work of significant writers and a reading public indifferent or hostile to their work, a hostility often administered to *épater le bourgeoisie*. This continues today, but it should not be exaggerated. Though true of many avant-garde or experimental writers, the fact remains that those whom posterity regards as the greatest writers of the century, Dickens, say, or Tolstoy, were also extremely popular (although Dickens's prodigious sales were far exceeded by the now unread Charlotte M. Yonge).

PAPER AND PRINTING

As in so many other aspects of life, the expansion of publishing was made possible by basic advances in technology. Industry stimulated population growth, which was concentrated in towns, and provided easier communication and the facilities for making reading matter widely available. More specifically, great advances were made in papermaking and printing, with results hardly less dramatic than the invention of printing with movable type in the 15th century.

Until the end of the 18th century, paper was made by hand. The first papermaking machine consisted of an endless wire-mesh web which, as it was turned, dipped into a vat of pulp and lifted out a layer of pulp. It was invented before 1800, but was not used commercially for some years to come. Further advances in papermaking included chlorine-bleaching and the adoption of

Above: **Papermaking machine** c.1853. **Paper-making and printing were revolutionized in the 19th century, leading to much new publishing.**

wood pulp rather than textile fibres as the basic raw material, permitting paper manufacture on a greatly increased scale.

The cylinder press was the first great advance in printing. An early, steam-driven commercial example was installed by *The London Times* and could print 1,000 sheets an hour. The first 'web-fed' press, which printed on a continuous roll of paper, was in use before 1840. New methods of printing included lithography, in which ink is applied to a water-absorbent stone on which the image to be printed is drawn in a greasy substance, and photoengraving, which exploited the discovery that certain chemicals harden and become insoluble in proportion to the amount of light to which they are exposed. Ingenious new devices, notably the linotype machine, successfully mechanized the time-consuming process of setting type.

LITERACY

At about the end of the 18th century, an English farmer's wife, annoyed at the opening of a village school, remarked that 'it was preordained that [the poor] should be ignorant'. Such an attitude, common then, had almost entirely disappeared 100 years later, when primary education was made compulsory in most countries of western Europe. Secondary education, especially for girls, was more patchy ('England's,' said Matthew Arnold, raging at aristocratic 'barbarians' and middle-class 'Philistines', was 'the worst in the world'), but the majority of the population, including manual workers, could read and write. The reforms that had brought this situation into being were not of course intended to bring the joys of literature to the working class, but rather to ensure that they could read the instructions on the machine or the voting paper, but the effect was still the same. Perhaps the chief result was to produce a vast amount of the sort of 'books we could do without', but it also created many thousands of new readers for Dickens and the Brontës.

LIBRARIES

Subscription libraries multiplied in the early 19th century, a notable event being the founding, thanks largely to the influence of Thomas Carlyle, of the London Library in 1841 and still going strong. A few public libraries had existed in England since the 17th century, but the first Act of Parliament authorizing the establishment of public libraries on a national scale was passed in 1850 (some American states were earlier). Due chiefly to inadequate funding, progress was rather slow for many years, and the sales of Victorian novelists continued to depend largely on the circulating libraries (see page 86), some of which continued in existence until the mid-20th century. A large number of public libraries were founded as memorials to Queen Victoria's jubilee (1887) and tremendous impetus was provided in the early years of the 20th century by the philanthropy of the Scottish-born steel magnate Andrew Carnegie, who presented thousands of library buildings to towns all over the British Empire and the U.S.A. Meanwhile, in addition to libraries such as the British Museum and the Bibliothèque Nationale of older foundation, national libraries of various kinds were established in most countries, as well as academic and privaely endowed specialist libraries.

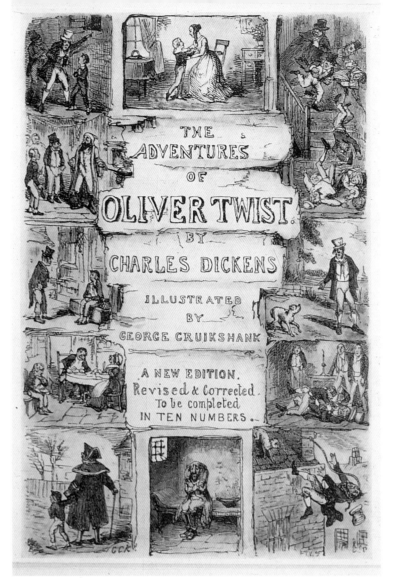

THE 19TH-CENTURY NOVEL

The development of the novel in the 19th century is an extraordinary episode in literary history. Less than 100 years separates Fanny Burney's *Evelina*, highly regarded by discerning judges of the time, from George Eliot's *Middlemarch*, but the cultural gap is similar to that between the Bronze Age and the Renaissance.

Above: **The serialisation of novels offered opportunities for artists too. George Cruikshank (1792–1878) illustrated** *Oliver Twist.*

Opposite: **Dickens reading** *A Christmas Carol* **to a group of literary friends. Alexander Dyce (extreme right), appears overcome.**

THE VARIETY OF THE NOVEL

The 19th century provided plenty of evidence for the idea that the novel is not so much a literary form amenable to categorization as the product of limitless aspects of popular culture. As the Russian critic Bakhtin remarked, the novel draws from 'that broadest of realms, the common people's creative culture . . .', and the 19th-century novel is so rich and various that it is impossible to characterize generically. The number of novels published in Britain alone during the course of the century has been conservatively estimated at 40,000. Few topics were excluded from their pages, few contemporary problems went unaddressed and, in judging 19th-century novelists, the social and political context is no less important than the purely artistic.

As for form or character, a profusion of '-isms' can be distinguished, which often represent contradictory trends. Many themes can be listed, however none can be said to encapsulate the spirit or character of the age. Melville's *Moby Dick* and Dickens's *David Copperfield* were published within a few months of each other; though both were novels, and were written in the same language, in nearly every other respect they were totally different works of art.

THE VARIETY OF NOVELISTS

Thomas Love Peacock (1785–1866) is an example of a novelist who belonged to no literary movement and obstinately avoids classification. A close friend of Shelley, he was also a satirist of Romanticism – and of most other contemporary styles, notions and fashions. Not much interested in characterization or plot, he set up ideas – and deftly demolished them – in ingeniously constructed dialogue.

After Scott, it was possible to be a successful professional novelist, even a comparatively rich one, but only for a very few; even those with the most compelling vocation were often forced to seek other means of support. Peacock was saved from penury by having a clerkship for most of his life in the East India Company, winning plaudits for designing an iron steamship.

A novelist such as Edward Bulwer Lytton (1803–73), who had an active political career and became a peer, exemplifies another way in which some 19th-century novelists elude accepted categories: sheer versatility. His novels, over 20 of them and in most cases very long, were only part of his huge literary output, but they embraced a vast range of forms – historical novels in the tradition of Scott, novels of social protest, of crime, or 'terror', and a Utopian novel *The Coming*

novels, as Trollope said, 'from the Prime Minster down to the . . . scullery maid'. The majority of readers (as well as a large proportion of the writers) were women – more middle-class wives than hard-worked scullery maids, no doubt – and it is ironic that, for most of the century, novelists male and female were seriously hampered by the need to follow Victorian notions of respectability, so that female characters had to be either virtuous or damned.

'Two nations between whom there is no intercourse and no sympathy; who are as ignorant of each other's habits, thoughts, and feelings, as if they were dwellers in different zones or inhabitants of different planets; who are informed by a different breeding, are fed by a different food, are ordered by different manners, and are not governed by the same laws.'
   'You speak of – ' said Egremont hesitatingly.
   'THE RICH AND THE POOR.'
Disraeli, *Sybil*, bk. ii, ch. 5.

Race (1871). He was a literary giant in his day, though he is all too seldom read now.

Social commentary is a major ingredient of 19th-century fiction, and many novelists became embroiled in public events, notably Zola in the Dreyfuss affair. The most remarkable exponent of politics combined with novel writing was Benjamin Disraeli (1804–81), British Prime Minister and international statesman. The political novels for which he is best known, *Coningsby*, *Sybil*, and *Tancred*, upholding his romantic, one-nation ideals, were written in the 1840s, before he achieved high office, but his last novel, *Lothair*, was published in 1870, between his two spells as prime minister. It was almost as lively as his first, the absurd (but amusing) *Vivien Grey*, published 44 years earlier.

NOVEL READERS

Although novel reading was often regarded as a frivolous activity, nearly everyone read

For most of the 19th century, novels in Britain were commonly published in three volumes and, priced at 55p, were beyond the means of many readers. However, the price of a couple of novels could buy a year's membership of a circulating library. Later, novels, including those of nearly all the major novelists, were published as monthly serials, either as slim single volumes published independently or, more often as time went on, in a weekly magazine such as Dickens's *Household Words*. These arrangements had important effects on the form that novels took. Mudie's, the largest of the circulating libraries, in practice exercised a kind of censorship by declining novels of which they disapproved: a refusal could have a disastrous effect on sales. Serial publication, like TV soap operas today, were inclined to end each instalment with a cliff-hanger to keep the readers' interest. Plots might be altered, popular characters written up, unpopular ones dropped, according to public reaction.

The difference between the two most distinguished novelists of the early 19th century was summed up in his *Journal* by one of them, Sir Walter Scott, in a comment on the other, Jane Austen: 'The Big Bow-Wow strain I can do myself like any now going; but the exquisite touch, which renders ordinary commonplace things and characters interesting, from the truth of the description and the sentiment, is denied to me.'

JANE AUSTEN

THE RECTOR'S DAUGHTER

The father of Jane Austen (1775–1817) was rector of Steventon in Hampshire until his retirement in 1801, when the family moved to the fashionable spa city of Bath, returning to Hampshire after his death in 1805. Jane Austen never went to school, but was taught by her father, who encouraged her to read widely. She never married, though she had several suitors, and continued to live with her mother and sister, Cassandra, until her death at 41. It was a remarkably uneventful life, but provided the material for a series of novels which, though not particularly successful in her own time, have held their readership ever since – and have recently proved extraordinarily popular in film and television adaptations. Her career coincided almost exactly with the era of Napoleon (her brother served in the Navy under Nelson at Trafalgar), but these were matters famously excluded from the world of her novels (as one of her characters complained about history, all

the men were good-for-nothings and there were hardly any women at all).

In spite, or because, of her remoteness from the literary world, Jane Austen had a clear idea of the scope of her own talent, and was never tempted to stray beyond it. Her novels were all set within the narrow circle of the country gentry and her plots were all concerned with courtship and marriage. At the time, largely as a result of the tales of terror and romance that supplied the circulating libraries, fiction was widely regarded as not entirely respectable, but the remark in *Northanger Abbey* that in the

Above: **Portraits of Jane Austen are scarce. This is based on a drawing by her sister, Cassandra.**

Opposite: **An illustration from** *Sense and Sensibility,* **which contrasts the way two sisters deal with the problem of love denied.**

novel 'the greatest powers of the mind are displayed', although characteristically ironic, nevertheless indicates a thoroughly serious approach. Like Fielding, Jane Austen saw the novel as an art form, demanding close study and careful planning. What appears a straight-forward story casually told, tempting the ill-informed into remarks about 'Regency soap opera', is in fact the result of hard-won preci-sion, all the more remarkable in the light of our knowledge that the later novels at least were written at the table in the family parlour, where concentration must have been difficult.

PRIDE AND PREJUDICE

Owing to the vagaries of publishers, Jane Austen's novels were not published in the order in which she wrote them; two, *Northanger Abbey*, known to be an early work, and *Persuasion*, were not published until after her death. Her first work, written at fifteen, was a burlesque of Richardson. She had no time for Richardson's high moral tone, nor for sentimen-tality either, which she mocked in other early exercises. Her satirist's eye was directed at the popular taste for the macabre; in *Northanger Abbey* the episode presented a perceptive view of how imagined horrors may work on the mind. It was sold to a publisher (for £10) in 1803, several years after it was written, but remained unpub-lished until 1818. *Pride and Prejudice* was first written in 1797 as 'First Impressions', and rejected by a London publisher. Revised and reti-tled, it appeared in 1813. It is probably Jane Austen's best-known, perhaps her best, book. The intelligent, headstrong Elizabeth Bennett, the author's favourite heroine, and the supercil-ious but romantic Mr Darcy provide the conflict between 'pride' (Darcy) and 'prejudice' (Elizabeth). Although there is a deepening subtlety in the later novels, *Pride and Prejudice* represents an author in full command of her art, and has a certain extra sparkle of youth. Some vivid minor characters are almost as familiar as the characters of Shakespeare or Dickens.

THE LATER NOVELS

There is a considerable interval in Jane Austen's work during roughly the first decade of the 19th century, probably caused by family matters and her father's death in 1805, when she abandoned work on her current book, *The Watsons*. *Sense and Sensibility* dated back to a sketch of 1795, and was rewritten twice before publication in 1811. After *Pride and Prejudice* there was little difficulty with publishers, and it was followed by *Mansfield Park* (1813) and *Emma* (1816), warmly reviewed by Scott. *Persuasion* was written in 1815 and her last book, *Sanditon*, was unfinished when she died of Addison's disease.

Jane Austen had many contemporary admir-ers, including the Prince Regent (later George IV), but also some critics, including Charlotte Brontë and Elizabeth Barrett Browning. Her cult status in English literature dates from the late 19th century, and her reputation has gone on rising, though many different views of her as a writer have been put forward, especially since the rise of feminist criticism.

'Where people wish to attach, they should always be igno-rant. To come with a well-informed mind, is to come with an inability of administering to the vanity of others, which a sensible person would always wish to avoid. A woman especially, if she have the misfortune of knowing any thing, should conceal it as well as she can.'
Jane Austen, *Northanger Abbey*, ch 14.

The novel in France underwent extraordinary development between about 1830 and 1880, with a succession of innovations introduced by novelists of genius. The central theme was the ascendancy of Realism. It has always been a thread through the novel, but it was used in a special sense of the French novel of the mid-19th century, influenced by the rise of science and the positivism of Auguste Comte (1798–1857).

THE NOVEL IN FRANCE

GEORGE SAND

The novels of George Sand (Amandine-Aurore Dupin, 1804–76) fall into two groups. The early novels, written in Paris in the 1830s, were Romantic tales of women struggling against social restrictions. The second, more popular today, were deceptively simple pastoral tales, set in the Berry countryside where she lived. They included autobiographical elements, including her liaisons with Chopin and the poet Musset.

STENDHAL

A prolific writer on many subjects, especially music and art, Stendhal (Henry Beyle, 1783–1842) was nearly always entertaining, if unreliable. His novels include two classics, *Le Rouge et le Noir* (*Scarlet and Black*, 1830) and *La Chartreuse de Parme* (*The Charterhouse of Parma*, 1839). They are generally regarded as

the precursors of Realism, highlighting social life in the provinces and political life in France and Italy (where Stendhal spent many years) during the post-Napoleonic era. They are remarkable for their psychological insights and the passions of the central characters.

HUGO

The first night of *Hernani* (1830), a verse drama by Victor Hugo (1802–85), provoked a riot involving the supporters of Hugo's Romantic doctrine – that human nature should be freed from the restraints of Classicism – and those loyal to the tradition of Corneille and Racine. Hugo is regarded as a great French lyrical poet, but is mainly remembered outside France for two great novels, *Notre Dame de Paris* (*The Hunchback of Notre Dame*, 1833 [1831 in Hutchison Encylopedia]), and *Les Misérables* (1862), written while Hugo was in exile as a republican. Returning in 1870, he found himself a national hero, who received a state funeral when he died.

DUMAS

The other great French Romantic, Alexandre Dumas (1802–70), is known as Dumas *père* to

Above: **A caricature of Honoré de Balzac, whose *Comédie humaine* was one of the most ambitious enterprises in literary history.**

Opposite: **The 1948 version of *The Three Musketeers*. This rattling adventure moves so fast that faulty plotting slips by unnoticed.**

distinguish him from his son Dumas *fils* (1824–95), author of *La Dame aux camélias* (*Camille*, 1848). In energy, ebullience and productivity (his *Complete Works* occupy over 300 volumes), Dumas *pere* challenged such giants as Hugo and Balzac. His novels of 16th and 17th century France, full of sudden twists and coincidences, were written over half a century. *The Three Musketeers* (1844–45), has been the most popular. *The Count of Monte Cristo* (1844), set in the Napoleonic era, has also proved a lasting favourite.

BALZAC

Henry James regarded Honoré de Balzac (1799–1850) as the greatest of novelists, whose influence on the novel has been huge. His *Comédie Humaine* (1842–48) was originally planned as 137 separate but interconnected novels and stories, of which Balzac completed 97, plus rough drafts of several more – all in under twenty years. Balzac's aim was to present in fictional terms a comprehensive picture of French society in the years after the Revolution; it was also to be a critical analysis, drawing on techniques similar to those of the scientist or the historian. He divided the novels into three groups: customs, covering social and political life; philosophical; and analytical, including aspects of the supernatural. Among the author's main interests were the working of human emotions, the relationship between the individual and the environment, and the effects of money, ambition and energy in social relations. The work glows with Balzac's formidable vitality (he was physically and metaphorically a giant) and includes more than 2,000 characters, some of whom reappear in different novels. Notwithstanding contemporary success, Balzac, who lived an eventful life in spite of intense work, was constantly in debt until he married a rich Hungarian countess in 1850, only to die months later.

FLAUBERT

In contrast with the prodigious output of Hugo, Dumas and Balzac, Gustave Flaubert (1821–80) published only five novels, plus some shorter works, in a working life of 37 years. His

first and most famous novel *Madame Bovary* (1857), the story of a doctor's wife oppressed by the dull restrictions of life in a small Normandy town who escapes through adultery and eventually suicide, is one of the most influential novels ever. Flaubert was tried for offences against public morals, and acquitted, the trial doing wonders for sales. Flaubert, who disliked the label 'Realist', was the supreme stylist. Plot and characterization interested him less, although, as befits an acute commentator on the art of the novel, he acknowledged their importance. He sought a style 'as rhythmic as verse, as precise as the language of science' and believed that the author must be 'like God . . . present everywhere but visible nowhere'. *Salammbô* (1862), set in a minutely researched ancient Carthage, restored him to favour with the Establishment, but his remaining novels (*A Sentimental Education*, 1869, *The Temptation of St Anthony*, 1874, begun 25 years earlier, and *Bouvard et Pécuchet*) were less successful.

Books are not made like children but like pyramids . . . and they're just as useless! and they remain in the desert! . . . Jackals piss at the base and the bourgeois clamber all over them.'
Flaubert, *Correspondence* (1857).

DICKENS

There are clearly generic differences between the English novel and the French, or the Russian, novel. Without entering too deeply into a subject where all generalizations are suspect, it can be said that one feature of the novelists of the English Victorian novelists is that they always recognized that part of their duty was to entertain. Dickens was the great entertainer, and at one time was regarded as almost exclusively that. More recently, his social criticism has been taken more seriously, and his darker, more complex, later works have attracted respectful attention from serious academic critics.

THE NOVELIST

Charles Dickens (1812–70) came from the poorest reaches of the middle class. His father was imprisoned for debt when Charles was twelve and he went to work in a warehouse at 30p a week. He became a reporter, recording Parliamentary debates in shorthand, and in 1833 sold the first of his 'Sketches by Boz' to a magazine. *Pickwick Papers* began in 1836, *Oliver Twist* the following year, and Dickens's triumphant career was off to a flying start. In less than 30 years, he produced 14 major novels and a number of lesser fictions. Yet this was only a part of his almost frenetic activity. Dickens was a driven man, who never let up, constantly busy editing magazines, organizing amateur theatricals, charitable projects and protest campaigns, entertaining and being entertained by a huge circle of friends, lecturing, travelling (two trips to America), and of course writing, and all with extraordinary energy. In his later years, he had huge popular success with public readings from his novels, one-man shows by a born actor, and these exhausting performances on tour are said to have hastened his death. His private life was less happy. His marriage ended, after 10 children in 20 years. Gossip linked him with his wife's sister; in fact he was in love with the actress Ellen Ternan, for a time his mistress.

THE NOVELS

Dickens's popular reputation rests on his humour, his spirited narration, and his ability to create larger-than-life minor characters. He was such a 'natural' that he never needed to rewrite, which partly explains the dynamism of his prose and the breathtaking vigour of his set-piece descriptions, such as his famous descriptions of

London, the city with which he was so strongly and ambivalently involved. His faults are also obvious: sentimentalism, the vapid nature of his heroines, and, to some extent, his heroes too. It can also be said that his highly original minor characters, are generally two-dimensional, more caricature than character.

Besides *Pickwick*, containing the immortal coachman Sam Weller, and *Oliver Twist*, with the two disparate villains Fagin and Bill Sykes, his outstanding novels are (dates given here are of first serial publication): *Nicholas Nickleby*

father); *Bleak House* (1852), Dickens's most impressive novel of social protest, especially for its devastating attack on the Court of Chancery; *Hard Times* (1854), an attack on soulless utilitarianism in the person of Mr Gradgrind (a typically inspired name); *Little Dorrit* (1855), including an attack on the absurdities of the system in which honest men (like Dickens's father) could be imprisoned indefinitely for debt, and emphasizing the responsibility of the individual; *A Tale of Two Cities* (1859), Dickens's untypical – it is histor-

'Fog everywhere, fog up the river, where it flows among green aits and meadows; fog down the river, where it rolls defiled among the tiers of ship-ping, and the waterside pollu-tions of a great (and dirty) city. Fog on the Essex marshes, fog on the Kentish heights. Fog creeping into the cabooses of collier-brigs; fog lying out on the yards and hovering in the rigging of great ships; fog drooping on the gunwales of barges and small boats . . .'
Dickens, *Bleak House*, ch. I.

(1838), a swingeing attack on private schools (Dotheboys Hall, Wackford Squeers, headmas-ter), but with many joyful and lively episodes; *The Old Curiosity Shop* (1840), containing the notorious tear-jerking scene of Little Nell's death, adored by the Victorians but not us; *Barnaby Rudge* (1841), set in the time of the anti-Catholic Gordon riots; *Martin Chuzzlewit* (1843), partly based on Dickens's experience of America (he was critical), but one of his funni-est; *A Christmas Carol* (1843), first of a projected Christmas series, in which miserable old Scrooge is redeemed by his Christmas dream; *Dombey and Son* (1848), written in Switzerland and taken as marking the begin-ning of a more serious approach by Dickens to his art; *David Copperfield*, partly autobio-graphical (Mr Micawber seems to owe some-thing to Dickens's likable but improvident

ical, set partly abroad and has little humour – novel of the French Revolution; *Great Expectations* (1860–61), many people's fav-ourite, with a more believable hero (also the narrator) whose development from selfish youth to humane young man is the unifying theme, some memorable descriptive passages, an espe-cially rich assortment of minor characters and, until he was persuaded to change it, a down-beat ending; *Our Mutual Friend* (1864), Dickens's most pessimistic novel, a dense, complex and, despite initial impressions, coherent picture of contemporary society. Dickens died suddenly in 1870 leaving *The Mystery of Edwin Drood* unfinished. The question who, if anyone, murdered Edwin Drood has exercised the ingenuity of surpris-ingly numerous writers since and spawned several attempts to complete the novel.

At the 1997 Booker Prize, the annual British award for fiction, someone drew up a short list that might have figured in 1847, had the Booker Prize existed then. On it were Dickens's *Dombey and Son*, Thackeray's *Vanity Fair*, Trollope's *The Macdermots of Ballycloran*, and novels by each of the three Brontë sisters, *Wuthering Heights* (Emily), *Jane Eyre* (Charlotte) and *Agnes Grey* (Anne). Suffice to say that all those authors, and most of the books, are more familiar to readers today than any one of the six authors or books nominated in 1997. A telling illustration of the standard and range of Victorian fiction.

ENTERTAINMENT
AND SOCIAL CONSCIENCE

THACKERAY

Had there been a prize awarded by popular vote in 1847, William Makepeace Thackeray (1811–63) would have won. *Vanity Fair* was greeted as a challenge to Dickens. Set a generation earlier, it is a sweeping satire of contemporary English mores, in particular the materialism of the industrial age. It contrasts the fortunes of two female friends, Amelia Sedley and the immortal Becky Sharp, poor, bright, cynical and, inevitably, on the make, whom Thackeray, compelling his readers to make their own moral judgements, cannot bring himself to consign to the unhappy end that convention demanded for less than virtuous women. It also contains one or two set pieces of scintillating humour. Thackeray wrote for a living, demanding a huge journalistic output. None of his other novels quite measured up to *Vanity Fair*, although *Henry Esmond* (1852) comes close, followed by *Pendennis* (1848) and *The Newcomes* (1853). He was an admirer of, and expert on, the novels of the 18th century, and shares the vigour and liberality of Fielding and his contemporaries.

'. . . for though the task of husband-hunting is generally, and with becoming modesty, intrusted by young persons to their mammas, recollect that Miss Sharp had no kind parent to arrange these delicate matters for her, and that if she did not get a husband for herself, there was no one else in the wide world who would take the trouble off her hands.'
Thackeray, *Vanity Fair*, ch. 3.

TROLLOPE

Anthony Trollope (1815–82) sat down every morning at 5.30 for three hours to write 3,000 words before leaving for his work in the Post Office. He bruised his reputation as an artist in his *Autobiography* (1883) by insisting that novel-writing is merely a craft. *Framley*

Parsonage (1860) was written in only six weeks in response to an offer of £1,000 for serial rights from Thackeray's *Cornhill Magazine*. Trollope's straightforward image disguised a penetrating knowledge of human nature and in his later works, notably *The Way We Live Now* (1874), he took a less optimistic view of society than the image of the genial, fox-hunting chronicler of Barchester would suggest. It was the first of the Barchester novels, *The Warden* (1855), that made him famous. They are probably still the most read, though closely followed by the Palliser series, in which the theme is political rather than ecclesiastical.

STEVENSON

Robert Louis Stevenson (1850–94) was once regarded as a children's writer and minor essayist – an entertainer then. In more recent times, Stevenson, a friend of Henry James, has come to be seen as a serious novelist and as an early exponent of modernism (his poetry and drama have not shared in this revival). Brought up in Edinburgh, as a child his lungs were weak, but fragile health did not prevent him travelling extensively; he is another example of the writer as wanderer. He finally left Britain for the Pacific in 1888, settling in Samoa, where he enjoyed a period of intense activity, much of it channelled into fierce attacks on European exploitation of the Pacific islanders. For most people, he is still pre-eminently the author of two classics: the children's tale of adventure, *Treasure Island* (1883), and the brilliant, resonant tale of horror, *The Strange Case of Dr Jekyll and Mr Hyde* (1886). Probably the best of his other novels are *Kidnapped* (1886) and *The Master of Ballantrae* (1889).

MEREDITH

A poet first, George Meredith (1828–1909) is today better remembered as a novelist. That he is not more popular is largely due to his convoluted style, cultivated in a prolonged attempt to develop a form of prose that shared the lyric intensity of poetry. His first novel, *The Ordeal of Richard Feverel*, was not published until 1859, but 'the sage of Box Hill' (Surrey) still had fifty years ahead of him. At regular inter-

Above: Captain William Dobbin and Miss Amelia Smedley, an illustration to *Vanity Fair* by the author.

Opposite: Anthony Trollope who, like his admired friend Thackeray, was a thoroughly professional writer although, unlike Thackeray, he declined to risk giving up his day job.

vals he published novels, short stories, poetry and criticism, notably *On the Idea of Comedy* . . . (1897). By general consent, his best novel is *The Egoist* (1879), which, in its cool examination of the absurd Sir Willoughby Patterne, also reveals Meredith's gift for comedy.

GISSING

The reputation of George Gissing (1857–1903) has risen in the past 30 years. Unlike Trollope or Meredith, he fits the image of the born artist, devoted to his art, alienated from society – Gissing was drawn to the working class from which he unsuccessfully picked two wives. In spite of his grim realism, he was relatively prosperous and productive. His subjects were human misery, poverty and failure, and what he described as 'the hideous injustice of our whole system of society'. In *New Grub Street* (1891), he contrasts the careers of two writers, the first facile, selfish and successful, the second a genuine artist, hampered by poverty and rejection.

WOMEN OF WORDS

With the 19th-century novel, men and women for the first time in any literary genre stood on equal footing. The majority of novel readers were women, and possibly the majority of novelists were too. Plots and settings were usually domestic – traditionally the woman's sphere – even if they were concerned with non-domestic themes, and intelligent middle-class women whose activities were severely constricted by social convention found opportunities to express themselves in writing fiction. As George Eliot remarked in her essay, 'Silly Novels by Lady Novelists', 'No restrictions can shut women out from the materials of fiction, and there is no species of art which is so free from rigid requirements.'

The literary significance of all this is hard to judge. Today, gender is perhaps exaggerated. Some feminist critics would say that there is no essential difference between male and female writers, and that to maintain otherwise is to perpetuate traditional prejudice.

ELIZABETH GASKELL

Mrs Gaskell, wife of a minister, began writing to distract herself after the death of her baby son. She attracted favourable attention from Dickens, and most of her work was first published in *Household Words* and its successor. A thoroughly admirable person, devoted wife and mother, friend (and biographer) of Charlotte Brontë among many others, she was a perceptive and sympathetic observer of human nature, a sound researcher (notably on the conditions of industrial workers) and a powerful force for greater social co-operation. In her day, she was very highly regarded, and her reputation, which dipped after her death, is now again high. One novel in particular has always remained popular: *Cranford* (1851), a charming picture of life in her native town, Knutsford, and a quiet affirmation of ordinary human decency.

THE BRONTËS

This extraordinary family grew up in the vicarage of Haworth, a bleak village on the Yorkshire moors and now one of the most visited literary shrines in Britain. They were never really happy anywhere else, though chiefly because life, and hereditary tuberculosis, gave them little chance to be. With their brother Branwell, the three girls, Charlotte (1816–55), Emily (1818–48) and Anne (1820–49), made up elaborate stories and fantasies and in 1846 published a combined collection of poetry as the brothers Bell. Charlotte, the eldest, then persuaded her sisters to publish the novels that all had by now written, and as a result her own *Jane Eyre*, Emily's *Wuthering Heights* and Anne's *Agnes Grey* all appeared in 1847, still under the names Currer, Acton and Ellis Bell, suspected by many of being one person. All too soon, private disasters crowded out their public success. Branwell, an alcoholic, died in 1848, followed within months by Emily and, after her second, better novel, *The Tenant of Wildfell Hall* (1848), by Anne. Charlotte remained to cope with her stricken father. Although shy and lacking self-confidence, she did begin to mix in literary circles, becoming a close friend of Mrs Gaskell, and in

1854 she married her father's curate. She died at 39 when pregnant with her first child.

Charlotte, having lived the longest, appears to be the most substantial novelist, though some regard Emily as the most brilliant. Charlotte's best novel after *Jane Eyre* is probably *Villette*, based on the traumatic nine months she spent in Brussels in 1842 where she fell in love with her middle-aged and married employer. However, Emily's only novel, *Wuthering Heights*, is probably the best known of the works of the Brontës, a passionate and powerful love story with a positively terrifying lover in Heathcliff, saved from toppling into melodrama by its solid Yorkshire roots.

GEORGE ELIOT

Virginia Woolf remarked that George Eliot (Mary Ann Evans, 1819–80) was the first English novelist to write exclusively for adults. Her powerful intellect and insight extended the novel's range and gave it greater seriousness, and, notably in *Middlemarch*, she displayed detailed comprehension of an enormous range of subjects, from medicine to politics. She began writing articles in about 1850 and in 1853 started an affair, which developed into a life-time partnership, with a married man, G. H. Lewes. Though very learned himself, he put her literary ambitions first, encouraging her to write novels and forsaking his own work, which included the standard work on Goethe in English, to take over the housework. She adopted a male pseudonym, though Dickens for one, writing a fan letter in 1858, correctly deduced her sex.

Eliot's 1859 novel *Adam Bede* confirmed the accuracy of Lewes's judgement that his partner was the greater talent; *The Mill on the Floss* (1860) and *Silas Marner* (1861) followed. Not everything came easily – *Romola* (1863), set in Renaissance Italy, turned her, she said, from a young woman to an old one in two years – but in 1871 she published what is generally regarded as her masterpiece, *Middlemarch*. The death of Lewes in 1878 was a shattering blow, but two years later she married a man 20 years younger, shortly before her own death.

Above: Branwell Brontë's famous portrait of his three sisters, left to right Charlotte, Emily and Anne.

Opposite: George Eliot, the most philosophical and perhaps the most intellectually respectable of 19th-century English novelists, from a sketch by Caroline Bray.

'At least eighty out of a hundred of your adult male fellow-Britons . . . are neither extraordinarily silly, nor extraordinarily wicked, nor extraordinarily wise . . . their brains are certainly not pregnant with genius, and their passions have not manifested themselves at all after the fashion of a volcano . . . Yet these commonplace people – many of them – bear a conscience, and have felt the sublime prompting to do the painful right; they have their unspoken sorrows, and their sacred joys . . . '
George Eliot, *Amos Barton* (1857), ch. 5.

Russia's arrival on the literary scene was sudden and dramatic. In general, the great Russians, although well versed in European literature, owed little to the West. Their situation was entirely different. They lived in a vast and backward country, where the mass of the population was illiterate and the educated élite was very small. They were, or were expected to be, committed. They were, in a sense, prophets, with serious purposes – social, political, philosophical or religious – and a novel was a manifesto. Under a reactionary regime, writing was a dangerous trade. A hint of subversion and there was a danger of being sent to Siberia, as Dostoevsky was. Suspicion remains that Pushkin (1799–1837), who was killed in a duel, was the victim of a tsarist plot. His early death cut short the career of a great poet and deprived the world of a potentially great novelist.

THE RUSSIANS

GOGOL

Sometimes regarded as the first Russian realist and a progenitor of modernism, Gogol (1809–52) also belonged obliquely to the Romantic movement, as the man who 'put the gargoyles on the Gothic tower of Romanticism'. An admirer of Sterne, he created a unique, fantastic, grotesque fictional world, aided by his formidable imaginative power and command of a language that was, like English in Shakespeare's time, young, vigorous and malleable. His famous play, *The Government Inspector* (1836), satirizes stupidity and corruption in a provincial town, representing Russian society, and his St Petersburg stories, including 'The Overcoat', take place in a surreal city. His masterpiece is the comic epic *Dead Souls* (1842), many years in the making. He subsequently underwent a long spiritual crisis, and burned the second part of *Dead Souls* shortly before his death.

TURGENEV

The most Westernized of the great Russians, Turgenev (1818–83) knew Flaubert, Dickens and George Eliot, and received an honorary degree from Oxford. The Goncourt brothers described him as 'a charming colossus . . . who looks like the good spirit of a mountain or a forest'. Once the most admired of the Russian writers, his reputation has declined partly because he is no great Russian wild man like Gogol or Dostoevsky, but an altogether gentler artist. His first large prose work, *Notes of a Hunter* (1847–51) is a neglected masterpiece. Turgenev's novels examine prevailing social, political and philosophical questions through the lives of individuals. The best known today is *Father and Sons* (1862), in which he introduced the word nihilist to describe the central figure, but the work probably most familiar today outside Russia is his play, *A Month in the Country* (1850), an influence on Chekhov, amongst others.

DOSTOEVSKY

It is hard to imagine two more different writers than Russian contemporaries, Turgenev, swanning around the literary salons of Paris and London, and Dostoevsky (1821–81) who, after a ghastly childhood, was condemned to four years in a hideous prison and four more in Siberian exile. He made use of these experiences in his first masterpiece, *Memoirs From The House of the Dead* (1860), first serialized in a magazine he started with his brother, in which he condemns as 'contaminated to its very foundation' a society that permits the brutality and savagery he

Above: Pushkin was criticised by Stalinists for being insufficiently revolutionary.

Above left: Dostoevsky admired Dickens who shared his concern for the sufferings of the innocent.

had witnessed. He travelled in Western Europe in 1862, and was appalled by the excesses of capitalist England. London's Crystal Palace (built for the Great Exhibition of 1851) appears as a symbol of the corrupt modern world in *Notes from Underground* (1864), the first of the works that support his huge reputation today: *Crime and Punishment* (1866), *The Idiot* (1868) and above all *The Brothers Karamazov* (1880). Dostoevsky was admired by every 20th-century thinker from Freud to Sartre, and his influence on the novel is hard to exaggerate. His greatest single quality is his understanding of the most complex depths of individual character.

'. . . he had dreamt that the entire world had fallen victim to some strange, unheard of and unprecedented plague . . . Some new kind of trichinae had appeared, microscopic creatures that lodged themselves in people's bodies. But these creatures were spirits, gifted with will and intelligence. People who absorbed them into their systems instantly became rabid and insane. But never, never had people considered themselves so intelligent and in unswerving possession of the truth as did those who became infected . . . each person thought that he alone possessed the truth . . .'
Dostoevsky, *Crime and Punishment*, vi, 11, (trans. David McDuff 1991).

TOLSTOY

Not everyone liked Dostoevsky. Henry James and D. H. Lawrence were notable dissidents. The Russian giant was not he but Tolstoy (1828–1910), author of probably the world's best-known novel, *War and Peace* (1863–69), a magnificent epic which traces the fortunes of three aristocratic families during the era of Napoleon's invasion. It was followed by the almost equally famous *Anna Karenina* (1873–77). Tolstoy's profound concern with moral questions led to a spiritual revolution in the 1880s and a dramatic change in the character of his work, as manifest in novels such as *The Death of Ivan Illich* (1886) and *The Kreutzer Sonata* (1889). His radical rejection of private property and of political and ecclesiastical authority led to his works being banned in Russia, but made him a revered sage and his home, a large inherited estate in central Russia where he lived all his life, a place of pilgrimage.

Fiction aside, 19th-century prose is so vast and varied that it becomes difficult to highlight the most important themes and developments, let alone the outstanding writers. The subjects of study, already expanding fast during the 18th century, multiplied further under the stimulus, in particular, of the Industrial Revolution and scientific advance, together with the political transformation heralded by the French Revolution and American democracy.

HISTORIANS AND CRITICS

SCIENCE AND SOCIETY

The most influential thinkers of the century had no literary pretensions, though their ideas had profound effects on society and therefore on literature. Charles Darwin's explanation of the workings of evolution in *The Origin of Species* (1859) shook the foundations of society by implicitly challenging fundamental religious doctrine and downgrading humanity's idea of its own importance. The works of Karl Marx and Friedrich Engels, which argued that social change was the result of conflict and that on economic factors were the controlling influence upon politics, were to affect thinkers in practically every discipline, though Marxism's most dramatic effects were delayed until the 20th century. At the very end of the century, the theory of the unconscious mind developed by Sigmund Freud was to overturn accepted views of human nature, with incalculable effects on modern literature.

Among other writers who belong more to the history of thought than the history of literature were the Utilitarian philosophers Jeremy Bentham, who measured right and wrong by the criterion of the hedonistic calculus, i.e. the principle of 'the greatest happiness of the greatest number', and John Stuart Mill. Perhaps the weightiest philosophy came from Germany. Marx himself owed his dialectic to Hegel, but he rejected Hegel's idealism, as did Nietzsche, whose idea of a 'superman' as a kind of saviour of society has been undeservedly blamed for Nazism. Nietzsche had more in common with the earlier Schopenhauer, whose grimly pessimistic view of the world was to influence Mann, Hardy and later novelists.

HISTORIANS

An admirer of German philosophy, the formidable Thomas Carlyle (1795–1881) was a historian (notably of the French Revolution) who was chiefly concerned with contemporary society. His first and most idiosyncratic major work was *Sartor Resartus* (1836), a partly autobiographical discourse on the transitory nature of human institutions written in his characteristic, ebullient style later known as 'Carlylese', often thunderous, sometimes obscure. His chief work on that popular subject the 'condition of England' (Carlyle's term, though he was a Scot) was *Past and Present* (1843), attacking the doctrine of *laissez-faire*, materialism and the cash nexus ('Men are grown mechanical in head and in heart, as well as in hand'). A Romantic anti-intellectual, Carlyle's distrust of democracy and his cult of the hero strike an unsympathetic note today, but in the late 19th century the 'Sage of Chelsea' was the most powerful intellectual influence in Britain.

Among less unorthodox historians, the best, or the best stylist, in English was Thomas Babington Macaulay (1800–59). A brilliant essayist, his greatest work was his unfinished *History of England* (1849–61), although the so-called 'Whig interpretation of history' for which he was largely responsible is now thoroughly defunct. Otherwise, in historiography, Germany again was at the forefront. Leopold von Ranke (1795–1886) pioneered the 'scientific' approach, stressing the importance of studying primary evidence, leading to increasing specialization. Otherwise, the works most read today belong to a more classical tradition, combining broad historical perspective with distinguished literary style, as in Jules Michelet (1798–1874) in France, Jakob Burckhardt (1818–97), Swiss historian of *The Civilization of the Renaissance in Italy*, and Macaulay himself.

CRITICS

Among Victorian polymaths, Matthew Arnold (1822–88) was a fine if melancholy poet ('Dover Beach' is probably best remembered), who turned to prose in his middle years. Like Carlyle, he combined a powerful intellect with a wider, more European outlook. Besides his stimulating *Essays in Criticism* (1865–88), his most notable work is *Culture and Anarchy* (1869), which attacks Victorian Philistinism and recommends culture, the pursuit of perfection through study of the greatest artists and writers, as the best resource against current dissatisfactions. John Ruskin (1819–1900) was also infected with the Victorian malaise induced by rampant materialism and the decline of religion. The latter, it seemed, he almost wished to replace with a kind of philosophy of aesthetics, and he is now remembered chiefly for his grandly phrased writing on art. His condemnation of shabby, commercial mass production and advocacy of traditional craftsmanship lived on in William Morris and the Arts and Crafts movement.

One of the most influential literary critics of the age was Charles Augustin Sainte-Beuve (1804–69), whose published works, such as *Port-Royal* (1840–59), began life as articles or lectures. Tolerant, humane and infinitely curious, he is regarded as one of the founders of modern criticism.

Alexis de Tocqueville (1805–59), an aristocratic French government official and politician, travelled to the U.S.A. to study the penal system in 1831–32. He subsequently produced his classic *Democracy in America* (1835–40), a lucid, accurate and still pertinent commentary in which, while commending American democracy, he also perceived its dangers, notably the threat of 'the tyranny of the majority'.

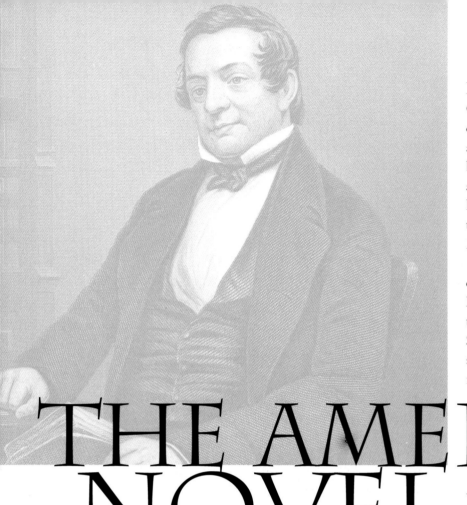

THE AMERICAN NOVEL

In the 1840s, Dickens's sales in North America were relatively as high as in Britain, but in the years before the Civil War he was increasingly challenged by American novelists. As in England there were many women novelists, no Jane Austens or George Eliots perhaps, but Harriet Beecher Stowe far surpassed them (and everyone else) in sales of her first book, the melodramatic but influential, anti-slavery novel, *Uncle Tom's Cabin* (1852). However, neither slavery nor the Civil War figured much in the work of the two great writers who, together with Walt Whitman, were chiefly responsible for the establishment of uniquely American literature on level terms with that of European countries.

Above: **Washington Irving, who set the fashion for the American cultural tour of Europe and was largely responsible for the folksy image of Europe that travel agents still find profitable to maintain.**

HAWTHORNE

Culturally, North America in the early 19th century lagged behind developments in Europe and, inasmuch as a dividing line can be drawn between Romanticism and Realism, it was situated in the Civil War, although the conflict had less of an effect than the rapid industrialization that followed. Both Hawthorne and Melville were rooted in Romanticism.

Nathaniel Hawthorne (1804–64) was descended from 17th-century Puritans in New England and one of his ancestors was among the persecutors of the accused witches of Salem, where Hawthorne was born. He had a solitary childhood with an eccentric widowed mother, read widely and in 1837 achieved fame with the publication of a collection of short stories in *Twice Told Tales*. He could not initially make a living from his writing (his first novel, *Fanshawe*, 1828, was published at his own expense), in spite of much hack editorial work and successful children's stories, such as *Tanglewood Tales* (1852–53), based on stories from classical mythology. He was influenced by Emerson and the Transcendentalists, although he took a far more pessimistic view of life, and spent some time at the Brook Farm community, the basis for his novel *The Blithedale Romance* (1852).

THE SCARLET LETTER

Hawthorne was concerned with the past, whereas the Transcendentalists were interested in nature and the present. *The Scarlet Letter* (1850) was set in 17th-century New England and its successor, *The House of the Seven Gables* (1851), though relating contemporary events, is rooted in the same period. The title of Hawthorne's masterpiece refers to the scarlet letter 'A' (for 'adulteress') which his heroine is forced to wear after she had produced a baby in her husband's prolonged absence and refused to name the father. It is a powerful allegory of the moral effects of sin and punishment, a subject

> 'The founders of a new colony, whatever Utopia of human virtue and happiness they might originally project, have invariably recognised it among their earliest practical necessities to allot a portion of the virgin soil to a cemetery, and another portion as the site of a prison.'
>
> Hawthorne, *The Scarlet Letter*, ch. I.

with which the dark genius of Hawthorne was so deeply, not to say neurotically, concerned. *The House of the Seven Gables* was based on a curse, tradition had it, pronounced on the Hawthorne family (disguised as the Pyncheons) when the author's great-grandfather was a judge in the Salem witch trials.

In his last decade, much of it spent as U.S. Consul in Liverpool, Hawthorne seems to have been less tormented, and though continuing to write, he produced nothing to compare with *The Scarlet Letter*.

MELVILLE

Like Hawthorne, Herman Melville (1819–91) was troubled by inner demons. After his father's bankruptcy and early death, Melville left school early, worked in assorted jobs and sailed as a cabin boy to Liverpool in 1839, gaining a lifelong love of the sea. In 1841, he sailed on a whaling ship to the South Pacific, jumped ship and lived on the Pacific Islands, working at one time as an agricultural labourer in Tahiti. He served a year on a U.S. warship, before returning to New England and embarking on a literary career, partly to support a growing family. His first five books were essentially pot-boilers, based on his varied experiences, and they, especially the first, *Typee* (1846), gained him a large readership and introduced him to literary circles. In 1847 he settled on a Massachusetts farm, and became a friend of Hawthorne.

MOBY-DICK

Melville's greatest work, *Moby-Dick*, or *The Whale* (1851), was dedicated to Hawthorne, who may have been partly responsible for his more ambitious approach to this new tale of the sea. The symbolic story of Captain Ahab's obsessive pursuit of the white whale responsi-

Right: **John Huston's film (1956) of Melville's classic which sadly miscast Gregory Peck as Ahab.**

ble for crippling him is America's greatest tragic epic. It is written in a variety of styles, ranging from nautical slang to Shakespearean bombast, and the narrative is often interrupted by extraneous tales and dissertations. The book received some admiring notices, especially in Britain, where Melville – to a lesser extent Hawthorne too – was more highly regarded than in America. The general public, however, preferred its sea stories in Melville's earlier, less demanding style, and, although he continued to produce both fiction and, increasingly, poetry (latterly printed privately), his popularity rapidly faded. Unlike Hawthorne, he was unable to land an appointment as a U.S. Consul and in his later years toiled as a customs officer in New York. On his death, which passed almost unnoticed in his own country, he left unpublished another minor masterpiece, *Billy Budd*.

In the very large and fast-growing country, regionalism became an important factor. A North-South divide existed in England, as Mrs Gaskell and many others were aware, but in the U.S.A. it was, of course, a much more momentous division. In the early 19th century, America's literary heartland lay in New England, especially Boston where, as Bret Harte remarked, if you shot an arrow into the air, you would probably hit a writer. Harte himself, chronicler of the California miners, was a regional writer. So were Ambrose Bierce, another Californian, and Kate Chopin, representing the South, the principal area of regionalism in the sense of an intellectual movement (though the greatest Southern writers belong to a later period). The first novel by an Afro-American published in America (William Wells Brown had been published earlier in England), was Harriet Wilson's *Our Nig* (1859). The greatest of regional novelists, and the greatest novelist, though of Southern origin, came from a perhaps less likely region, the Old West of the central Mississippi valley.

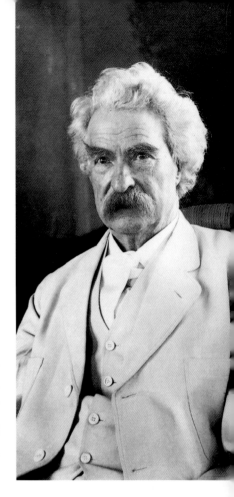

Above: Mark Twain (1835–1910) in his trademark white suit, from a photograph taken after misfortunes had made their mark on him.

AMERICAN HUMOUR

HUMOURISTS

A rich vein of humour runs through the American novel, no less than the British, though it runs a different course. One early ingredient is the curious folklore of the frontier (though much of it is not very authentic as folklore), exemplified in the tales of super heroes such as the mythical lumberjack Paul Bunyan (possibly of French-Canadian origin), or the originally real-life frontier hero Davy Crockett. The humour often depends on deadpan, self-generating exaggeration, the conning the gullible and an ear for the telling anti-climax. The short story by Mark Twain (1835–1910), 'The Celebrated Jumping Frog of Calaveras County' was based on one of these tales. Uncle Remus's anecdotes of Br'er Rabbit and his constantly outsmarted enemy Br'er Fox derive from the tales of the Afro-American workers on the plantations. The 'Sayings' of Artemus Ward exploited supposed traits of the mountain men (including bad spelling).

It was common for 19th-century humourists to adopt pseudonyms, and Mark Twain's real name was Samuel Langhorne Clemens. Uncle Remus was a Georgia journalist named Joel Chandler Harris, and Artemus Ward was the sadly short-lived Charles Farrar Browne. Mr Dooley, the Irish bartender whose spiked wit convulsed the country around the end of the century was the alter ego of Chicago journalist Peter Finley Dunne.

SAMUEL CLEMENS

Sam Clemens grew up in the riverside town of Hannibal, Missouri, apparently enjoying an enviably unfettered, frontier childhood, and he began writing for his brother's newspaper

HUCKLEBERRY FINN

Mark Twain's most famous works are his novels of boyhood, *The Adventures of Tom Sawyer* (1876) and its sequel, *The Adventures of Huckleberry Finn* (1884), which drew heavily on the author's experience and painted a vivid picture of life on the Mississippi frontier. *Huckleberry Finn* is his masterpiece and probably the best-known and most loved of all American novels. Relating Huck's picaresque adventures with a runaway slave on a raft down the Mississippi, it is a marvellous adventure story that is also a powerful commentary on American society and institutions, brilliantly conveyed through the observations of simple and naive characters. It is told in exuberantly racy and realistic language, employing local dialect that is entirely convincing without hindering the progress of the story. Some critics have called it the first

An illustration from *Huckleberry Finn*. **At the end of the story, Huck heads for the West in fear of being 'sivilized... I can't stand it. I been there before.'**

lecturer, and was married and settled in the New England town of Hartford, Connecticut.

when apprenticed to a printer. Printing soon bored him, and he became a river pilot on the Mississippi steamships, an important character-forming experience, shortly before the railways made the magnificent old stern-wheelers redundant. He drew his pen name from the call of the leadsman sounding the depth, and years later gave a fascinating and knowledgeable account of *Life on the Mississippi* (1879), a minor classic. His early writing was encouraged by Artemus Ward and Bret Harte, with whom he collaborated. The volume of 'sketches' headed by the 'Celebrated Jumping Frog' in 1867 made him famous, and his popularity increased even further with his personal, irreverent accounts of his travels, *The Innocents Abroad*, 1869), *Roughing It* (1872), and *A Tramp Abroad* (1879). By that time he was a well-established and extremely popular

modern American novel; it certainly marked a great shift in language.

In 1894, as the result of the failure of a firm in which he had invested heavily, Twain was forced to declare himself bankrupt, though within four years, by dint of hard work including a world lecture tour, he paid off his debts. However, that experience, followed by the deaths of his daughter and his wife, encouraged the growth of the misanthropic element that was always evident in his character, as it is in that of most great humourists. There is a bitter note in his allegorical satire, *A Connecticut Yankee in King Arthur's Court* (1889) and his story 'The Man That Corrupted Hadleyburg' (1898) takes a jaundiced view of human nature. His later writings, including two disappointing stories about Tom Sawyer, fell far short of his best work.

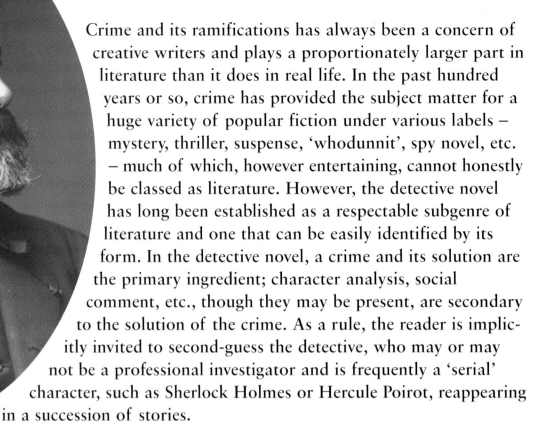

Crime and its ramifications has always been a concern of creative writers and plays a proportionately larger part in literature than it does in real life. In the past hundred years or so, crime has provided the subject matter for a huge variety of popular fiction under various labels – mystery, thriller, suspense, 'whodunnit', spy novel, etc. – much of which, however entertaining, cannot honestly be classed as literature. However, the detective novel has long been established as a respectable subgenre of literature and one that can be easily identified by its form. In the detective novel, a crime and its solution are the primary ingredient; character analysis, social comment, etc., though they may be present, are secondary to the solution of the crime. As a rule, the reader is implicitly invited to second-guess the detective, who may or may not be a professional investigator and is frequently a 'serial' character, such as Sherlock Holmes or Hercule Poirot, reappearing in a succession of stories.

THRILLERS AND WHODUNNITS

POE AND COLLINS

It is generally agreed that Edgar Allan Poe, pioneer of the modern horror story, originated the classic model of detective fiction with his stories of 'ratiocination' involving the French detective, C. Auguste Dupin. The best known is probably *The Murders in the Rue Morgue*. Like Sherlock Holmes later, Dupin is a brilliant eccentric whose somewhat blockheaded friend is the narrator of the story.

In Britain, the prototype of the full-length detection novel was Wilkie Collins's (1824–29) *The Moonstone* (1868). His early work consisted of articles written for the magazines of his friend Charles Dickens, and his first novel, *Antonina* (1850) was set in ancient times. *The Woman in White* (1860), a 'mystery' – related to the Gothic romance, rather than a detective novel – falls into the category that literary historians call the 'novel of sensation'. With its gripping opening scene based on a real-life experience, it demonstrated Collins's mastery of suspense and skilful plotting.

T. S. Eliot described *The Moonstone* as 'the first, the longest, and the best of modern English detective novels'. Brilliantly plotted, with a notable twist in the investigator's discovery that he himself was responsible for the disappearance of the eponymous stone, it is also sharply characterized: the gloomy Sergeant Cuff is a memorable detective. Collins wrote many more novels, but the standard declined and his narrative gift was latterly almost submerged by his engagement with social issues, but he continued to command large sales, not only in English-speaking countries, but also in translation.

CONAN DOYLE

The most famous fictional detective of all time is without doubt Sherlock Holmes, the violin-playing, drug-taking intellectual of 221B Baker

> 'Is there any other point to which you would wish to draw my attention?'
> 'To the curious incident of the dog in the night-time.'
> 'The dog did nothing in the night-time.'
> 'That was the curious incident,' remarked Sherlock Holmes.
> Conan Doyle, *The Memoirs of Sherlock Holmes*, 'Silver Blaze'.

Street, the creation of Arthur Conan Doyle (1859–1930). Like Holmes's friend and narrator, Dr Watson, Conan Doyle was a physician, a G.P. who began writing stories when short of patients. The first Sherlock Holmes story, *A Study in Scarlet*, appeared in a Christmas magazine in 1887, but his extraordinary popularity dates from the short stories that appeared in *The Strand Magazine* from 1891 and were later published in two volumes as *The Adventures of Sherlock Holmes* (1892) and *The Memoirs of Sherlock Holmes* (1894). The first person to tire of Holmes was his creator, but when he attempted to kill him off in 'The Final Problem', the outcry was such that he had to resurrect him. The author never did shed the character with whom he came to be irritatingly (to himself) identified, but he wrote many other books. Non-Holmesian novels included *The Lost World* (1912), featuring another 'serial' protagonist, Professor Challenger, the progenitor of many science-fiction stories on the 'extinct monsters' theme.

Above: What was supposed to be Sherlock Homes's last moment, as he plunges with arch-villain Professor Moriarty over the Reichenbach Falls. Public demand forced Doyle to retrieve him.

Opposite: Jules Verne, one of the pioneers of science fiction.

'GOLDEN AGE'

The success of Holmes encouraged others. Among the most notable was Father Brown, the insignificant but astute priest invented by G. K. Chesterton (1874–1936). The short story was still the usual vehicle (there were only four Sherlock Holmes novels). A classic of the detective novel was E. C. Bentley's *Trent's Last Case* (1912), which refined the form of the genre and led to the 'golden age' of the 1920s–1940s, dominated by women writers such as Dorothy L. Sayers, Margery Allingham, Ngaio Marsh, and the 'queen' of the detective novel, Agatha Christie (1890–1976). The creator of Hercule Poirot and Miss Marple was one of the biggest international bestsellers of the century, but she was a writer whom it is hard to imagine working effectively in any other milieu.

MEAN STREETS

A different form of the detective novel, the 'hard-boiled' school, is associated almost exclusively with the U.S.A., though an early progenitor was Émile Gaboriau in France. The first American master was Dashiell Hammett (1894–1961), author of *The Maltese Falcon* and *The Thin Man*. He was closely followed by the British-educated Raymond Chandler (1888–1959), whose wisecracking, streetwise hero Philip Marlowe first appeared in *The Big Sleep* (1939). Chandler was popular with ordinary readers (and film producers), but equally with highbrow critics, and W. H. Auden insisted that his books should be judged 'not as escape literature, but as works of art'.

CHILDREN'S LITERATURE

Although books for children were written as early as the 17th century, their purpose was generally didactic rather than entertaining. Children might find entertainment in adult books, such as *Aesop's Fables* or the travel tales of a Defoe or a Swift, but not until the late 18th century, under the influence of Rousseau and other educational reformers, did books appear that were written to amuse them, and a strong moral purpose still remained in many children's stories throughout the 19th century. Practically all the classics of children's literature date from the past 150 years.

CHAPBOOKS AND FAIRYTALES

Chapbooks were crudely printed pamphlets including versions of old romances and tales such as 'Dick Whittington' and 'Jack the Giant-Killer', illustrated with rough woodcuts. They circulated from the Renaissance to the 18th century. They sometimes included an alphabet, but were not exclusively designed for children. The name is modern, deriving from 'chapmen', the itinerant pedlars who sold them.

Fairytales may be read by children purely for amusement, but they generally have a moral purpose and, in the present century, they have been subject to 'deconstruction', especially under the influence of Freud. That there was more to fairytales than mere amusement was realized long before. In the 19th century their suitability for children caused lively argument. The most influential early collection, based on French folk tradition, was published by Charles Perrault in 1697, and in English translation as *Mother Goose Tales* in 1729. It included such favourites as 'Cinderella'. The brothers Grimm published their famous collection of German fairytales in 1812–15 (English translation 1823). Some lesser-known tales – including an incident in which someone is rolled downhill in a barrel with inward-projecting spikes – seem hardly suitable for children. Nothing so repulsive is to be found in the haunting Danish tales of Hans Christian Andersen (1805–75), which were mostly based on Danish tradition ('The Ugly Duckling', 'The Emperor's New Clothes').

FAMILIES, ANIMALS, ADVENTURES

Demand for children's stories of quality developed rapidly in the 19th century. Among the earliest forms were the family saga, (popular-

Probably the most famous children's story of the century was *Alice's Adventures in Wonderland* (1865) by Lewis Carroll, the pseudonym of a somewhat cranky Oxford mathematician, C. L. Dodgson (1832–98). Like Lear, Dodgson was awkward in adult society and adored little girls, adapting the book from stories he told the daughter of a colleague. It blends humour and fantasy, set against a very down-to-earth heroine, and includes memorable comic verse, often parodying Victorian party pieces. The sequel, *Through the Looking*

Left: Child abuse is a prominent theme of folk stories: Hansel and Gretel about to enter the gingerbread house.

Opposite: Illustration by the author from Lear's 'The Owl and the Pussycat' who 'went to sea in a beautiful pea-green boat'.

ized by J. D. Wyss, *The Swiss Family Robinson* (1813), animal stories (e.g. Anna Sewell, *Black Beauty*, 1877), school stories (Thomas Hughes, *Tom Brown's Schooldays*, 1857), fantasy (Charles Kingsley, *The Water Babies*, 1863) and adventure tales (Captain Marryat, *Masterman Ready*, 1841 and, notably, R. L. Stevenson). By the middle of the century, although didactic elements had not disappeared (Kingsley's classic being an example), many writers set out merely to please children without telling them how to behave. Some contemporaries explained the success of Lewis Carroll's 'Alice' stories on their absence of teaching or preaching.

HUMOUR

A Book of Nonsense (1845) by Edward Lear (1812–88) exploited children's love of the sound of words, regardless of meaning, and included many limericks of which Lear was the master, although not the inventor. Lear, who was an accomplished watercolourist, illustrated his own books. Since adult novels were often illustrated, children's stories naturally were too, but pictures were generally subsidiary, at least until the time of Beatrix Potter (1866–1943) in whose tales text and illustrations carry equal weight.

Glass (1871) is almost equally good, but Carroll's later children's story, *Sylvie and Bruno* (1889–93) is less memorable. His nonsense poem, 'The Hunting of the Snark' (1876), employs the same mad logic typical of dreams, in which Alice's adventures are set. Like most of the best children's books, the Alice stories appealed as much to adults as to children. They have remained hugely popular both in English and, in spite of obvious problems of translation, other languages.

ENGLISH CLASSICS

The generation after Lewis Carroll produced several classics of English children's literature. Like Beatrix Potter's Peter Rabbit and company, the characters were often anthropomorphized animals, though in Kipling's stories they are authentic animals and in A. A. Milne's *Winnie the Pooh* (1926) they are toys, the central character being a human child, Christopher Robin. Kenneth Grahame's *The Wind in the Willows* (1908) owes its continued appeal chiefly to the thoroughly 'human' character of the ineffable Mr. Toad. Other stories, notably those of E. Nesbitt (1858–1924), are about children, the greatest example being *Peter Pan*, originally a play (1904), the masterpiece of J. M. Barrie.

Naturalism, an allegedly more exact and 'scientific' extension of Realism, is associated in particular with Zola and the Goncourt brothers. It was influential primarily in French, German and European literature, to some extent in America but perhaps least of all in Britain. It never formed anything like a school or a movement in the English novel, though its influence is evident in the novels of Gissing, Arnold Bennet and especially the less well-known Arthur Morrison, author of the crusading novel of London's East End, *Child of the Jago* (1896).

NATURALISM

ZOLA

Émile Zola (1840–1902), who described his ideas in *The Experimental Novel* (1880), saw human beings as creatures determined by heredity and environment. He was influenced by contemporary scientific ideas, especially the work of Prosper Lucas on heredity, and the writings of the determinist historian Hippolyte Taine, author of a notable history of English literature. He saw the novelist's task as akin to that of an experimental scientist, taking characters of distinctive temperaments, placing them in apposite social circumstances and observing the results. At heart he was a social reformer, and his characters generally belong to the lower or middle classes.

Zola's ideas were first deployed in *Thérèse Raquin* (1867), but were more fully expressed in his ambitious cycle of twenty novels under the general title *Les Rougon-Macquart* (1871–93), in which he traced the 'natural and social history' of two branches of a particular family. Overall, he presents a wide-ranging prospect of mid-19th century social life, pain-stakingly researched, with the customary realist emphasis on the more grimmer aspects of human

behaviour. Zola's individual novels deal with particular communities or topics, and the general pessimism is relieved by lyrical passages and, despite the overall impression of human beings as 'weasels fighting in a hole', by Zola's faith in the possibility of improvement. That emerges more strongly in his later, unfinished sequence, *Les Quatres Evangiles* (*The Four Gospels*, 1899–1902). The third (and last) of these deals with the Dreyfuss Case, in which he had made a momentous intervention on behalf of justice with his open letter to the French president, *J'accuse* (1898), published in the newspaper *L'Aurore*.

HAUPTMANN

The leading exponent of German naturalism was the young Gerhart Hauptmann (1862–1946), epic poet and novelist but most famous as a playwright, in which role he was strongly influenced by Ibsen. The best known of his novels, at least in his naturalistic phase, is *Signalman Thiel* (1888), and his first major theatrical success, *Before Sunrise* (1889), depicting peasant life, was a landmark in the development of the naturalistic German theatre. His most famous play, proclaimed a masterpiece by James Joyce, is *The Weavers* (1892) based on a weavers' revolt in his native Silesia in 1844, in which the protagonist is the group rather than an individual. A humane social critic, Hauptmann's work varied widely in style, form and subject matter, attracting comparisons with Goethe. Besides his social realism, he manifested profound spiritual yearnings, which are most evident in later works, where naturalism has long given way to poetic symbolism. The late works are also marked by his horror at what had happened to Germany under the Nazis – who, of course, had no time for him.

BLASCO IBÁÑEZ

The vigorous, politically orientated Vicente Blasco Ibáñez (1867–1928) spent much of his life outside Spain, due partly to natural restlessness, partly to his political activities. An early republican poem landed him in prison, his support for the Cuban nationalists in 1896 resulted in a period of exile and, after serving 22 years in the Cortes, he left Spain for good when Primo de Rivera became dictator (1923). His literary reputation rests on his early novels, set in his native Valencia, in particular *La Barraca* (*The Cabin*, 1898) and *Cañas y barro* (*Reeds and Mud*, 1902). He describes the grim lives of farmers and fishermen with uncompromising realism, with strikingly powerful characterization and vivid descriptions of nature. After 1902, ideology got the upper hand and, though he wrote several powerful novels on social affairs, his work went into severe critical decline, though his sensational, energetic stores were enormously popular. His biggest success was the World War I blockbuster, *The Four Horsemen of the Apocalypse* (1916), which earned enough for a palace on the Riviera.

AMERICAN NATURALISM

Although influenced by Zola, American Naturalism arrived later than in Europe and was less rigid in conception, placing more emphasis on environment than heredity, and

Above: Rag pickers in Paris, 1897. Naturalist writers took great pains to record the lives of the poor in accurate detail.

Opposite: Gerhart Hauptmann as a young man. His naturalistic work portrayed peasant life with unparalleled sympathy.

owing much to the native regional novel. An early example was *Maggie, Girl of the Streets* (1893) by Stephen Crane, best known for his Civil War novel, *The Red Badge of Courage*. The most thoroughly naturalistic of American novels is *An American Tragedy* (1925) the masterpiece of Theodore Dreiser (himself a child of the slums), in which the failures of the weak-willed hero are blamed on the social environment and, implicitly, on the capitalist system. Naturalism is an element in the work of many other American writers, especially in its disposition in favour of the weak and oppressed. John Steinbeck's *Grapes of Wrath* (1939) is probably the most acclaimed work in this tradition.

One of the most popular books in mid-Victorian Britain was *Missionary Travels* (1857) a charmingly misleading account of African travel by the explorer, David Livingstone. Travel books had been popular since the days of Defoe, and 19th-century writers were keen travellers (or vice versa). The figure of Phileas Fogg, Jules Verne's hero in *Around the World in 80 Days*, circulating the globe with aplomb, was a recognizable British type. It was possible to travel through much of the world without leaving British soil, and the Empire added a further note of romance. Imperialism peaked towards the end of the century with the 'Scramble' for Africa (Livingstone would have been shocked), followed by the South African War, which threw some doubt on the whole notion.

BARDS OF THE EMPIRE

INDIA

The British had controlled most of India since the mid-18th century. They were not at first interested in power, merely in trade, but as time went by the imperialist ideal took hold, and India became 'the jewel in the [imperial] crown'. In spite of the 'Mutiny' (as the British described the Indian rebellion of 1857), India assumed an almost mythical status for the British. Yet India's inspiration on English literature was late in arriving. There was not even an equivalent of Rider Haggard's romances set in Africa, such as *King Solomon's Mines* (1885). About that time, however, Kipling's stories began to appear in the Lahore *Civil and Military Gazette*.

KIPLING

Born in India, but educated in England, Rudyard Kipling (1865–1936) returned in 1882 as a journalist on the Lahore *Gazette*. His early stories were collected as *Departmental Ditties* (1886), *Plain Tales From the Hills* (1888), etc. Together with his poems, published as *Barrack-Room Ballads* in 1892, they established him in literary circles after he returned to England in 1889. In 1892, having married an American, he moved for some years to Vermont, where he wrote the classic *Jungle Book* and its sequel. By 1897, the family were back in England, eventually settling in Sussex though Kipling spent long visits in South Africa, where he wrote some of the *Just So*

FRANCIS FORD COPPOLA
Apocalypse Now x
Released by COLUMBIA EMI WARNER Distributors Limited
EMI

'I am sick o' wastin' leather on these gritty
pavin'-stones,
An' the blasted English drizzle wakes the fever
in my bones;
Tho' I walks with fifty 'ousemaids outer
Chelsea to the Strand,
An' they talks a lot o' lovin', but wot do they
understand?
    Beefy face an' grubby 'and—
    Law! wot do they understand?
    I've a neater, sweeter maiden in a cleaner,
greener land!
    On the road to Mandalay . . .'
Kipling, 'Mandalay'.

Stories (1902). In 1911 he became the first English writer to win a Nobel Prize.

KIM

Kipling's masterpiece is his novel, *Kim* (1901, illustrations by the author's father) in which the loyalties of the boy-hero are divided between an old Tibetan lama (representing the contemplative life) and the British spymaster Colonel Creighton (representing the life of action). The real interest of the novel lies in its panoramic picture of India and the characters encountered along the Grand Trunk Road. Most Indian and British critics agree that it is the best British novel about India, though admittedly a winner in a small field.

Kipling's reputation faded before his death, some critics finding him too facile. It suffered later because of his identification with British imperialism, but has recovered recently. Kipling is the inventor of many great characters, several of them boys (Mowgli, Kim), and some of them animals (Bagheera the panther, Rikki-tikki-tavi the mongoose). 'Tommy Atkins' (the ordinary soldier) and 'the white man's burden' are among his contributions to the language. His output was huge (so were his sales) and he was extraordinarily fluent, especially in verse, with a good ear for colloquial speech. He knew intimately the everyday life of India, ordinary people of all sorts, Afghan horse traders and Bengali clerks, as well as British (and Irish) soldiers, the ways of the jungle and the military camp.

CONRAD

A more shadowed, psychologically more subtle view of Empire is presented in the works of Joseph Conrad (1857–1924). He was born in the Ukraine of Polish parents, who both died before his 12th birthday. He spent 20 years in the French and British merchant navies before becoming a writer – in English, his third language. In his early novels, including *An Outcast of the Islands* (1896), which were set in Malaya and the South Pacific, there is an occasional suggestion of strain, but by the time of *The Nigger of the Narcissus* (1897) he was in full command of the language, of an elaborate, rhythmical style and of a distinctive sense of form. Conrad had once captained a river steamer in the Congo, providing background for the novella *Heart of Darkness* (1899), an allegory of the takeover of the Belgian Congo, in which Conrad's concern with the corruptibility of the individual is taken to a shocking conclusion. This theme, of man's susceptibility to evil influences, is evident in *Lord Jim* (1900) and in the powerful *Nostromo* (1904), set in South America and regarded by some critics as his greatest work.

Conrad's novels were slow to engage the approval of either critics or readers, although his brilliance was swiftly recognized by contemporaries such as Henry James and Edward Garnett, Jonathan Cape's near-legendary publisher's reader. By the time of his death he was established as a leading Modernist (see page 144).

THE NOVEL AT THE TURN OF THE CENTURY

During the last decade of the 19th century, when it was apparent that Britain's reign as the leading world power was not permanent, there was a reaction against Victorian moral values. The so-called decadents represented one aspect of the reaction: sex and gender – the advent of the New Woman – were an intrusive element.

Above: Thomas Hardy in 1893. He came from a poor but cultured family and was an architect prior to *Far from the Madding Crowd*.

Right: Henry James, unlike Hardy, was deeply committed to the novel as an art form.

BUTLER

An important though isolated part in this revolt was played by the polymath Samuel Butler (1835–1902). A misfit rather than a rebel, he rejected his destined profession in the Church, and spent time farming sheep in New Zealand before returning to London and becoming a writer. His Utopian novel *Erewhon* (1872) is a Swiftian critique of the mechanization of 19th-century life: the sick are treated as criminals; churches are banks. No publisher would touch it, so Butler published it himself. His masterpiece is *The Way of All Flesh* (1903), a posthumous time-bomb 'waiting to blow up the Victorian family [the Pontifex family was modelled on his parents'] and with it the whole great pillared . . . edifice of the Victorian novel' (V. S. Pritchett).

HARDY

Thomas Hardy (1840–1928) regarded himself as a poet first and a novelist second, since reversed by posterity. England's pre-eminent regional novelist, he was born and lived most of his life in Dorset, the locale of many of his novels, though he preferred to call it Wessex, the name of the Anglo-Saxon kingdom. Torn between architecture and writing, he chose the latter and gained wide popularity with his second novel, *Under the Greenwood Tree* (1872), an amiable tale of the rustic villagers who were to feature in later novels. Thereafter he became progressively more serious and

'You left us in tatters, without shoes or socks,
Tired of digging potatoes, and spudding up docks;
And now you've gay bracelets and bright feathers three!' –
'Yes: that's how we dress when we're ruined,' said she.
Hardy, 'The Ruined Maid'.

more sombre. *Far From the Madding Crowd* (1874), in which a bright country girl is forced to choose between suitors representing different social milieus, was a major success, and it was followed by a succession of fine novels, *The Return of the Native* (1878), *The Mayor of Casterbridge* (i.e. Dorchester – Dorset is peppered with Hardy's fictional place names) and, perhaps his greatest novel, *Tess of the D'Urbervilles* (1891). Tess is an innocent girl who bears an illegitimate child and later murders her seducer. It caused considerable consternation among the middle-class reading public, and they were completely alienated by the bleakly pessimistic *Jude the Obscure* (1895), publicly burned by an irate bishop. Hardy was so disgusted by the reaction to *Jude* that he forsook novel-writing altogether, but in his later years, after his second marriage in 1914, he became something of a Tolstoyesque sage in his self-designed – and very ugly – house at Max Gate, south of Dorchester.

Hardy was a countryman. It is generally agreed that he is at his best on his native heath, which drew from him his richest descriptive writing and his deepest characters. Fundamentally, however, Hardy is at odds with a hostile universe. A frequent theme is the conflict between the old and the new, and the advance of the city upon the countryside. Apart from higher living standards, he would take little comfort in what has happened to his 'Wessex' since his death.

JAMES

The sales of Henry James (1843–1916) were far less than Hardy's and, except for his famous ghost story *The Turn of the Screw* (1898), he was not very widely read (recent Hollywood adaptations have revived public interest), but his critical reputation was far greater (a famous biography of James by Leon Edel runs to five volumes). The novelist's

novelist, he was virtually the first English speaking writer to give serious consideration to the novel as an art form, and his sheer craftsmanship has created such enthusiasm among critics that it is easy to forget that James was a born story-teller.

He came from a New England family of intellectual heavyweights, but disliked the current commercialism of American society and found the older culture of Europe more rewarding. He settled in England in 1876 and eventually became a British subject. Nevertheless, he remained closely engaged with America, and his novels, especially those of his first period – including *Roderick Hudson* (1875), *The American* (1877), *The Europeans* (1878), *Daisy Miller* (1879) and the finest of them, *Portrait of a Lady* (1881) – are largely concerned with the conflict between the old and new civilizations.

In the 1890s he turned his attention to English society and he also made serious efforts in drama, but his plays were painfully unsuccessful. James was a man of deep human sympathy – 'be kind' was his advice to his young nephews – but in his second period his style became more indirect and sometimes obscure. Nor are his last three great novels, *The Wings of the Dove* (1902), *The Ambassadors* (1903) and *The Golden Bowl* (1904), in which he returned to the ever-fascinating question of Euro-American contrasts, easy reading. Among other notable examples of his fiction are *Washington Square* (1881), *The Bostonians* (1886), *The Aspern Papers* (1888) and *What Maisie Knew* (1897). His travel writing, critical essays (Balzac was his favourite) and fragments of autobiography are full of interest.

'It is art that makes life, makes interest, makes importance, for our consideration and application of these things, and I know of no substitute whatever for the force and beauty of its process.'
James, Letter to H.G. Wells, July 1915.

CHAPTER NINE
MODERNISM

The dramatic changes that took place in literature between 1900 and 1930 can justly be called a revolution. In rejecting the traditional forms and values of 19th-century literature, Modernism included the adoption of new subject matter as well as new style and new technique. The visual arts were affected no less, more obviously in fact, than literature, and some movements, such as Dada and Surrealism, Italian Futurism, and English Vorticism, spanned both art and literature. Like most such convenient labels, however, 'Modernism' is elastic. The first great modernists in the English novel – James, Conrad – were in action well before 1900, and they were strongly influenced by still earlier writers such as Balzac, Hawthorne and George Eliot.

1900
Sigmund Freud publishes *The Interpretation of Dreams*

1907
The first volume of Sir James G. Frazer's *The Golden Bough* is published

1914-18
First World War

1917
The Hogarth Press is founded by Leonard and Virginia Woolf

1922
T. S. Eliot's poem *The Waste Land* and James Joyce's *Ulysses* **are published**

1924
André Breton produces the *Manifeste du surréalisme*

1936
William Faulkner publishes *Absalom, Absalom!*

1941
Virginia Woolf commits suicide

The period between the 1890s and the First World War was a period of transition. Writers were acutely aware of changes in society, particularly those relating to science and technology, and to human consciousness. The certainties of the Victorian era were lost, and the modern age loomed as a frightening, unknowable future. However, such insecurity was not exactly new. It had activated the often-noted malaise that affected so many 19th-century writers, including such pillars of the Victorian age as Tennyson or Matthew Arnold. Literary historians see the 'modern' revolution as two movements, the first, relatively optimistic phase, which ended in 1914, and a second, pessimistic phase in the wake of the First World War and the Bolshevik Revolution of October 1917.

EXPERIMENT

Like every new movement in the arts, Modernism was antagonistic to the tradition it displaced. It was hostile not only to 19th-century moral values, but also to 19th-century techniques, the general structure of rational narrative, description and resolution. Instead of the omniscient narrator, for example, novelists preferred to convey personality through unspoken thoughts and feelings in the 'stream of consciousness' technique (the phrase originated by the American philosopher William James, brother of Henry). Modernism was self-consciously and determinedly experimental, which is one reason why it is hard to categorize as a 'movement'. Incidentally, it represented a further widening of the division between the upper reaches of literature and the

NEW DIRECTIONS

Above: The bohemian Latin Quarter of Paris in the late 19th century.

Opposite: Old Town Square in Prague, capital of Bohemia, alleged home of the gypsies, the original 'Bohemians'. Henri Murger defined Bohemians as people 'whose main business is to have no business . . .'.

lower slopes occupied by the reading public. Poetry, in particular, was to become an increasingly a minority interest.

MODERNISTS AND 'EDWARDIANS'

Of course not all writers of the early 20th century were modernists. In English literature, critics draw a distinction between modernists and Edwardians – broadly, those who followed the realist tradition, such as Arnold Bennett (1867–1931), John Galsworthy (1867–1933) or H. G. Wells (1886–1946). It is today increasingly evident that this distinction is far from straightforward, and that the most revered names among the modernists (James, Conrad, the early D. H. Lawrence, even Joyce) often wrote in an 'Edwardian' way. The influential novelist and critic Ford Madox Ford (1873–1939), a major figure in contemporary thinking about literary form, who scoffed at amateurish 'nuvvles', nevertheless published, as editor of the *English Review*, Bennett and Galsworthy, as well as James, Conrad, the Vorticist Wyndham Lewis and Ezra Pound. His four-volume masterpiece, *Parade's End* (1924–28), though employing many characteristic

'The myth of King Oedipus, who killed his father and took his mother to wife, reveals, with little modification, the infantile wish, which is later opposed and repudiated by the barrier against incest. Shakespeare's Hamlet is equally rooted in the soil of the incest-complex, but under a better disguise.'
Freud, *Five Lectures on Psycholanalysis*, IV.

modernist experimental devices, can be seen as a direct successor of the old, three-decked, 'condition-of-England' type novel. Altogether, Modernism was more pragmatic than is often assumed.

PSYCHOLOGY

Probably no one had more influence on modern literature than the Viennese psychologist and founder of psychoanalysis, Sigmund Freud (1856–1939). In an elegy written on Freud's death, W. H. Auden called him, without exaggeration, 'no more a person now but a climate of opinion'.

Freud's ideas arose from his study of neuroses. Freudian criticism, though perhaps not Freud himself, sees creativity as a form of sublimation, typically deriving from traumatic experiences in childhood, and art as a pathological phenomenon. In the words of the critic Lionel Trilling, 'the poet is a poet by reason of his sickness as well as by reason of his power'. The greatest impact of Freud himself resulted from his theories of the unconscious mind and the nature of repression, his study of the development of sexual instincts in young children, and his 'interpretation of dreams' (the title of his first great book). Many of his ideas have given rise to popularised conceptions with which everyone is now familiar: for example, the Oedipus Complex, the sexual rivalry between a son and father for the mother (whence the Electra Complex, rivalry between daughter and mother for the father); the death

wish; phallic symbols, the significance, conscious or unconscious, of any penis-shaped object as a symbol of male sexuality; penis envy, the desire of a girl for such an organ. The latter doctrine in particular has aroused outrage amongst feminists, and in fact very little of Freud's teaching is now accepted without considerable qualification. However, that does not lessen its impact on the modernists.

Freud would have been less influential had he not also been a fine writer. Some of his case studies are true works of art, and he was also a penetrating literary critic, his writings on Hamlet, Oedipus and other characters marking the beginning of a long, continuous, tradition of Freudian biography.

ANTHROPOLOGISTS

After the writings of Freud, the most influential work was *The Golden Bough* of the British anthropologist, Sir James G. Frazer (1854–1941), the first volume of which was published in 1907. It is a monumental comparative study of myth and religion, the fundamental thesis of which is that humanity progresses from magic, through religion, to science. Frazer's eloquent style added to its appeal. His work inevitably relied on secondary sources and his ideas have long been overtaken, but his description of primitive society and his discussion of such matters as fertility rites, sacrifice, the dying god, etc. had a profound effect on writers – which was in fact a greater effect than they had on anthropologists.

CRAFT OF THE NOVEL

The novel thrived in the early years of this century, and so did the idea of the novel which, among the modernists, was turning into a very different creature. According to the literary theories of Flaubert and Henry James, style and form were everything, or almost everything, and subject matter was unimportant. The novel was an autonomous aesthetic creation, not an imitation of life, on which the creator – the novelist – should not intrude. Aesthetic considerations of this kind were the chief concern of the greatest novelists of the period, including Proust, Joyce, Woolf and Faulkner.

PROUST

Marcel Proust (1871–1922) was physically frail, an asthmatic, who as a young man moved freely in Parisian high society. There he acquired the material for his single great masterpiece, *A la recherche du temps perdu* (published in seven sections between 1913 and 1927), translated as *Remembrance of Things Past*. The work became practically his only interest during his latter years when he lived as a recluse, seldom venturing outside in daytime, an existence only partly prescribed by deteriorating health. The subject of this seminal novel, which ran to about 3,000 pages, is *Time and Memory*. The authentic past can only be recaptured through involuntary memory, triggered by an apparently insignificant incident or object. Through such 'privileged moments', the past is recaptured. All traditional ideas of narrative are abandoned, and events and feelings are fed through a narrator figure, Marcel (not, in spite of similarities, an alter ego). Proust's precision in describing human consciousness echoes Henry James and Joyce; his idea of insignificant past incidents assuming later importance is found in Virginia Woolf, and his notion of human relationships forming a pattern like a piece of music was adopted by Anthony Powell in *A Dance to the Music of Time* (1951–75).

JOYCE

Born and raised in Catholic Ireland, James Joyce (1882–1941) set all his fiction in his native city of Dublin, although from 1904 he abandoned country and religion and lived abroad. His first, autobiographical novel, *A Portrait of the Artist as a Young Man*, published, largely due to the enthusiasm of Ezra Pound, in 1916, throws light on his early life and his discovery of his vocation. It adopts a stream-of-consciousness narrative reflecting the hero's development and foreshadows the astonishingly original use of language that characterises his greatest work, *Ulysses* (1922; not published in Britain until 1936 due to alleged obscenities). Ostensibly it covers a single day in the life of three characters in Dublin (Leopold and Molly Bloom and Stephen Daedalus, the hero of *Portrait of the Artist*). Its 18 episodes roughly

'Can't hear with the waters of. The chittering waters of. Flittering bats, fieldmice bawk talk. Ho! Are you not gone ahome? ... Dark hawks hear us. Night! Night!. My ho head halls. I feel as heavy as yonder stone ... Beside the rivering waters of, hitherandthithering waters of. Night!'
Joyce, *Finnegans Wake*.

reflect equivalents in the *Odyssey*, and this mythic structure contributes to the creation of an epic from superficially mundane material. Past and present interact, trivial events acquire sometimes profound significance, and extreme erudition mingles with coarse humour. Joyce's highly allusive style, including parodies of various literary forms, does not make for easy reading, and his last book *Finnegans Wake* (1939) is inaccessible to the ordinary reader without a comprehensive gloss. Newcomers to Joyce, possibly the most influential novelist of the century, wisely start with his early short stories, *Dubliners* (1914), which are relatively conventional in technique.

FAULKNER

Place is no less important in William Faulkner (1897–1962), whose mythical Yoknapatawpha County reflects Lafayette County in Mississippi where his family had long been established and where he lived nearly all his life. The history and legends of the South, including his own family, furnish the material for most of his books and all of the better ones. Encouraged by Sherwood Anderson (1876–1941), a leading naturalistic writer famous for his stories of Winesburg, Ohio, he began writing fiction while working as a journalist in New Orleans. His first two novels were based respectively on his experiences as a trainee pilot in the Royal (British) Air Force and bohemian life in contemporary New Orleans.

Moving back to his home town of Oxford (Jefferson in the novels), Faulkner began to write the remarkable novels that presented a fictional illustration of the doom-laden history of the South, containing plenty of tragedy and horror but also much humour. Though his literary career was long and productive, Faulkner's

Above: James Joyce. Though born and raised in Ireland, Joyce abandoned his homeland and lived most of his life abroad.

Opposite: Posthumous caricature of Proust. Proust's seminal work, *A la Recherche du Temps Perdu*, dealt with issues of time and memory.

fame rests chiefly on the novels written in the late 1920s and early 1930s, persistently experimental in style and earning him recognition as a leader of Modernism (a slightly later development in North America). *The Sound and the Fury* (1929) has several narrators, one of them mentally disabled. *As I Lay Dying* (1930) brilliantly employs the stream-of-consciousness technique. *Light in August* (1932), the immense and complex *Absalom, Absalom!* (1936) and *Intruder in the Dust* (1940) consolidated his reputation. Faulkner also wrote short stories, including the classic 'The Bear' which is an episode in *Go Down, Moses* (1942), and two volumes of poetry. By the time he won the Nobel Prize in 1949, his best work was some years behind him, though his last novel, *The Reivers* (1962) is genial and entertaining.

Bloomsbury is an area of west London containing the University, the British Museum (and Library), many publishers, bookshops, and residential Georgian streets and squares which, in the early years of the century, were home to many mutually acquainted literary and artistic people. 'Bloomsbury', in the sense of an intellectual social circle, extended much further. It represented the essence of the post-Victorian, modernist culture, extending from literature and art to sex, family life and international relations. Bloomsbury in this sense had a profound effect on Britain, although its truly international figures were few, the most notable being the economist John Maynard Keynes (1883–1946) and the novelist Virginia Woolf. Today, Bloomsbury has become a cult, and an apparently inexhaustible subject of books. Tourists have worn a path along the bank of the River Ouse in Sussex to the spot where Virginia Woolf committed suicide in 1941.

Above: **D. H. Lawrence: ferociously anti-intellectual, Lawrence could not escape – a common dilemma among artists – the fact that he was an intellectual himself.**

BLOOMSBURY

WOOLF

Virginia Woolf (1882–1941) came from a prominent literary family. Her father, Leslie Stephen, was the originator of the (British) *Dictionary of National Biography*, and her mother was a Duckworth, the publishing family. Her sister Vanessa Bell was, like her husband Clive, an artist, who designed jackets for the Hogarth Press, set up by Virginia and her husband Leonard in 1917. Virginia, a woman of ethereal beauty and, like so many of the Bloomsbury group, bisexual, married Leonard, social reformer and author, in 1912.

Woolf, whose life was punctuated by nervous breakdowns, was an experimental novelist often compared with Joyce. Besides her own work, she was a stimulating commentator in her luminously intelligent essays and in her feminist criticism, for example, *A Room of One's Own*, 1929. Her early novels, *The Voyage Out* (1915, but written earlier) and *Night and Day* (1919) were relatively realistic. The interval between them was largely occupied with the Hogarth Press, which published Katherine Mansfield and T. S. Eliot, among others.

Her reputation as England's leading modernist author was established in the 1920s by *Jacob's Room* (1922), based on the life and death of a beloved brother; *Mrs Dalloway* (1925), a classic using the stream-of-consciousness technique; *To the Lighthouse* (1927), employing the same technique to explore male-female conflict and based on her parents; and *The Waves* (1931), her most boldly experimental (and difficult) novel, and considered by some critics to be her masterpiece. The eponymous *Orlando* (1928), is alternatively male and female through four centuries. Something of a departure, it was her most successful novel and dedicated to Vita Sackville West, a woman of shared affinities. Her last novel *Between the Acts* (1941) returns to the stream-of-conscious-

Connect ... ', signifying his commitment to sympathetic relationships as the foundation of a civilized existence. During the rest of his life he wrote only two more novels: *Maurice* (1971), celebrating a homosexual relationship, which he declined to publish during his lifetime, and his most famous, *A Passage to India* (1924), the fruit of two visits to the subcontinent that cemented his hatred of imperialism. Sexual deviance, then highly improper, no doubt contributed to Forster's humane liberalism (he was the first president of the National Council for Civil Liberties). Besides his few but intensely evocative novels, he wrote short stories and fine and accessible commentaries on English literature, notably in *Aspects of the Novel* (1927).

LAWRENCE

As the son of a Nottingham miner, the connections of D. H. Lawrence (1883–1930) with Bloomsbury were remote, though when living in London he became friendly with several of the group, including the critic David Garnett, the new Zealand short-story writer Katherine Mansfield and the philosopher Bertrand Russell. He was a born – and prolific – writer, of poetry, criticism, travel, plays, essays and short stories, as well as novels. His first novel, *The White Peacock* (1911), was published thanks to Ford Madox Ford, who had been impressed by his early poetry. *Sons and Lovers* (1914), based on his childhood, exemplified the intensity of Lawrence's passions, but *The Rainbow* (1915), one of his best, ran into trouble through alleged obscenity and for some time he was unable to find a publisher for *Women in Love* (privately printed 1920).

In 1912, Lawrence ran off with Frieda, the German wife of a Nottingham professor, and from 1919 they lived a peripatetic life. Australia provided the setting for *Kangaroo* (1923) and Mexico for *The Plumed Serpent* (1926). Although the real subject of his last novel is the destructive effects of industrialism on human consciousness, Lawrence's frank treatment of sex prevented publication of *Lady Chatterley's Lover* until 30 years after his death from tuberculosis at the age of 44.

ness technique and celebrates traditional English values in the shadow of war.

FORSTER

Technically, E. M. Forster (1879–1970) was a more traditional novelist. The novel, he famously said, 'tells a story'. He established his reputation with *Where Angels Fear to Tread* (1905), *The Longest Journey* (1907), *A Room With a View* (1907) and, conclusively, with *Howard's End* (1910), a brilliant encapsulation of contemporary middle-class mores, which ends with Forster's famous motto, 'Only

Poetry of the modern period, as one literary historian put it, 'has not escaped the atmosphere of controversy.' Few groups of poets have endured such censure as the English 'Georgians' (1920s), seen as artificial and shallow. French symbolism remained an important influence, especially in Germany, where it stimulated one of the finest lyric poets of the century, Rainer Maria Rilke (1875–1926) and the Austrian Hugo von Hofmannsthal (1874–1929), while in France Surrealism, a term coined by the 'evangelist of Modernism', Guillaume Apollinaire (1880–1918), aimed, under the vigorous leadership of André Breton (1896–1966), to overturn all accepted doctrine in poetry and the arts. Other influential movements included German Expressionism and Italian Futurism.

The last note of English Romanticism was sounded by A. E. Housman (1859–1936), and a powerful influence was exercised, not for the best, by the highly original work of Gerard Manley Hopkins (1844–89), almost unknown before 1918. The exotic appeal of the East surfaced in James Elroy Flecker (1884–1915); Walter de la Mare (1973–1956), champion anthologist, wrote technically distinguished lyrics untouched by modern fashion. In short, variety, like controversy, was not lacking. Nevertheless, poetry in English in the first half of the 20th century was largely dominated by an Irishman, Yeats (see page 156), and an American, Eliot.

T. S. ELIOT

WASTELANDS

WAR POETS

The First World War had a dramatic effect on literature. All the great works of Modernism, if not actually concerned with the War, are affected by it. The term 'war poets' signifies a disparate group in whose work the War plays the major part, often because, sadly, the poet himself did not survive it.

Rupert Brooke, a young Georgian, was probably the most popular with – civilian – readers, though not with critics. He died early (April 1915), before the hideous experience of the trenches had obliterated the curiously exalted spirit in which, at the outset, war was regarded as a liberating, cleansing experience.

Julian Grenfell (fatally wounded May 1915) also died before disillusion led Edmund Blunden (a survivor) to the realisation that only 'the War had won, and would go on winning'. Other survivors included Siegfried Sassoon, Robert Graves, a major though idiosyncratic writer, and Ivor Gurney. Among non-survivors were Edward Thomas, Isaac Rosenberg and Wilfred Owen.

ELIOT

Born and raised in St. Louis, Missouri, and educated at Harvard, where he wrote some of the satirical poems in *The Love Song of J. Alfred Prufrock* (1917), T(homas) S(tearns)

Eliot (1888–1965) left the U.S.A. in 1914 and settled in London, eventually becoming an influential publisher at Faber and Faber. Like many others, he was encouraged by Ezra Pound, to whom *The Waste Land* (1922) is dedicated. Among other important influences were Dante, the Elizabethans/Jacobeans, especially Donne, and Christian mystics (Eliot joined the Anglican Church in 1927). *The Waste Land*, the most influential (though not the most read) poem of the century, is a pessimistic view of the desolation of European civilization after the war. In five books, mainly in free verse, it is uncompromisingly intellectual, full of complex and learned references which are not much clarified by Eliot's notes (for further elucidation of a transcription from the Sanskrit *Upanishads*, the reader is advised to consult a scholarly work in German).

'April is the cruellest month, breeding
Lilacs out of the dead land, mixing
Memory and desire, stirring
Dull roots with spring rain.
Winter kept us warm, covering
Earth in forgetful snow, feeding
A little life with dried tubers.'
Eliot, *The Waste Land*, 'The Burial of the Dead'.

Right: British soldiers on the Western Front during the First World War. Slaughter on a vast scale galvanized feelings of horror.

Opposite: Caricature of T. S. Eliot, 'one of the major voices of the age, proclaiming its disgust and despair, its guilt and angst, its struggle to find a faith.'

Eliot's poetic drama, 'Sweeney Agonistes' (published in the 1936 *Collected Poems*, but written ten years earlier) turned him towards the theatre. His most successful verse play, often revived, was *Murder in the Cathedral* (1935), about the murder of Thomas Becket in Canterbury Cathedral and first staged there. *The Cocktail Party* (1950) was also a popular and critical success. The work that some critics think challenges *The Waste Land* as Eliot's masterpiece is the sequence *Four Quartets* (1943), 'Burnt Norton', 'East Coker', 'The Dry Salvages' and 'Little Gidding'. It is suffused with Anglo-Catholic mysticism, dwells on time, memory and consciousness and offers some hope of reconciliation that is hardly discernible in *The Waste Land*. Eliot also wrote several volumes of profound and original social and literary criticism, not forgetting humorous verses for children about cats.

POUND

Another American exile, Ezra Pound (1885–1972) lived in London, Paris and, mostly, Italy. He was leader of the experimental movement known as Imagism, characterised by new verse forms, complex imagery and everyday speech. Adherents included the poets H. D. (Hilda Doolittle), Amy Lowell and Richard Aldington. Pound also promoted the work of Robert Frost, advised Eliot, and was associated with the brief Vorticist movement. Hugely well-read, witty, complicated, his own creative effort went into his *Cantos*, a modern epic that occupied most of his life. This, plus his influence on others and his many volumes of criticism, make him one of the masters of Modernism. Pound's support for Fascism led to his incarceration for 13 years in a US mental hospital after World War Two where he completed *The Pisan Cantos* (1948), controversially awarded the Bollingen prize for poetry.

CHAPTER TEN

20TH CENTURY DRAMA

In drama, the 20th century was far more fruitful than the 19th, and original playwrights more numerous. Although Realism remained the predominant mode in Western theatre for the fifty years after the deaths of Ibsen and Chekhov, new movements, styles, techniques and influences multiplied. Playwrights in the 20th century have certainly been eclectic – there is not much similarity between *Peter Pan*, a children's fantasy, and *Krapp's Last Tape*, a dying man's monologue, other than both are works written for the stage.

1897
Moscow Art Theatre is founded by, among others, Konstantin Stanislavsky

1921
Pirandello writes *Six Characters in Search of an Author*

1949
Bertolt Brecht founds the Berliner Ensemble/Arthur Miller writes *Death of a Salesman*

1955
Samuel Becket's *Waiting for Godot*

1956
The first performance of John Osborne's *Look Back in Anger*

1983
Tennessee Williams dies

1997
Dario Fo is awarded the Nobel Prize

Perhaps the most important ingredient in the recipe for the 20th century's rich dramatic pudding, besides the basic dough of the texts, was the new independent, specialised theatres. Among them were the theatre Strindberg founded to present his own plays in Stockholm, the Moscow Art Theatre that pioneered Chekhov, the Abbey Theatre in Dublin, and the Provincetown Players in Massachusetts and New York.

THEATRES AND ACTORS

THEATRES

The rapid rise in population in the 19th century resulted in an increase in the number of theatres and in the entertainments – music hall or vaudeville, melodramas – put on to fill them. Popular actors became stars (Sarah Bernhardt was known all over the world). Directors acquired greater importance. Authenticity in set design was diligently sought, and sometimes taken to extremes (real rabbits in the Forest of Arden). The great majority of theatres still adhered to the Italian, proscenium-arch stage, but the influence of designers such as Gordon Craig (1872–1966), of directors such as Max Reinhardt (1873–1943), and of traditional Oriental theatre, encouraged experiments with the thrust or apron stage and 'theatre in the round'. The biggest technical improvement within the theatre was in lighting, first gas, which produced 'limelight' among other effects, then electricity. In 1881, the Savoy Theatre in London installed the first electric lighting, and by the end of the century it was practically universal.

STANISLAVSKY

Konstantin Stanislavsky (1863–1938) was one of the founders of the Moscow Art Theatre in 1897, whose first big success was Chekhov's *The Seagull* in 1898 (a seagull is still the symbol of the Theatre). Stanislavksy's career launched the era of the all-powerful director, and his pursuit of psychological truth – 'the truth of feeling and experience' – was to prove of great and lasting influence. Sets and effects were painstakingly realistic, and actors were required to prepare intensively for their role, with many long and demanding rehearsals. It was necessary not only to act, but also to identify so closely with the character that his or her very emotions would be felt by the actor. Stanislavsky also encouraged the use of some idiosyncratic gesture to suggest the essence of the character. He described his 'Method' in several books, and it was the inspiration for later innovators, including Lee Strasberg, director of the famous Actors Studio in New York (1948-82), who put great emphasis on improvisation and exercises to assist the actors' emotional identification.

BRECHT

The poet, playwright and theoretician Bertolt Brecht (1898–1956) evolved theories of production very different from those of Stanislavsky, and they had great impact in the years after he founded the Berliner Ensemble in 1949. A committed, if rather unconventional Marxist, he threw out Realism in favour of stylised, 'epic' drama in which the actors are self-consciously performers. The response demanded from the audience is not emotional but rational, and Brecht employed rhetorical and other devices to alienate the audience in the interests of maintaining their objectivity.

Brecht's early work was in the Expressionist mode pioneered by Strindberg and Frank Wedekind (1864–1918). His most popular work by far is *The Threepenny Opera* (1928), with music by Kurt Weill. This fruitful partnership was abandoned as Brecht became more interested in didactic drama, linked with the interests of the Communist party (which he never joined). His plays, of which the most often performed, include *Man is Man* (1927), *The Life of Galileo* (1937), *Mother Courage* (1939), *The Resistible Rise of Arturo Ui* (1941) and *The Caucasian Chalk Circle* (1945), take the form of linked episodes, without great climaxes, including songs that comment on the action. They had a dramatic effect on the work of avant-garde playwrights in the 1950s and 1960s and his techniques have been of universal influence.

ORIENTAL THEATRE

'Theatre' in some form, often religious or ritualistic, is common to all cultures, and although Far Eastern drama has had little effect in the West, Asian theatrical traditions have had some influence in the 20th century. In his famous 1970 production of *A Midsummer Night's Dream*, Peter Brook introduced acrobatics, juggling and other elements characteristic of Chinese theatre, and his ten-hour production of a Hindu epic, *The Mahabharata*, in 1985 was another milestone.

The three Japanese traditions, No drama, Bunraku and Kabuki (all still maintained), are more familiar in the West. Yeats, at the Abbey Theatre, was one who sought inspiration in the ancient No drama, introduced to him by Ezra Pound. Like most forms of Asian performance art, they are intensely symbolic: in No, actors (all male; actresses were banned in the 17th century) are masked; in Bunraku they are puppets. Kabuki was developed in the late 16th century and is less stylized, incorporating song and dance, fantastic costumes, exaggerated make-up, and complex stage machinery that includes a revolving stage (copied much later in Europe) and a walkway from the back of the theatre to the stage, bringing the actors close to the audience. The best-known Japanese playwright, Monzaemon Chikamatsu (1653–c.1725), wrote for both Bunraku and Kabuki theatres.

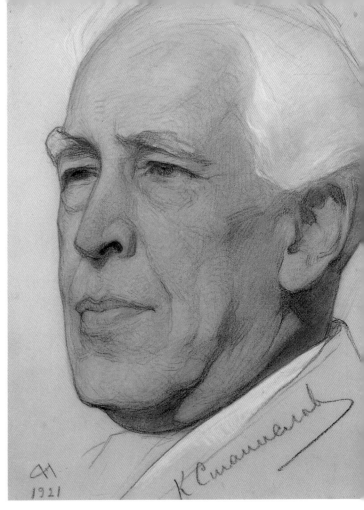

Above: **Post–Second World War opinion was divided over Bertolt Brecht, partly because of his political background, partly because of his controversial dramatic theories.**

Top: **Stanislavsky (real name Alexeev), the father of modern Russian theatre, in 1921.**

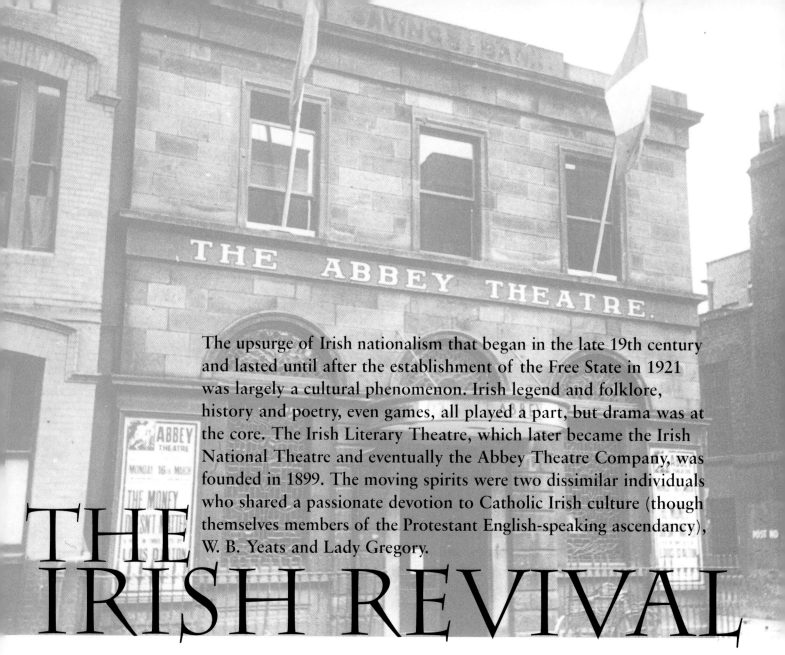

THE IRISH REVIVAL

The upsurge of Irish nationalism that began in the late 19th century and lasted until after the establishment of the Free State in 1921 was largely a cultural phenomenon. Irish legend and folklore, history and poetry, even games, all played a part, but drama was at the core. The Irish Literary Theatre, which later became the Irish National Theatre and eventually the Abbey Theatre Company, was founded in 1899. The moving spirits were two dissimilar individuals who shared a passionate devotion to Catholic Irish culture (though themselves members of the Protestant English-speaking ascendancy), W. B. Yeats and Lady Gregory.

'Had I the heavens' embroidered cloths,
Enwrought with golden and silver light,
The blue and the dim and the dark cloths
Of night and light and the half-light,
I would spread the cloths under your feet:
But I, being poor, have only my dreams;
I have spread my dreams under your feet;
Tread softly because you tread on my dreams.'
Yeats, 'He wishes for the Cloths of Heaven'.

YEATS

Son and brother of successful painters, W(illiam) B(utler) Yeats (1865–1939) gave up art in favour of literature in his twenties, his early publications including studies of Blake and Spenser. A convinced Irish nationalist, he was fascinated by Irish folklore and from an early age was powerfully attracted by mysticism and the supernatural, a significant influence and potent source of symbol in his work. He founded an Irish Literary Society in London (1891) and later Dublin, and his dream of a national theatre began to take concrete shape when, through a Catholic landowner, Edward Martyn, he met Augusta, Lady Gregory, widow of an ex-governor of Ceylon. His play, *The Countess Cathleen*, based on a story in his first collection of Irish folk tales, was staged in Dublin in 1892, an event taken as marking the beginning of the Irish Revival.

Yeats's most successful play was *Cathleen ni Houlihan* (1902) with Maud Gonne, the beautiful revolutionary nationalist and subject of his love poetry, in the title role as a personification of Ireland. In spite of all his work for the Irish theatre, Yeats was essentially a poet, not a playwright, though Ireland is the theme of all his creative writing. Often described as the greatest poet in English of the century, Yeats went through many reincarnations, from the Romantic, Pre-Raphaelite poems of his early years, to a tougher, more refined style under the influence of Synge, Pound and others, to the dense symbolism of *The Tower* (1928) and *The Winding Stair* (1933). What lends him great stature is the blend between his life and his work, his noble, if sometimes faulty (he flirted with Fascism in the 1930s), effort to make the world fit his imaginative pattern.

SYNGE

Although both Yeats and Lady Gregory wrote many plays for the company, it was another director of the Abbey Theatre, John Millington Synge (1871–1909), who, in a career cut short by cancer, showed the greatest dramatic gifts. From a middle-class, Protestant background, Synge spent long periods in the Aran Islands, at Yeats's suggestion, writing about peasant life. By listening to the idioms and cadences of everyday speech, he came to create his distinctive, rhetorical dialogue, every line 'flavoured like a nut'. Two one-act plays, *In the Shadow of the Glen* (1903) and the poetic tragedy *Riders to the Sea* (1904), appeared at the Abbey Theatre, followed by his masterpiece, *The Playboy of the Western World* (1907). Hard to categorize, it relates how villagers shelter a young fugitive who tells them he has killed his father, but they turn against him when the father turns up with only a bump on the head. The idea that Irish people should be tolerant of patricide and a frank (women's underclothes are mentioned!) attitude to sex caused a riot and the play had to be taken off. *The Tinker's Wedding*, a comedy disrespectful to the clergy, was staged in London (1909, written earlier), rather than Dublin.

O'CASEY

The Abbey's other great playwright, Sean O'Casey (1880–1964), not only provoked the touchy Dubliners but, touchy himself, eventually fell out with the Abbey when it rejected *The Silver Tassie* (1928). A Dubliner from a poor Protestant family, O'Casey had little formal education and worked for ten years as a labourer, becoming involved in nationalist organizations and amateur dramatics. His first approaches to the Abbey were unsuccessful, but Lady Gregory was encouraging and *The Shadow of a Gunman* was accepted in 1923. It was followed by his two great plays, *Juno and the Paycock* (1924) and *The Plough and the Stars* (1926). They were set among the Dublin poor, where O'Casey's deepest sympathies lay, in the time of the struggle for independence and civil war. In a style of heightened realism, they dealt with violent death and the way weak men are sustained by nationalist bravado and by their stronger women. They contain richly comic episodes as well as grim horrors. *The Plough and the Stars*, by its jaundiced view of nationalist heroes, provoked a ferocious response and O'Casey, hostile to the Church and increasingly a Communist sympathizer, settled permanently in London. In *The Silver Tassie* he began to experiment with non-Realist, Expressionist techniques, which characterize his later, less successful plays. Yeats, like many others, preferred his naturalistic style. In his later years O'Casey also wrote six discursive, entertaining volumes of his imaginative autobiography.

Above: Not only was Yeats a great poet, he was a strong, even formidable character, who was able to exploit the advantages of his own genius and circumstances.

Opposite: The Abbey Theatre opened in 1904 with three one-act plays, two by Yeats and one by Lady Gregory. It burned down in 1951 and reopened in 1966.

Realism in drama encouraged Realism in the theatre – in sets and stagecraft, as well as acting. Among the leaders in this development were Sir Henry Irving at the Lyceum Theatre in London, where he induced nightly fainting fits with his highly detailed production of the famous melodrama, *The Bells* (1871); Duke George II of Saxe-Meiningen, who with his actress-wife formed a touring company in which the actors spoke rather than enunciated; and the American impresario David Belasco, a truly 'theatrical' personality, famous for special effects of which his own popular plays were often the vehicle (*Madame Butterfly* and *The Girl of the Golden West*, attained greater fame as Puccini operas).

NATURALISM
AND ITS OPPONENTS

A RIVAL MEDIUM

Belasco's lavish, brilliantly-lit interiors could not be equalled by what appeared in the 20th century as a potential rival to the theatre – film. Few theatre people were worried by this dim innovation. It had no colour and, crucially, no dialogue. But in spite of these drawbacks (and it has been suggested that silent movies in America actually gained thereby, since many of the audience were immigrants with an imperfect command of English) the impact was soon felt. Even the primitive early silent movies, especially Hollywood's action spectaculars which even Belasco could hardly imitate on stage, had a dramatic effect on theatre attendance. In the U.S.A. between 1900 and 1920, a fertile period for drama as it happened, the theatre lost a large percentage of its audience. It would never regain them.

ANTI-REALISM

The most obvious casualties were the 'popular' theatres and music halls which catered to the working class, but they were not the only ones. The middle classes were also deserting the theatre. For this, however, the cinema was only partly to blame. From Ibsen and on, people simply did not like the new drama: it broke cherished taboos and demanded that they think

Above: Strindberg's psychological dramas, such as *Miss Julie*, employed an original brand of naturalism, but he later moved beyond it into a more subjective, semi-mystical form of drama.

Opposite: The Red Sphinx, 1910, by Odilon Redon (1840–1916), whose halucinatory paintings are often based on literary inspiration.

for themselves, something they had no desire to do. With the arrival of Modernism, in its various anti-Realist guises, all the old conventions appeared to have been abandoned, and anarchy, it seemed, strode the stage. Experimental drama did not provide 'a good night out', and theatres contracted to adjust to their reduced audience.

SYMBOLISM

The reaction against experimental drama was noticeable in France as early as the 1850s; a dramatisation of Zola's *Thérèse Raquin* was booed off the stage. Zola was a Symbolist only in the rather general sense in which symbolism is a characteristic of nearly all literature. More specifically, Symbolism refers to certain French writers and artists around the turn of the century, perhaps to a group of Russians somewhat later and sometimes to Modernism in Latin America.

The most influential figure was Mallarmé (see page 95) whose advice to depict not the thing but the effect is a kind of Symbolist motto. He advocated a new drama portraying the mental life, not the world of the senses. For the Symbolists, art is a means of understanding rather than feeling, and since they despised mundane reality, the Symbolists were antagonistic towards Realist drama. Symbolist drama tends to be learned and decidedly static.

The Art Theatre founded in the 1890s by the poet Paul Fort, was at the centre of the movement, set up largely in reaction against the predominantly Realist Théâtre Libre of the actor-director André Antoine, a friend of Zola. Playwrights patronized by the Art Theatre included Maurice Maeterlinck (1862–1949), best known for *Pelléas et Mélisande* (1892, later the basis of Debussy's opera) and *The Blue Bird* (1908), Hoffmansthal (1874–1929), Paul Claudel (1869–1955) and the young Yeats, whose interest in the occult the Symbolists shared. The influence of Symbolism was widespread, not only in Russia and Latin America, but also on Pound, Joyce, Eliot, Rilke and Virginia Woolf.

EXPRESSIONISM

As J. B. Priestley remarked 'it is a waste of time trying to find an exact definition of

Expressionism in drama'. In its most forceful, revolutionary phase, it belonged to the Berlin theatre of the early 1920s, more broadly to Central Europe in the first quarter of the century, and more broadly still to much non-Realist drama. The term was first used of painting in which the painter 'sought to express emotional experience rather than impressions of the physical world'. The young Expressionist playwrights had large ambitions, seeking a spiritual transformation of society, and, in terms of the drama, abandoning objectivity and attempting to capture the subjective depths of modern poetry and the greater scope of, significantly, the cinema (where Expressionism had powerful effects). Rebelling against most current values, Expressionist playwrights turned to oncetaboo subjects such as sex and class. The typical Expressionist 'hero' (always male) is not involved in a plot but in some kind of inward odyssey, and the mood is often violent, always extreme. Stage designers were influenced by Expressionist art, with atmospheric lighting, fierce colours, and jagged lines. Beyond Central Europe, the Expressionist influence was not great, though an exception might be made for Eugene O'Neill.

Above: Tennessee Williams at the Savoy Theatre, London, for the British opening of *The Night of the Iguana*, a drama of three disparate characters in a remote Mexican hotel.

Opposite: Arthur Miller and the Hollywood goddess Marilyn Monroe, his wife during a strange and short-lived alliance.

AMERICAN PLAYWRIGHTS

North America in the 19th century was not short of theatrical entertainments, from vaudeville and burlesque through melodrama to serious plays, but native American drama made little impression on the world stage until the early 20th century. Its flowering then is associated largely with O'Neill and the development of an American equivalent of the European independent art theatre. O'Neill was unique, but there were other dramatists worthy of serious consideration, such as Maxwell Anderson (1888–1959), Thornton Wilder (1897–1976), remembered especially for his evocation of provincial life in *Our Town* (1938) and his best-selling novel *The Bridge of San Luis Rey* (1927), Lilian Hellman (1907–84), who caused a sensation with her first play, dealing with lesbianism, *The Children's Hour* (1934), and, later and greater, Tennessee Williams and Arthur Miller.

O'NEILL

Son of an actor, Eugene O'Neill (1888–1953), as with so many American writers, knocked about in various colourful jobs (gold prospector, seaman, etc.) before beginning to write plays, mainly naturalistic dramas based on his maritime experience, while confined in a tuberculosis sanatorium. He became involved with the Provincetown Players, a group of actors and writers who founded an art theatre in a converted New England fishing shack in 1915, and the company produced his early plays. With *Beyond the Horizon*, a full-length realistic drama, and the Expressionist *The Emperor Jones* (both 1920), about the rise and fall of a black adventurer, he achieved national recognition. Although O'Neill is generally known for only a handful of plays, he was at this time extremely prolific: between 1920–22 he produced nine plays. He was widely recognized as America's first great playwright, and became a major influence on later American drama.

Influenced by Ibsen, Strindberg and Greek tragedy, O'Neill was an experimental dramatist who did not find his true voice until comparatively late. The New England tragedy *Desire*

under the Elms (1924) is naturalistic in form. Strange Interlude (1928) is an experiment in the dramatic use of the stream-of-consciousness technique, and Mourning Becomes Electra (1931) is O'Neill's rewriting of Aeschylus set in the American Civil War. After Ah, Wilderness! (1933), uncharacteristically a nostalgic comedy, and the unsuccessful Days Without End (1934), no new play appeared for twelve years, due largely to ill health, although he did not stop writing. His final period began with The Iceman Cometh (1946), a long, naturalistic tragedy of the pipe-dreaming no-hopers in a saloon on New York's Bowery. His masterpiece, Long Day's Journey into Night (1956) was written in the early 1940s and first performed posthumously. It recounts a day in the lives of the troubled, mutually destructive Tyrone family, based on his own. A Moon for the Misbegotten (1957) concerns the self-destruction of the elder brother of the family after the mother's death.

TENNESSEE WILLIAMS

Like O'Neill, Tennessee (Thomas Lanier) Williams (1911–83) had many one-act plays performed by obscure groups before establishing a reputation for his deeply felt, partly autobiographical drama The Glass Menagerie (1944). Williams was born in Mississippi and Southern culture and families form the major component of his plays. His sympathy for the lost, tormented individual (a description that, judging from his Memoirs, 1975, might be applied to him) was evident also in A Streetcar Named Desire (1947), set in New Orleans and concerned with the destructive – or destroyed – illusions of a faded Southern belle. None of his later plays had quite the resounding success of these two. They included: The Rose Tattoo (1950), a comedy; the symbolic, experimental Camino Real (1953);

'Alfieri: "Most of the time now we settle for half and I like it better. But the truth is holy, and even as I know how wrong he was, and his death useless, I tremble, for I confess that something perversely pure calls to me from his memory – not purely good, but himself purely, for he allowed himself to be wholly known and for that I think I will love him more than all my sensible clients. And yet, it is better to settle for half, it must be! And so I mourn him – I admit it – with a certain … alarm."'
Miller, A View From The Bridge, act II.

Cat on a Hot Tin Roof (1955), a psychological family drama; Sweet Bird of Youth (1956), and The Night of the Iguana (1959).

ARTHUR MILLER

The finest plays of Arthur Miller (born 1915) were written by the time he was 40, although his reputation has continued to climb, especially in Britain. His first Broadway play in 1944 closed within a week, but All My Sons (1947), a drama of disillusion in the tradition of Ibsen (an important influence), was a big success, and his masterpiece, Death of a Salesman (1949), an even greater one. An American classic, it concerns an ordinary, well-meaning man destroyed by the false values of society. Miller's famous essay on 'Tragedy and The Common Man' was written the same year. The Crucible (1953) is a powerful, if flawed, drama about the witch trials of 17th-century Salem, but clearly reflected McCarthy's persecution of alleged Communists in contemporary America. A View from the Bridge (1955), set among Sicilian longshoremen (dockers) in Brooklyn, is again concerned with tragedy brought upon a simple family by contemporary values. Perfectly constructed, it features in many 'Eng. Lit.' syllabuses. After a long silence, Miller's next play was the controversial After the Fall (1964), apparently based on his marriage to Marilyn Monroe. Incident at Vichy (1964) concerned the persecution of the Jews; The Price (1968), more widely admired, returned to his old theme of the destruction of family relationships; Broken Glass (1994) won the Olivier Best Play Award.

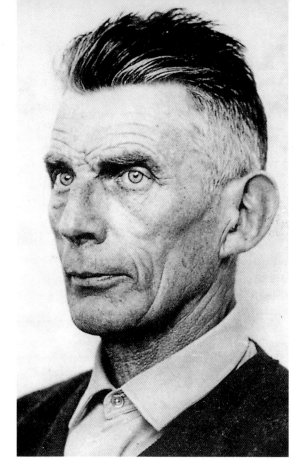

THE THEATRE OF THE ABSURD

This term describes the work of a number of avant-garde playwrights during the middle of the 20th century, including Edward Albee (born 1928), Beckett and Pinter. The philosophical idea of the Theatre of the Absurd was the result of contemporary interest in the absurdity of the human condition deriving partly from Albert Camus, especially from his essays *The Rebel* and *The Myth of Sisyphus*, first published in English in 1953 and 1955 respectively. Its antecedents, however, were much older, going back at least to Alfred Jarry (1873–1907), whose *Ubu roi*, the first of several 'Ubu' plays, was produced at the anti-Naturalistic Théâtre de l'Oeuvre in Paris in 1896. Jarry was an eccentric humorist, inventor of pataphysics, 'the science of imaginary solutions', but hostile to the social order, and Ubu, a caricature of the bourgeoisie, is unpleasant as well as absurd. Jarry was a

AVANT-GARDE DRAMA

The rise of the independent 'art' theatre, the rejection of Naturalism and the resulting experimentalism in drama spawned a variety of novelties. Some caused a brief flutter and disappeared as suddenly as they arose. Others carried more intellectual weight and, although contemporaries may have seen them as passing curiosities, they proved to have unexpected staying power and influenced the later development of drama.

Above: In Beckett, there is humour in despair: '...where I am I don't know, I'll never know, in the silence you don't know, you must go on, I can't go on, I'll go on.' (*Malone Dies*, 1958).

Opposite: Harold Pinter about the time of *The Caretaker*, which confirmed his distinctive gift for conjuring the sinister and disturbing from the mundane.

major influence on the Surrealists as well as the Theatre of the Absurd.

Another influence on post-1945 drama and an early opponent of Naturalism was the Italian Luigi Pirandello (1867–1936), whose plays – *Six Characters in Search of an Author* (1921) being probably the best known – questioned the reality of appearances and explored the breakdown of personality in a manner anticipating Beckett.

FRENCH ABSURDISTS

Romanian-born Eugène Ionescu (1912–94) was an admirer of Jarry and also found comedy in the absurd, notably in *The Bald Prima Donna* (1948), constructed largely from the banal phrases of a French phrase book. His later 'anti-plays', often featuring a bewildered author-figure, fuse humour with grim and tragic elements, even despair. In his most successful play, *Rhinoceros* (1959), human beings are turned into rampaging pachyderms by an increasingly totalitarian society.

The rough early life, much of it spent in prison, of the 'saintly monster' Jean Genet (1910–86) furnished material for his plays, notably *The Maids* (1947), *The Balcony* (1957) and *The Blacks* (1958). Illusion battles with reality, and bizarre, often violent fantasies are played out in a dream-like atmosphere that, in spite of Genet's declared amoral and hedonistic principles, approaches religious ritual. This was something like the form of drama, misleadingly called the 'Theatre of Cruelty', advocated by the actor-director Antonin Artaud (1896–1948).

BECKETT

The idea that the world is absurd, mysterious beyond comprehension, naturally gives rise to pessimistic sentiments, bewilderment and a sense of purposelessness. Representing these themes in drama can have enervating effects. Plots become more illogical or non-existent, dialogue minimal and obscure. Theatregoers for whom the naturalistic drama is the norm naturally complain of these difficulties. Compensations include humour, an important element in Beckett's renowned play *Waiting for Godot* (1952, first performed in English in 1955), which had a massive impact on modern drama and is chiefly responsible for Beckett's reputation as the most innovative, influential writer of his time.

Samuel Beckett (1906–89) was born near Dublin, went to Paris, where he later settled permanently, and met Joyce, a lifelong friend and subject of his first book. Most of his work was written in French, sometimes translated into English by himself. His later stage plays include *Endgame* (1957), *Krapp's Last Tape* (1958) and *Happy Days* (1961). With *Come and Go* (1966), containing 121 words, and *Breath* (1969), lasting 30 seconds, he took minimalism as far as possible. He also wrote novels, stories and poems. Although Beckett's work is despairing, it is illuminated by black humour: some of the two tramps' exchanges in *Godot* amount to an intellectual comic patter, and the play overall has a strangely exhilarating effect.

PINTER

Born into a Cockney Jewish family, Harold Pinter (born 1930) was writing poetry in his teens. He became a professional actor, later a notable theatrical director, and aroused interest with his second play, *The Birthday Party* (1958). It contained many of the characteristics of Pinter's distinctive style: set in a single room, whose occupant is vaguely and inexplicably threatened by mysterious intruders, the dialogue inconsequentially conversational, with pauses more meaningful than words. In *The Caretaker* (1960), which established Pinter as a major playwright internationally, a derelict who may or may not be named Davies, seeks to gain possession or occupancy of a room which may or may not belong to one or both of two brothers. The prevailing air of menace is hard to account for. Of his other plays, perhaps the best is *The Homecoming* (1965), a black and sinister 'comedy' superficially about the effects of introducing a woman into a male household. Later plays lacked the impact of the early ones, and Pinter became involved with various other projects, e.g. directing plays and writing film scripts.

'Vladimir: "That passed the time."
Estragon: "It would have passed in any case."
Vladimir: "Yes, but not so rapidly."'
Becket, *Waiting for Godot*.

DÜRRENMATT

Swiss playwright Friedrich Dürrenmatt (*born* 1921), a prolific writer who first gained attention abroad in the 1950s through his existentialist detective novels, considered, in the wake of the horrors of 1939–45, that it was no longer possible to make moral judgements since the world was devoid of moral values. 'Tragedy' is therefore no longer appropriate, but his disillusioned, absurdist plays are very black comedies. *The Marriage of Mr Mississippi* (1952) concerns two people whose zealous pursuit of justice ends in their justification of murder, and the infinite corruptibility of human beings underlies *The Visit* (1956) and *The Physicists* (1962). Dürrenmatt's later plays show signs of mellowing and are more conventional in technique.

THE 'KITCHEN SINK' SCHOOL

The drama in Britain underwent a minor revolution in the 1950s as the result of the work of a group of young playwrights in reaction against the staple fair of the London theatre of the time, dominated by conventional, middle-class plays by writers such as – the subsequently underrated – Terence Rattigan. The pivotal moment was the opening of the appropriately named *Look Back in Anger* (1956) by John Osborne (1929–94), set in a grubby flat in a Midlands town rather than a Kensington drawing room. It was essentially a naturalistic family drama, with a powerfully written central character (Osborne displayed a mastery of invective) and a psychologically acute

Above: **John Osborne, 'a great man for raging', in 1959.**

Opposite: **A scene from the film version of** *Look Back in Anger* **with Richard Burton and Mary Ure, whose marriage to the playwright ended as stormily as the marriage in the play.**

A great deal of modern literature is concerned with making some kind of protest, even if only against other forms of literature. Criticism of society had been a prime ingredient of the 19th-century novel, and later made its way into drama. The Theatre of the Absurd can be said to be making a fundamental protest about life itself, while at the other extreme, documentary drama or the so-called 'Theatre of Fact' makes very specific charges against alleged political or social evils. The public nature of a theatrical performance makes the drama well suited to such purposes.

PROTEST PLAYS

study of a love-hate relationship. Osborne became a leader of the so-called 'Angry Young Men', and in later plays such as *The Entertainer* (1957) and *Inadmissible Evidence* (1964) proved himself the best playwright of the 'Kitchen Sink' school, which included Arnold Wesker and Shelagh Delaney, both, unlike Osborne, sprung from working-class roots.

CLASS, RACE AND SOCIETY

Edward Bond (1934–90) was also of working-class origin and left school at 14. Like other avant-garde British writers, he was taken up by the Royal Court Theatre in Chelsea and his second play, *Saved* (1965), about the dire effects of cultural deprivation, made him notorious when it was banned because of a scene in which some youths stone a baby. His third play suffered a similar fate. Bond's plays sometimes attacked the injustices of capitalist society in the guise of historical abuses, and often employed extreme shock tactics, as in his brutal version of *Lear* (1971).

The plays of the South African Athol Fugard (born 1932) were largely concerned with personal and social conflicts exacerbated by the doctrine of apartheid. He co-operated closely with black South African actors and writers, and most of his plays were banned in his own country. Among the most notable are *Boesman and Lena* (1968), in which the central characters are a coloured (mixed-race) couple of migrant workers, *Sizwe Bansi is Dead* (1972), *A Lesson from Aloes* (1980), the partly autobiographical *Master Harold . . . & the Boys* (1982) and *The Road to Mecca* (1984).

The German novelist and playwright Peter Weiss (1916–82) achieved international renown with his play *The . . . Assassination of . . . Marat as Performed by the Inmates of the Asylum of Charenton under the Direction of the Marquis de Sade* (1964), a piece of 'total theatre' set in the mental asylum where Sade was confined in 1808, a metaphor for modern society. It was the subject of a memorable production by Peter Brooke for the Royal Shakespeare Company. Weiss, also a painter and film-maker, was influenced by Kafka and the Theatre of the Absurd, as well as by Artaud and, of course, by Brecht, whose alienation technique he adopted in later plays.

THE THEATRE OF FACT

Weiss was a significant figure in documentary drama associated with the German director Erwin Piscator (1893–1966), who was responsible with Brecht for forging 'epic' theatre in the 1920s. Weiss's play, *The Investigation* (1965), directed by Piscator, includes genuine testimony from guards and victims at Auschwitz. The same techniques were employed by Rolf Hochhuth in his controversial plays *The Deputy* (1963), also directed by Piscator, and *Soldiers* (1967), which attacked the Pope and Winston Churchill.

The German political theatre had some effect in other countries. In the U.S.A., where the documentary novel was also popular, a number of controversial political topics or individuals (Malcolm X, the myth of the American West, etc.) were the subjects of dramas in the late 1960s and 1970s.

RICHARD BURTON
CLAIRE BLOOM
MARY URE

Blick zurück im Zorn
LOOK BACK IN ANGER

Nach dem bekannten Theaterstück von
JOHN OSBORNE

Regie: Tony Richardson

'Jimmy: "Was I really wrong to believe that there's a – a kind of – burning virility of mind and spirit that looks for something as powerful as itself? The heaviest, strongest creatures in this world seem to be the loneliest. Like the old bear, following his own breath in the dark forest. There's no warm pack, no herd to comfort him."'
Osborne, *Look Back in Anger*, act 3.

CHAPTER ELEVEN

LITERATURE SINCE THE 1920S

The nearer the present age approaches, the more difficult it becomes to take a balanced view about the literature. Apart from the overall growth in the sheer number of authors, controversy is more easily aroused and judgements are inevitably more subjective – and they are increasingly likely to be overturned in the near future. We are often surprised by the ideas of earlier generations on literature and other matters, and we can be certain that future generations will be equally surprised by ours. In any case, it serves little purpose in so short a space to attempt to encompass the leading novelists or poets of the age, whether judged by general critical acclaim, popular success or simple personal preference, as the end result would be simply a list, no more informative than a telephone directory.

1925 Kafka's *The Trial* is published posthumously

Margeret Mitchell's *Gone with the Wind*, the world's best-selling novel

1936 The Spanish Civil War

1936-39

1939-45 The Second World War

George Orwell's *Nineteen Eighty-Four*

1949

1956 Allen Ginsburg's poem 'Howl'

1974 Solzhenitsyn is exiled from the Soviet Union

1989 Iranian *fatwa* decrees death for Salman Rushdie

1998 Ted Hughes's poems about his life with Sylvia Plath, *Birthday Letters*, published

All writers reflect their times, but a writer's engagement with society varies, not only for personal reasons but also by the extent to which contemporary problems demand attention. Great events normally influence writers' general view of society. Political developments in the Thirties had a more direct effect. The rise of the formidable rival ideologies of Communism and Fascism (and their clash in the Spanish Civil War), combined with the apparent failure of the capitalist system in the Great Depression, convinced many writers of the importance of reflecting immediate experience and compelled them to take sides in historical events. A by-product of this impact was the revitalization of Realism.

THE THIRTIES

EXILES

Eliot, the English American, was a great influence on a younger group of English poets (including Louis MacNeice and Stephen Spender) of whom the leader was W[ystan] H[ugh] Auden (1907–73), an Englishman who settled in America. He also spent some time in Berlin with his childhood friend Christopher Isherwood (1904–86), remembered best for his Berlin novels (*Mr Norris Changes Trains*, *Goodbye to Berlin*), and they later co-operated on three plays. Auden drove an ambulance in the Spanish Civil War and emigrated to America with Isherwood in 1939. His great technical virtuosity was apparent in his early *Poems* (1930). His left-wing political beliefs and interest in Freudian psychology were powerful forces in his early work, but the Anglo-Catholic faith in which he had been brought up re-emerged strongly in later years.

Thomas Mann, (1875–1955), another American resident, was acknowledged as the greatest contemporary German novelist since the publication of *Buddenbrooks* (1901). German-Jewish writers naturally left their homeland in droves – the only alternative was destruction.

SPAIN

Good writers tended to belong to the political Left than the Right. Among new voices in France in the 1930s the novelist Louis Ferdinand Céline (1894–1961) represented the Right, whereas the multi-gifted André Malraux (1901–76), who helped organize the Republicans' air force in Spain, represented the radical Left.

As the focus of the world struggle between Left and Right, the Spanish Civil War (1936–39) dominated European literature in the 1930s, and impelled José Ortega y Gasset in *Toward a Philosophy of History* (1941) to the conclusion that Communism and Fascism were responsible for the collapse of Western civilization. Many writers were drawn to Spain, some as volunteers in the Communist-organized International

Brigades. They included the French Communist poet and one-time Surrealist Louis Aragon, the Hungarian novelist Mata Zalka (who was killed), and the British novelist George Orwell (who survived a bullet through the neck), as well as over twenty from Germany alone. Amongst the journalists were French novelist Antoine de Saint-Exupéry and the Americans John Dos Passos and Ernest Hemingway (1899–1961).

Hemingway's novel For *Whom the Bell Tolls* (1940) is the best-known English novel of the Civil War. Generally considered at his best in the short story, Hemingway developed a distinctive, pared-down style that was to influence post-war novelists.

One of the millions of Spanish victims of the war was the poet Federico García Lorca (1898–1936), now regarded as one of Spain's greatest playwrights (*Blood Wedding*, *The House of Bernarda Alba*). He was murdered by General Franco's Nationalists in Granada.

DEPRESSION

As F. Scott Fitzgerald, the 'laureate of the Jazz Age', recognized in his novel *Tender is the Night* (1934), the Wall Street Crash of 1929 ended an era by demonstrating the fragility of the American Dream. The classic America novel of the Depression is John Steinbeck's *Grapes of Wrath* (1939), a tale of the trek of ruined poor whites from Oklahoma to California, but it affected all American literature, not least drama. Richard Wright's famous protest novel, *Native Son* (1940), told the tale of poor blacks in country and city. President Roosevelt's Works

Progress Administration funded the arts and many young writers were employed in the Federal Writers' Project.

EXISTENTIALISM

In *Nausea* (1938), Jean-Paul Sartre (1905–80) explained the tenets of existentialism, but its influence on French and European literature was delayed by the Second World War. Existentialism was not a doctrine but a group of loosely associated ideas, whose proponents included Martin Heidegger and Karl Jaspers in Germany and Gabriel Marcel in France. It placed emphasis on the autonomy of the individual and was hostile to general laws or principles of human nature and to all efforts to explain the universe rationally.

Sartre's radical form of existentialism made the individual his own moral judge, a deed being justified by the sincerity with which it is committed. Other writers associated with existentialism in France were Albert Camus, especially in his novels *The Outsider* and *The Plague*, and Sartre's close friend Simone de Beauvoir (1908–86), best known otherwise for her influential feminist work, *The Second Sex*. The influence of existentialism was less, or less direct, in Britain and America.

'Tomorrow for the young the poets exploding like bombs,
The walks by the lake, the weeks of perfect communion;
Tomorrow the bicycle races
Through the suburbs on summer evenings. But today
the struggle.'
Auden, 'Spain 1937'.

According to legend, the denunciations of the poet Archilochus against his enemies were so effective that they committed suicide. By the mid-20th century, poets and their work had lost that kind of impact. Perhaps the last poet who really believed in poetry's influence on public events was Yeats, who agonized that his play *Cathleen ni Houlihan* was responsible for the deaths of the leaders of the Easter Rising in Dublin ('Did that play of mine send out/Certain men the English shot?'). Modern poets are more of the mind of Auden (in his elegy to Yeats): 'poetry makes nothing happen'.

Opinion polls show that a large number of people have written a poem at some time, and published poets are more numerous than ever, though very few make a living from their poetry. Modern poetry since Eliot has often been too 'difficult' for the average reader. However, a handful of poets in the late 20th century have achieved a huge popular following as well as the respect of the critics.

FROST

The popular image of Robert Frost (1874–1963) is of the poet of New England, its birch trees and farmland, the heir of Wordsworth and the Transcendentalists. His early poetry was published in old England, where he lived with his family in 1912–15 after a period of profound depression caused partly by the deaths of two children. He formed a close friendship with the English poet, Edward Thomas, killed in the First World War, who shared his love of the traditional and the colloquial. He subsequently settled on a New Hampshire farm, though neither farm nor poetry absolved him from the need to teach. By the time of *Collected Poems* (1930), Frost's 'woodland philosophy' – and the accessibility of his work – had made him an American icon, but there was something deeper and darker in him. This bitter, destructive element is more evident in the dramatic, blank-verse poems of the 1940s, which explore the relationship of the individual to God in the modern world.

LOWELL

Robert Lowell (1917–77) also came from old New England stock, though similarities to Frost end there. The intellectual qualities, complex, multi-layered imagery, subtle irony and sophisticated technique of Lowell's poetry could hardly command such popular affection, but *Lord Weary's Castle* (1946), his second collection, won a Pulitzer Prize. *Life Studies* (1959), *For the Union Dead* (1964) and *Near the Ocean* (1967) confirmed his reputation as the greatest American poet of his time, but his public fame derived rather from his opposition to the Vietnam War and the disasters of his private life, frankly revealed in *The Dolphin* (1973).

DYLAN THOMAS

Hugely popular during his lifetime, Dylan Thomas (1914–53) has come to be regarded with suspicion by some critics, who suggest that his extraordinary verbal exuberance and elaborate style mask superficiality and insincerity. Even in Wales, some regard him as a showman, exploiting Welshness. However, a few of his poems are among that select number familiar to nearly everyone. In general, his poems need to be read aloud, and no one read them better than himself. Best of all is his radio play, *Under Milk Wood* (1952), a picture of a Welsh fishing village in language that bridges the division between prose and poetry. His exhausting American tours, combined with frail health and an addiction to wild living, combined to cause his early death.

LARKIN

For thirty years librarian at the University of Hull, Philip Larkin (1922–85) knew from youth that he was a writer, but he did not find his true voice until about 1950, and first attracted widespread attention with *The Less Deceived* (1955). His other major collections are *The Whitsun Weddings* (1964) of which the title poem is his best known, and *High Windows* (1974). Conservative, anti-modernist, working with traditional forms and conventional subject matter but in subtly new ways, Larkin, if not a major artist – his total output was small – seems to exemplify the first-rate poet who yet remains in touch with and appeals to ordinary people.

HUGHES

Ted Hughes (born 1930), who succeeded the much-loved John Betjeman as Britain's Poet Laureate in 1984, is a very masculine poet, vital, even violent, whose best-known work is probably *Crow* (1970), a sequence of poems linked by the image of the dark, crafty, predatory crow. Hughes's view of the animal world, his chief subject, emphasizes the alienation of modern society from its natural origins. He has also written extensively for children and for the theatre. Hughes was married to the distinguished American poet Sylvia Plath (1932–63), whose subsequently much-discussed suicide (before most of her work was published) has obstructed objective judgment of her work and may (or may not) be connected with Hughes's ambiguous attitude to women.

HEANEY

Hughes co-operated on two notable anthologies with Seamus Heaney (born 1939), the pre-eminent representative of a rich crop of contemporary Irish poets, whose early work had similarities with Hughes's nature poetry. Later work engages with the problems, past and present, of Ireland. Volumes such as *Wintering Out* (1972), *North* (1975) and *Field Work* (1979) established his reputation as a profound and brilliantly accomplished poet, and his stature on an international level was acknowledged by the award of the Nobel Prize (1996).

THE POLITICAL NOVEL

Some engagement with political concerns marks most novelists, at least indirectly. The more direct engagement with current events of recent times is basically political, and in some countries, such as Russia under Stalinism, virtually all serious literature is political; there is no escaping it, even in a book of nursery rhymes. The Hungarian-born Arthur Koestler's *Darkness at Noon* (1940) is a classic anti-Stalinist novel. But there is really no identifiable category of 'the Political Novel', and whatever links Kafka, Orwell and Solzhenitsyn, it is not similarity of form or style.

KAFKA

The novels of Franz Kafka (1883–1924) are 'political' largely in retrospect. The real subject of his unsettling tales is the alienation of the individual in a hostile, uncomprehending, inexplicable world. A German-speaking Jew from Prague, tubercular and mentally troubled, he was hardly known in his lifetime, his three novels and most of his short stories being published posthumously through his friend and executor, Max Brod, who disregarded Kafka's suggestion that they should be burned.

Kafka's novels, *The Trial* (1925), *The Castle* (1926) and *Amerika* (1927), are fragmentary, and the last is unfinished. The first sentence of *The Trial* suggests the flavour: 'Someone must have slandered Joseph K. because, one morning, without his having done anything wrong, he was arrested.' The central character, whose surname is never elucidated, is persecuted and eventually executed by various incomprehensible agencies working on behalf of a mysterious judicial body. In *The Castle*, the central character strives heroically and fruitlessly to secure recognition of his existence from the authorities in the castle. These novels predated the Stalinist terror and came to acquire greater resonance as a result of it. But the labyrithine complexities, the sinister absurdities, the oppressive atmosphere of intense anxiety that characterize Kafka's decidedly unsettling world are described, astonishingly, in pearl-like language, lucid and concise.

Few novelists have inspired more interpreters, but no interpreter satisfactorily explains Kafka's vision.

ORWELL

Old Etonian and veteran of the Burma Police, George Orwell (1903–50) acknowledged that he was not a true novelist. A gifted journalist and essayist, he was inspired by hatred of political injustice, and the novel sometimes proved the most suitable means to express it. Among his best books are his factual account of unemployment in the north of England, *The Road to Wigan Pier* (1937), and his account of his experiences as a Republican volunteer in the Spanish Civil War, *Homage to Catalonia* (1938), but he is chiefly remembered for two works of fiction.

A socialist but a democrat, Orwell's target in both *Animal Farm* (1945) and *Nineteen Eighty-Four* (1949) is Soviet totalitarianism. *Animal Farm* belongs to that select group of parables that can be read as a children's story. The farm animals rebel against the exploitative farmer and set up a republic in which 'All animals are equal'. The popular revolution is taken over by the pigs, led by Napoleon, the other animals are subjected to still worse suppression, and to their democratic slogan is added '. . . but some animals are more equal than others'. *Nineteen Eighty-Four* is a dystopia of a futuristic totalitarian state, owing something to Koestler, in which the Party rewrites history and the dictionary in its efforts to control the very thoughts of the people, who are watched over by the ubiquitous image of Big Brother. The Cold War made it seem all the more topical, but Orwell's tour de force also signifies his loss of faith in human nature.

AGAINST STALIN

The relationship between the writer and the state is the – hidden – subject of Mikhail Bulgakov's masterpiece *The Master and Margarita*, written in the 1930s, published in 1966. Stalin and his colleagues drew no distinction between literature and propaganda. The sign of literary worth was expulsion from, not admission to, the Writers' Union. After Stalin's death, the Party's attitude see-sawed. Boris Pasternak thought he could get away with *Doctor Zhivago* (published abroad in 1957, written earlier). It earned him a Nobel Prize, but the outraged authorities refused to allow him out of the country to receive it.

Under Khrushchev, it was possible to publish *One Day in the Life of Ivan Denisovich* (1962), which exposed the horror of the Stalinist prison camps. The author was the then-unknown Aleksandr Solzhenitsyn (born 1918), who became a thorn in the side of the more repressive Brezhnev regime. In 1965 the writers Andrei Sinyavsky and Yuli Daniel were sentenced to hard labour for publishing abroad, but the days of the terror were over: people were less easily intimidated, protests grew, and a stream of writers moved to the West, including, much against his will, the heroically Russian Solzhenitsyn in 1974. Some sort of a literary nadir was reached with the award of the top literary prize to Brezhnev himself, for his memoirs. The long-overdue collapse of the system in the late 1980s, in Russia and in the other countries that had languished under the Stalinist yoke since the 1940s, brought artistic freedom, but also the problem, similar to that faced by armies after the end of a war, of motivation. Returning to his beloved homeland from alien exile, rumbling now against Western materialism, Solzhenitsyn seemed a figure from a completely different age.

Above: Orwell, whose real name was Eric Blair, was a war correspondent for the BBC during the Second World War.

NORTH AMERICAN FICTION

'There was only one catch and that was Catch-22 . . . Orr would be crazy to fly more missions and sane if he didn't, but if he was sane he had to fly them. If he flew them he was crazy and didn't have to; but if he didn't want to he was sane and had to.'
Heller, *Catch-22* Chapter 5.

In the 1930s U.S. writers shared the concerns of Europeans: perhaps the best novel spawned by the Spanish Civil War, was Hemingway's *For Whom the Bell Tolls* (1940). Others chronicled American society, among them Steinbeck; Sinclair Lewis, most notably in *Main Street* (1920) and *Babbitt* (1922); John Dos Passos in his trilogy *U.S.A.* (1930–36), and James T. Farrell in his *Studs Lonigan* trilogy (1932–35). F. Scott Fitgerald too, though moving in different social circles, was essentially a chronicler of 20s high life. The acerbic critic H. L. Mencken (1880–1956), savaged European cultural predominance and upheld the colloquial American language, while condemning 'literary standards derived from the *Ladies' Home Journal*'.

In more recent times, North American literature has been divided among special-interest social groups (blacks, women, homosexuals, etc.) and with often contradictory theories. Older traditions still survive, especially the identification of the writer with the cause of reform.

SHORT STORIES

Two features of recent fiction writing in the U.S.A. frequently remarked on are the tendency for novelists to write one very good book whose quality is never repeated, and a fondness, especially among 'regional' writers, for the short story. The former has sometimes been ascribed to a surfeit of early critical praise, or material profit, taking the edge off a writer's 'hunger'; the latter partly to the influence of *The New Yorker* magazine. Among the many outstanding practitioners of the short story are the Polish-born Isaac Bashevis Singer (1904–91), who wrote originally in Yiddish; the once very popular John O'Hara (1905–70); Flannery O'Connor (1925–64) and Carson McCullers (1917–67), exponents of what is called 'Southern Gothic'; Mississippi-born Eudora Welty (born 1909); and the highly esteeemed Raymond Carver (1938–88). John Updike (born 1932), best known for his 'Rabbit' novels, is another exponent.

AFTER THE WAR

Expectations of a literary revival after the Second World War comparable with that of the First, were largely disappointed. Big changes in outlook and interesting developments in many spheres were occurring, but by and large, the writers who held centre stage were those of the previous generation, such as Fitzgerald, Hemingway, Faulkner, and on a lesser plane, James Gould Cozzens. However, James Jones (*From Here to Eternity*, 1951) and Norman Mailer (*The Naked and the Dead*, 1948), made their names as war novelists. Jones, arguably, never quite repeated his early success, but Mailer became increasingly famous, through his not-so-private life as well as his varied and uneven writings. The most successful war novel, eight years in the writing and a bestseller of huge dimensions, was Joseph Heller's surreal black comedy, *Catch-22* (1961). The title is now a familiar term for an absurd and insoluble dilemma.

The novel of the 1950s most widely admired by younger readers was J. D. Salinger's *Catcher in The Rye* (1951), with its 16-year-old narrator, Holden Caulfield, seeming in retrospect a herald of 1960s youth culture. Salinger's later works were less impressive and Robert Penn Warren, a respected poet and critic, is also remembered primarily for a single novel on similar lines, *All the King's Men* (1946), about a corrupt, power-hungry Southern politician. Ralph Ellison's memorable, Kafkaesque story of a Southern black in *New York, Invisible Man* (1952) will similarly ensure his niche in literary history.

THE BEAT GENERATION

The group of laid-back, anti-intellectual, faintly subversive American writers of the 1950s–1960s who were influenced by Zen Buddhism and native American cults, was so named by Jack Kerouac (1922–69). His novel *On the Road* (1957) is one of the group's most notable productions. Other 'Beat writers' include the anarchic, experimental William Burroughs, best known for *The Naked Lunch* (1959), and the poets Allen Ginsburg, whose bardic rage against American materialism was best expressed in *Howl* (1956), Gregory Corso and Lawrence Ferlinghetti, founder in 1953 of the City Lights bookstore, San Francisco, a centre for the Beats. Haughty critics have remarked that the Beats created more headlines than literature.

Opposite: A scene from Mike Nichol's film of *Catch 22*. Heller's later novels, beautifully observed and written, were inevitably disappointing after his masterpiece of a war novel.

Right: A scene from Steven Spielberg's film of Alice Walker's Pulitzer Prize-winning 1983 novel, *The Color Purple*. (see page 185).

AMERICAN-JEWISH

Although a doubtful category, the fact is that many of the most distinguished modern American novelists are Jewish and write – though not exclusively – about American-Jewish experience. Among the most admired are: Bernard Malamud (1914–86), famous especially for *The Fixer* (1967), set in Tsarist Russia; Nobel prizewinner Saul Bellow (born 1915), whose *Herzog* (1964) describes the inner torments of a Jewish intellectual ('The soul requires intensity' – Bellow's watchword); and Philip Roth (born 1933), best known for the controversial *Portnoy's Complaint* (1969) and his sequence featuring Nathan Zuckerman, a Jewish novelist.

Not all first or second-generation immigrants, of course, were Jewish. One of the finest masters of style was the wonderfully imaginative, bilingual, Russian-born Vladimir Nabokov (1899–1977), who achieved fame with *Lolita* (1955) but wrote many perhaps better books.

AFRO-AMERICAN

There was little black American fiction (meaning not only by blacks but about blacks) before the Harlem Renaissance of the 1920s. Richard Wright is best known for *Native Son* (1940), a bitter attack on race prejudice. The leading figure in the next generation was James Baldwin, whose non-fiction *The Fire Next Time* (1963) was a powerful blow in the movement for civil rights. More recently, outstanding black women writers making artistic use of autobiographical experience have emerged.

JAMES BOND IS BACK IN ACTION!

EVERYTHING HE TOUCHES

TURNS TO EXCITEMENT!

ALBERT BROCCOLI
and HARRY SALTZMAN

SEAN CONNERY
as AGENT 007 in

IAN FLEMING'S

GOLDFINGER

GERT FROBE as GOLDFINGER HONOR BLACKMAN as PUSSY GALORE

SHIRLEY EATON RICHARD MAIBAUM and PAUL DEHN HARRY SALTZMAN and ALBERT R. BROCCOLI GUY HAMILTON

TECHNICOLOR UNITED ARTISTS

The term literature originally meant all written language. In the case of fiction, however, an obvious distinction has arisen between what is, broadly, seen as art and what is seen as pure entertainment. The distinction is, superficially, obvious enough, and a glance around the airport bookstall is instructive in this respect. Nevertheless, the grey area is extensive. Clearly, all literature is in some way entertaining, and it could be argued that what is by general consent classed as 'literature' is on the whole more entertaining than the vast production of pulp fiction tailored to a target readership and aiming merely to entertain or secure large sales.

ALTERNATIVE MODES

GENRE

The idea of genre in literature describes works in categories distinguished by certain conventions, which are followed by the author and expected by the reader or audience. If you go to see a Greek tragedy, even if you don't know the play, you know it will have the certain characteristics that place it in the genre of the Classical tragedy. The term genre fiction is now often applied to the many and varieties of the popular novel, such as 'sex and shopping', 'romances', 'bodice-rippers', 'westerns', and many others, all visible on that airport bookstall. They do not generally aspire to the title of literature although some – a few – novels that fall within these genres are not only far from aesthetically worthless, they occupy the same aesthetic plane as the most high-flown works of postmodernism. Some serious novelists have found in these genres a rewarding (in more ways than one,

perhaps) 'alternative mode' of writing. Many learned scholars have, for example, written lightweight detective fiction.

THE SPY NOVEL

The spy novel has roots in the adventure stories of John Buchan (1875–1940), and Erskine Childers's *The Riddle of the Sands* (1903) is an early classic. Its golden age coincided with the Cold War, and its most adept practitioners were often former officers in intelligence services, such as Graham Greene (1904–91). Greene was one of the most distinguished British novelists of the century who, incidentally, divided his fiction into novels and 'entertainments', his spy stories (e.g. *The Confidential Agent*, *The Human Factor*) falling into the latter category. The most popular spy stories of the period were those of Ian Fleming's (1908–64) hero James Bond, the inspiration for a seemingly endless series of blockbusting films. The supreme exponent of the Cold War spy novel, however, is John Le Carré, whose *The Spy Who Came In From the Cold* (1963) was described by Greene as 'the best spy story I have ever read'. Le Carré's thorough research, subtle plots and vivid characterization were displayed in a series of gripping, often bleak novels.

HORROR

Like its ancestor, the 19th-century 'Gothic' novel, the horror novel exploits human fear of the unknown, and has been praised for offering 'insights we might prefer not to admit we have'. Modern horror fiction more often specializes in violent sensationalism offering no discernible insights beyond the most obvious. The most successful modern exponent has been Stephen King, whose first novel, *Carrie* (1974), built on the extraordinary popularity of William Peter Blatty's *The Exorcist* (1971). A perhaps more thoughtful writer in this genre, and a fine stylist, is another American, Peter Straub (born 1943).

SCIENCE FICTION

American writers were also prominent in the 'golden age' of science fiction, after the Second World War. Science fiction, variously defined, describes stories set in an imaginary, usually future world where more or less feasible scientific advances have created a different society. Although much earlier prototypes could be cited, modern science fiction is generally held to have begun with Jules Verne (1928–1905), author of numerous 'scientific' adventures (e.g. *Journey to the Centre of the Earth*, *Twenty Thousand Leagues Under the Sea*), H. G. Wells (1866–1946), whose SF novels (*The Time Machine*, *The War of the Worlds*, etc.) represented but one of the interests of an extraordinary polymath and social reformer, and Karel Capek (1890–1938), who coined the term 'robot'.

Aldous Huxley's dystopia, *Brave New World* (1932) helped to make SF more respectable, but in the postwar era it varied greatly in literary quality, much of it not aspiring to a level above pulp fiction. The legendary

Science fiction is one of the more secluded parade grounds where private fantasy and public event meet . . .

Science fiction is no more written for scientists than ghost stories are written for ghosts. Most frequently, the scientific dressing clothes fantasy. And fantasies are as meaningful as science. The phantasms of technology now fittingly embody our hopes and anxieties.
Brian W. Aldiss, *Billion Year Spree* (1973), Introduction.

editor of *Astounding Science Fiction*, John W. Campbell, was a powerful influence in extending the genre and raising standards. Among the most popular American SF writers in that era were Isaac Asimov, Frederick Pohl, C. W. Kornbluth, Walter M. Miller, Philip K. Dick and Ursula Le Guin (women SF writers were comparatively rare), and among the British, (Sir) Arthur C. Clarke (who forecast communications satellites), John Wyndham, Brian Aldiss and Michael Moorcock. The latter's novels straddled the nebulous boundary between SF and 'Fantasy' fiction, another modern variant of the Gothic.

With the nuclear age, SF entered the literary mainstream. The British novelist and poet Kingsley Amis was the first to write a serious study of SF (*New Maps of Hell*, 1961), and writers such as J. G. Ballard (born 1930) and the inimitable Kurt Vonnegut (born 1922) could not be placed in what was traditionally regarded as an inferior category; in fact, much of their work was not strictly science fiction.

Above: **Art Deco cover of** *Brave New World.* **Huxley's book was an example of science fiction as the vehicle for the novel of ideas.**

Opposite: **Poster for an early James Bond film. As portrayed by Sean Connery, Bond was more popular in the cinema than in print.**

Some critics have seen a decline in the British novel since the poweful impulse of modernism was absorbed – a post-imperial, insular tendency to match the national decline – and it has been compared unfavourably with the vigour of the American novel. The truth may have more to do with its very disparate character, its sheer variety, and the corresponding absence of some great central theme relevant to the times. British writers have not universally abandoned experiment (nor political commitment for that matter), but on the whole they have been less affected by modern literary theories inspired, largely, by French thinkers.

BRITISH FICTION

interests are rape, ultra-violence and Beethoven

STANLEY KUBRICK

CLOCKWORK ORANGE

From Warner Bros [W] A Warner Communications Company
Released by Columbia-Warner Distributors Ltd   Original Soundtrack recording on Warner Bros. K46127

Above: A Clockwork Orange, **thanks partly to Kubrick's film, was the best-known novel of the astoundingly productive writer, Anthony Burgess.**

CATHOLICS

Novelists of the 1930s continued to dominate the immediate post-war period. Greene was perhaps the most notable, his best novels, such as *The Power and the Glory* (1940) and *The Heart of the Matter* (1948), dominated by his powerful sense of evil and moral decay. He was a Catholic, and although there was no such thing as a 'Catholic school' in British fiction, a striking number of good novelists were Catholics. Of at least equal distinction was Evelyn Waugh (1903–66), best known now for his satirical comedies of the 1920s and 1930s and the nostalgic *Bridehsead Revisited* (1945), though his best work was his war trilogy *Sword of Honour* (1952–61). Malcolm Lowry (1909–57), not a Catholic, is known chiefly for a single, highly regarded novel, *Under the Volcano* (1947), which belongs essentially to modernism in the tradition of Joyce.

THE 1950S

There was a new spirit abroad in the 1950s, the era of the Angry Young Men (a meaningless nickname) typified by Osborne's Jimmy Porter. William Golding, a future Nobel prizewinner, began his literary career at 43 with the arresting *Lord of the Flies* (1954), a parable about a school choir marooned on a tropical island.

Another memorable anti-Utopian novel was Anthony Burgess's *A Clockwork Orange* (1962). Notable first novels of 1954, besides Golding's, were *Under the Net*, an existential comedy by the Oxford philosopher Iris Murdoch, and *Lucky Jim*, an uproarious, rebellious comedy set in a provincial, 'red-brick' university, by Kingsley Amis. It was the first British 'campus novel', a comedic genre richly exploited later by Malcolm Bradbury (born 1932) and David Lodge (born 1935). Lodge was another Catholic, and so, by conversion, was Muriel Spark, the first of whose wry comedies, *The Comforters*, was published in 1957. Doris Lessing arrived from Rhodesia to begin the first of her ambitious novel sequences with *The Grass is Singing* (1950).

The first of Anthony Powell's twelve-volume sequence *A Dance to the Music of Time*, a Proustian pageant of English life in literary and

Above: **One of the most successful modern British films was *Trainspotting*, based on the novel by the gifted Scottish writer, Irvine Welsh.**

upper-class society, was published in 1951. It would head many lists of the best English fiction of the century, but risks being underrated because so much of it is extremely funny.

Among a later generation of novelists, many of them, like V. S. Naipaul, Salman Rushdie, Timothy Mo and Hanif Kureishi, from different cultural backgrounds, the most

eminent included Margaret Drabble and her sister A. S. Byatt, Angela Carter, Fay Weldon and John Fowles. The writer who most successfully combined commercial success and critical approval was Martin Amis, son of Kingsley, and similarly eclectic, though best known for blackish satire.

BEYOND THE METROPOLIS

Although it sometimes seemed so, British literary life was not confined to London. William Cooper's affectionate comedy *Scenes from Provincial Life* (1950) is set in Leicester, though his characters, civil servants, gravitated to Whitehall later, where they might have met the characters of C. P. Snow, another Leicester-bred civil servant, though his best-known novel is set in a Cambridge college (*The Masters*, 1951). Alan Sillitoe represented Nottingham, David Lodge declined to leave Birmingham, and several good quality novelists, including John Braine and David Storey, not to mention the older J. B. Priestley, came from Yorkshire.

Ireland, as ever, swelled with literary talent – and literary rows. The troubles in the North, as troubles often do, motivated many fine writers. In the *Republic*, Flann O'Brien (1911–66) mocked rural nostalgia; John McGahern's second novel, *The Dark* (1965), lost him his teaching post; and short-story writer Frank O'Connor (1903–66) feelingly advised Irish writers to cultivate the hide of a rhinoceros and to live near the sea. The Irish government encouraged writers with tax concessions, but some, like Joyce, preferred to move out, including the Belfast-born Brian Moore (born 1921). Seamus Deane's huge *Anthology of Irish Writing* (1991) indicated the vast range of Irish talent, north and south.

It is common to speak of a Scottish literary renaissance in the late 20th century. It was centred largely on Glasgow and its populist tradition, and is exemplifed in Alasdair Gray, whose prodigious *Lanark* (1981) was immediately hailed as a masterpiece. On a smaller scale, the sometimes painful work of James Kellman, notably *How Late It Was, How Late* (1994), may prove equally influential.

There is no doubt that it is easier for writers to gain fame and popularity if their native language is English. In any other language, even French, it is more difficult, and in, for example, Armenian, it is exceedingly difficult. Style is another consideration. The writer from any culture who is best known internationally may or may not be the best writer. Much depends on ease of translation. Some books are almost impossible to translate (though it's amazing what can be done, even with *Finnegan's Wake*). It is sometimes suggested that the immense popularity of certain writers, for example the Italian Italo Svevo, author of *The Confessions of Zeno* (1923), is partly due to his translatability.

FRANCE

Literary Paris after the war was dominated by the circle of the Existentialists who revolved around Camus. Although it never quite regained the spirit of the 1930s, Paris became again a pre-eminent centre for ideas and an attraction to immigré writers, notably black Americans such as James Baldwin and Richard Wright. And the bars still hummed with literary feuds. Another American, Peter Matthiessen, founded the *Paris Review*, a literary magazine that became an institution. The Olympia Press of Maurice Girodias, notable mainly for pornography, published William Burroughs's *The Naked Lunch* (1959), as well as Nabokov's *Lolita* and the first novel of the American, later Irish-based, J. P. Donleavy, *The Ginger Man* (1955), books that more orthodox publishers shied away from.

Another publisher, Les Éditions de Minuit, patronized the experimental group of exponents of the *nouveau roman* ('new novel'), a term applied to a variety of writers who found the traditional form of the novel inadequate, broadly for the reasons outlined by Alain Robbe-Grillet (born 1922): that the presence of an omniscient narrator imposes order and significance on life where, in fact, they do not exist. Other proponents of the *nouveau roman* included Nathalie Sarrault (born 1902), who bombarded her readers with tropisms, i.e. the vague sensations and indefinable influences that are responsible for a person's actual words and actions, and Marguerite Duras (born 1914), author of the screenplay *Hiroshima Mon Amour* (1959) and of an autobiographical work which she claimed to have no memory of writing. Eventually, theorists such as Roland

7

Left: Gunter Grass (left) was born in Danzig (Gdansk). His first and most famous novel, *The Tin Drum*, has been described as 'a kind of "sick" Grimms' fairy tale for adults'.

Opposite: Sean Connery, moving on from James Bond, as the English monkish investigator, William of Baskerville (an allusion to a Sherlock Holmes story), in the film of *The Name of the Rose.*

EUROPEAN FICTION

Barthes, Jacques Derrida and Michel Foucault became more famous than any mere practitioner of fiction. Their theories, which belong to the academy and mean little to the ordinary reader, served to keep France in her traditional place as leader of the avant-garde.

ITALY

Neo-realism, so powerful a force in Italian post-war cinema, also affected literature, the most notable exponent being Alberto Moravia (1907–90), a fierce critic of the moral apathy of bourgeois society, which he regarded as responsible for Fascism. Perhaps his best novel, *Two Women* (1956), is set in Italy at the time of the Allied occupation towards the end of the Second World War. His exploration of sex and psychology in human affairs was partly and incidentally responsible for the great popularity of his novels and short stories.

Umberto Eco (born 1932), a professor of semiotics and more of a cultural hero than a novelist, posed sophisticated intellectual puzzles in books such as *The Name of the Rose* (1981), a historical thriller and international bestseller that operates on many levels, and the equally complex *Foucault's Pendulum* (1988). The inspirational Primo Levi (1919–87), a chemical engineer and (like Moravia) a Jew, survived Auschwitz (because his ability as a chemist made him useful) and made something extraordinary from the experience in his three-volume autobiography (1946–75). Other works interestingly mix autobiography, history and science. Italo Calvino (1923–85), though he began as, more or less, a neo-realist (e.g. *The Path of the Nest of Spiders*, 1947, an outstanding novel of the Italian Resistance), developed into a great exponent of myth, fable and fantasy, especially in his trilogy *Our Ancestors* (1952–62), and is often compared with Jorge Luis Borges. Calvino is said to have selected his titles with an eye to their effect in translation, though his reputation as perhaps the most influential of all late 20th-century Italian writers rests on more solid foundations. Sicily's problems inspired Leonardo Sciascia (1921–89) and produced one of the great novels of the age in *The Leopard* (1958) by Giuseppe Tomasi di Lampedusa.

GERMANY

The Nazis virtually killed off all forms of German literature: writers who survived were exiles. Some later returned, a few, like Anna Seghers and Arnold Zweig to the communist East. The leading literary movement in the West was Group 47, founded and miraculously sustained by Hans Werner Richter, and attracting both German and Austrian writers. Leading German novelists who gained international reputations – Heinrich Böll (1907–85), Gunther Grass (born 1927) and Uwe Johnson (1934–84) – received early encouragement from the Group. Böll explored the moral and social problems of Germany in the post-Nazi era in a series of novels, besides dealing sensitively with contemporary issues. Grass, a more humorous, and more determinedly experimental novelist, won immediate international acclaim for *The Tin Drum* (1959). Johnson also made his name with his first novel, *Speculations about Jacob* (1959), moving from East Germany to the West in order to get it published. Arno Schmidt (died 1979), though his later work is dense and obscure and thus little known abroad, was especially influential in Germany.

The things that the novel does not say are necessarily more numerous than those it does say and only a special halo around what is written can give the illusion that you are reading also what is not written.
Calvino, *If on a Winter's Night a Traveller*, Chapter 10.

Common characteristics of the regions summarized here are a strong sense of place and a heritage influenced by Europe. The exciting recent developments represent the achievement of independence and equality; the influence now travels in both directions. Another result is the questioning of the whole Western literary hierarchy, in which Afro-American authors, among others, have also played an important part.

'POST-COLONIAL' FICTION

CANADA AND AUSTRALIA

Until the upsurge of literary talent in the 1960s, Canadian writing was largely under British or U.S. influence. Robertson Davies (1913–95), whose best work was produced comparatively late, concentrated, often satirically, on Canadian themes in his three trilogies. Among others who have achieved international fame are Margaret Atwood (born 1939), whose primary concerns are feminism and Canadian nationalism, though her themes range widely, and Michael Ondaatje (born 1943 in Sri Lanka), best known for *The English Patient* (1992).

Australian writers have often tended to move to Europe. Notable early Australian writers included Henry Handel Richardson (Ethel Florence, 1870–1946) but the first of world stature was Patrick White (1912–90), best known for Australian epics such as *Voss* (1957). He was followed by Thomas Keneally (born 1935), a highly eclectic writer probably best known for *Schindler's Ark* (1982), though many of his novels deal with Australian themes, and Peter Carey (born 1943), influenced by magic realism and firmly rooted in Australia, who commands a unique mixture of the comic and the sinister.

AFRICA AND THE CARIBBEAN

South African literature has been inevitably concerned with problems of race. Before 1945, the best-known books from Africa were probably Olive Schreiner's *The Story of an African Farm* (1883) and the Kenyan stories of Isak Dinesen (Karen Blixen, 1885–1962). An international sensation was caused by Alan Paton's *Cry, the Beloved Country* (1948), a passionate plea for racial harmony. Nadine Gordimer (born 1923) was concerned with the relationship between private life and politics in South Africa, her vision growing bleaker with time. Other highly regarded South Africans include the inventive Dan Jacobson (born 1929), André Brink (born 1935), who wrote in both Afrikaans and English, and J. M. Coetzee (born 1940), who co-operated with Brink in editing *A Land Apart: A South African Reader* (1986).

A strong European influence on Black African writers has been combined with the effort to recreate the purely African past, utilizing mainly oral sources. Apart from the Francophone poet Leopold Senghor (born 1906), the most famous recent writers of fiction are the two Nigerians Wole Soyinka (born 1934), best known as a playwright, the first African to win a Nobel prize for literature, and Chinua Achebe (born 1930), whose best book is perhaps his first, *Things Fall Apart* (1958). Like other writers in parts of black Africa, both were forced into exile. The troubled question of authenticity when writing in English was highlighted by Ngugi wa

Making our way in this West stuffed with money, power and things, this North that taught us how to see from its privileged point of view. But maybe we were the lucky ones; we knew that other perspectives existed. We had seen the view from elsewhere. Rushdie, *The Jaguar Smile* (1987).

Thiong'o (born 1938), who wrote originally in English as James Ngugi, but later turned to his native Kikuyu.

Many Caribbean writers lived and worked in Europe or North America, though one of the best known, the poet Derek Walcott (born 1930), is a notable exception. Francophone writers were the first to make an impact on the wider world. Aimé Césaire (born 1913) developed, with Senghor, the important concept of négritude. Rastifarianism has been a more recent influence in creating a uniquely Caribbean literature. Of expatriate West Indians, the most famous is V. S. Naipaul (born 1932, to a Brahmin family in Trinidad). His masterpiece is probably *A House for Mr Biswas* (1961), which, among other features, is a lament for the disintegration of society under the seductive pull of Europe.

INDIA

English literature has flourished remarkably in India since independence. As elsewhere, the best-known writers are native English-speakers. The most famous is undoubtedly Salman Rushdie (born 1947), resident in Britain. His magic-realist *Midnight's Children*, provided an exuberant portrait of Bombay, India's main literary fulcrum. Among other outstanding novelists, the best-known in the West include Anita Desai (born 1937), Rohinton Mistry (born 1952), chronicler of the Parsees, and Vikram Seth (born 1952), whose enormous, cheerful *A Suitable Boy* was a runaway best-seller in 1993.

LATIN AMERICA

Latin America encompasses many different cultures, making all generalizations dubious. The continent has, however, had great influence on world literature in modern times, largely through the genre known as 'magic realism', implying a realistic story invaded by elements of fantasy and the supernatural. It can be traced to the great Argentinian Jorge Luis Borges (1899–1986), one of the greatest – and strangest – short-story writers of the century. Other early exponents were the Cuban Alejo Carpentier (1904–79), notably in *The*

Top: **García Marquez, discovering a new literary device, was a Jesuit-educated journalist who started writing novels while in Europe. He was awarded the Nobel Prize for Literature in 1982.**

Above: **V. S. Naipaul, still smiling, although his recent work has been increasingly marked by pessimism. His themes of violence and alienation have prompted comparisons with Conrad.**

Kingdom of This World (1949), the Brazilian Jorge Armado (born 1912) and the Colombian Gabriel García Márquez (born 1928), especially in *One Hundred Years of Solitude* (1967), a classic of the genre. Carlos Fuentes (born 1928), intensely influenced by the Mexican Revolution, combined myth and history in novels such as *The Death of Artemio Cruz* (1962). The novels of Mario Vargas Lhosa (born 1936) painted a merciless picture of Peruvian society.

SEX RACE AND CENSORSHIP

Literature of the past is constantly revalued in each new generation. New ideas invite reassessment of past authors and movements. Intellectual fashions change, and present changes throw new light on past events. The popularity of authors rises or falls according to their relevance to contemporary beliefs and prejudices. Victorian authors could scarcely discuss sex except in highly indirect ways; the lively contemporary field of 'gay literature' would have been unthinkable. Censorship, official or indirect, plays an important part in the process. Even in the most liberal society, there are some things that cannot be published without jeopardy.

FEMINISM

So-called special-interest groups have in recent times led to serious questioning of the established literary tradition. Undeniably, Western literary traditions are founded predominantly on the work of, as denigrators put it, dead white males. If you belong to a non-Western culture, if you are neither dead, white nor male, it is not surprising that you should question the values of the traditional literary hierarchy.

A major influence in the last generation or so has been the rise of modern feminism. The idea of a distinction between 'masculine' and 'feminine' writing may be questionable (and even, from a feminist point of view, counterproductive), but there are certainly qualities of style and thinking that are commonly so described. Feminist criticism, however, has had two main effects. The first is in reassessing earlier literature, often in opposition to the prevailing culture of its time. This has led to interesting new views of, in particular, 19th-century novels. The second is in rediscovering or reassessing neglected female writers of earlier times. In this endeavour feminist publishers, such as Virago in Britain, have played a major role.

RACE

English, and to a lesser extent French and other European literature, has long been a worldwide

THE BOOK IS BANNED!

How did they ever make a movie of LOLITA?

NOT SUITABLE FOR CHILDREN

METRO-GOLDWYN-MAYER presents in association with SEVEN ARTS PRODUCTIONS

JAMES B. HARRIS and STANLEY KUBRICK'S **LOLITA** Starring JAMES MASON · SHELLEY WINTERS PETER SELLERS as "Quilty" and Introducing SUE LYON as "Lolita"

phenomenon, but until recently it was largely confined to the British and their cultural descendants in North America and the old dominions. No longer. In recent years nominees, sometimes winners, of the chief annual British literary award, the Booker Prize, have included many Asian and African authors. However, the biggest impact has been made by Afro-American writers, who have blossomed since the civil-rights movement of the 1960s. Several of the best of them happen to be women and belong, more or less closely, to the feminist movement also. The outstanding figure is probably the novelist Toni Morrison (born 1931), who won the Nobel Prize in 1993. Alice Walker's (born 1944) *The Color Purple* was a huge international bestseller. A poem by Maya Angelou (born 1928) was read at President Clinton's inauguration. Another healthy sign is a growing tendency for black writers to extend their interests beyond the Afro-American experience.

CENSORSHIP

Censorship of publications has existed in all societies and no doubt always will exist, though developments in information technology appear to be making the laws difficult to enforce. Historically, the invention of printing seemed to present similar threats. During the English Reformation, Henry VIII established a licensing system that, in principle, controlled all printed matter: 'popish' propaganda was then the chief concern. It was this opprobrious system that led to one of the earliest defences of the freedom of the press, Milton's *Areopatigica* (1644, published without licence) and the subsequent abolition of the system. (Nevertheless, all plays for public performance in Britain had to be approved by an official called the Lord Chamberlain until 1968.) In the 18th century the

political press, with its often scurrilous attacks on public officials, was dealt with under laws against 'seditious libel'. In the 19th century obscenity, or just plain sex, became the main worry. Early ages being less pernickety, this raised a multitude of problems (as libertarians often pointed out, the Bible contains plenty of sex and violence). Dr Bowdler formed a Society for the Suppression of Vice in 1802 and himself produced a 'bowdlerized' edition of Shakespeare, removing all 'indecencies'. Parliament passed an *Obscene Publications Act* in 1857, contributing to the thriving business of underground pornography. Famous victims of the act and its successor of 1959 included Joyce's *Ulysses*, the entire first edition of which was confiscated in 1923, and Lawrence's *Lady Chatterley's Lover*, subject of a famous case in 1960, when Penguin Books, who had risked publishing the first unexpurgated edition in Britain, won acquittal.

The terms of all such legislation are necessarily vague and open to inerpretation. Writing deemed blasphemous (in Britain, to Christians only) or seditious is also liable to prosecution. The modern equivalent of Dr Bowdler is 'political correctness', an insidious, informal kind of censorship which, if often understandable or even desirable, can lead to absurdities, such as the banning from public libraries books which contain words now seen as racial epithets.

An recent example of censorship was provoked by Salman Rushdie's novel *The Satanic Verses* (1988), which many Muslims regarded as blasphemous. The extremist leader of Iran published a *fatwa* or religious decree demanding the author's death, and as a result Rushdie was forced to live in hiding under police protection.

Left: Publishers fought shy of *Lolita* because of its theme. Eventually it proved such a success that Nabokov, aged 59, was at last able to give up teaching and become a full-time writer.

Right: Angry Muslims in the Yorkshire city of Bradford burn copies of Salman Rushdie's *The Satanic Verses*.

PRIZE WINNERS

NOBEL PRIZE

Nobel prize was instigated by Alfred Bernhard Nobel (1833–96) a Swedish chemist and inventor of dynamite (1867) and cordite (1888). In his will he bequethed an annual award in five areas – literature, physics, chemistry, physiology or medicine and furtherance of international peace. The prize for literature has been awarded by the Swedish Academy since 1901 to those who produce 'the most outstanding work of an idealistic tendency'. Since its inauguration two people, Boris Pasternak (1958) and Jean-Paul Satre (1964), have declined the prize.

1901 Sully-Prudhomme, French poet
1902 Theodor Mommsen, German historian
1903 Bjørnstjerne Bjørnsen,
    Norwegian novelist, poet and dramatist
1904 José Echegaray, Spanish dramatist/Frédéric
    Mistral, French poet
1905 Hernryk Sienkiexicz, Polish novelist
1906 Giosue Carducci, Italian Classical poet
1907 Rudyard Kipling, British poet and novelist
1908 Rudolf Eucken, German philosopher
1909 Seima Lagerlöf, Swedish novelist
1910 Paul von Heyse,
    German poet, novelist and dramatist
1911 Maurice Maeterlinck,
    Belgian poet and dramatist
1912 Gerhart Hauptmann,
    German novelist poet
    and dramatist
1913 Rabindranath Tagore,
    Indian dramatist and poet
1914 No award
1915 Romain Rolland, Fench novelist
1916 Verner von Heidenstam, Swedish poet
1917 Karl Gjellerup, Danish novelist/Henrik
    Pontoppidan, Danish novelist
1918 No award
1919 Carl Spitteler, Swiss poet and novelist
1920 Knut Hamsun, Norwegian novelist
1921 Anatole France, French novelist
1922 Jacinto Benavente y Martínez,
    Spanish dramatist
1923 William Butler Yeats,
    Irish poet and dramatist
1924 Wladyslaw Reymont
1925 George Bernard Shaw, Irish dramatist
1926 Grazia Deledda, Italian novelist

1927 Henri Bergson, French philosopher
1928 Sigrid Undset, Norwegian novelist
1929 Thomas Mann, German novelist
1930 Sinclair Lewis, American novelist
1931 Erik Axel Karlfeldt, Swedish poet
1932 John Galsworthy,
    British novelist and dramatist
1933 Ivan Bunin,
    Russian-born prose writer and poet
1934 Luigi Pirandello, Italian dramatist
1935 No award
1936 Eugene O'Neill, American dramatist
1937 Roger Martin du Gard, French novelist
1938 Pearl Buck, American novelist
1939 Frans Eemil Sillanpää, Finnish novelist
1940 No award
1941 No award
1942 No award
1943 No award
1944 Johannes V. Jensen,
    Danish essayist and novelist
1945 Gabriela Mistral, Chilean poet
1946 Herman Hesse, German novelist
1947 André Gide, French novelist and essayist
1948 T. S. Eliot,
    American-born poet and dramatist
1949 William Faulkner, American novelist
1950 Betrand Russell, British philosopher
1951 Pär Lagerkvist, Swedish novelist
1952 François Mauriac,
    French poet, novelist and dramatist
1953 Sir Winston Churchill,
    British statesman and historian
1954 Ernest Hemingway, American novelist
1955 Halldór Laxness, Icelandic novelist
1956 Juan Ramón Jiménez, Spanish poet
1957 Albert Camus, French poet
1958 Boris Pasternak,
    Russian novelist and poet, declined prize
1959 Salvatore Quasimodo, Italian poet
1960 Saint-John Perse, French lyric
1961 Ivo Andric, Yugoslavian novelist
1962 John Steinbeck, American novelist
1963 George Seferis, Greek poet
1964 Jean-Paul Satre, French philosopher,
    dramatist and novelist, declined prize
1965 Mikhail Sholokhov, Russian novelist
1966 S.Y. Agnon, Israeli novelist/Nelly Sachs,
    German-born poet
1967 Miguel Angel Asturias,
    Guatamalan novelist and poet

1968 Kawabata Yasunari, Japanese novelist
1969 Samuel Beckett,
    Irish dramatist, poet and novelist
1970 Aleksander Solzhenitsyn, Russian novelist
1971 Pablo Neruda, Chilean poet
1972 Heinrich Böll, German novelist
1973 Patrick White, Australian novelist
1974 Eyvind Johnson, Swedish novelist/Harry
    Martinson, Swedish novelist and poet
1975 Eugenio Montale, Italian poet
1976 Saul Bellow, American novelist
1977 Vicente Aleixandre, Spanish poet
1978 Isaac Bashevis Singer, American novelist
1979 Odysseus Elytis, Greek poet
1980 Czeslaw Milosz,
    Polish-born poet, essayist and novelist
1981 Elias Canetti, Bulgarian-born novelist,
    dramatist and essayist
1982 Gabriel Garcia Márquez,
    Colombian novelist
1983 Sir William Golding, British novelist
1984 Jaroslav Seifert, Czechoslovakian poet
1985 Claude Simon, French novelist
1986 Wole Soyinka,
    Nigerian dramatist and poet
1987 Joseph Brodsky,
    Russian-born poet and essayist
1988 Naguib Mahfouz, Egyptian novelist
1989 Camilo José Cela, Spanish novelist
1990 Octavio Paz, Mexican poet
1991 Nadine Gordimer, South African novelist
1992 Derek Walcott, St Lucian poet
1993 Toni Morrison, American novelist
1994 Kenzaburo Oe, Japanese novelist
1995 Seamus Heaney, Northern Irish poet
1996 Wislawa Szymborska, Polish poet
1997 Dario Fo, Italian dramatist

BOOKER PRIZE

Started in 1969 The Booker McConnell Prize for Fiction is awarded to the best full-length novel published in the past year. The entrants come from the British Isles, Eire, the Commonwealth and South Africa.

1969 P. H. Newby, *Something to Answer For*
1970 Bernice Rubens, *The Elected Member*
1971 V. S. Naipaul, *In a Free State*
1972 John Berger, *G*
1973 J. G. Farrell, *The Siege of Krishnapur*

1974 Nadine Gordimer,
    The Conservationist
    /Stanley Middleton, *Holiday*
1975 Ruth Prawer Jhabvala, *Heat and Dust*
1976 David Storey, *Saville*
1977 Paul Scott, *Staying On*
1978 Iris Murdoch, *The Sea, the Sea*
1979 Penelope Fitzgerald, *Offshore*
1980 William Golding, *Rites of Passage*
1981 Salman Rushdie, *Midnight's Children*
1982 Thomas Keneally, *Schindler's Ark*
1983 J. M. Coetzee,
    Life and Times of Michael K
1984 Anita Brookner, *Hôtel du Lac*
1985 Keri Hulme, *The Bone People*
1986 Kingsley Amis, *The Old Devils*
1987 Penelope Lively, *Moon Tiger*
1988 Peter Carey, *Oscar and Lucinda*
1989 Kazuo Ishiguro, *The Remains of the Day*
1990 A. S. Byatt, *Possession*
1991 Ben Okri, *The Famished Road*
1992 Michael Ondaatje, *The English
    Patient*/Barry Unsworth, *Sacred Hunger*
1993 Roddy Doyle, *Paddy Clarke Ha Ha Ha*
1994 Jame Kelman, *How late It Was, How Late*
1995 Pat Barker, *The Ghost Road*
1996 Graham Swift, *Last Orders*
1997 Arundhati Roy, *The God of Small Things*

PULITZER PRIZE

Joseph Pulitzer (1847–1911), was a
Hungarian-born American who became a
wealthy newspaper proprietor. Similar to
Nobel, Pulitzer left a bequest in his will that
his part of his fortune should be awarded
each year for achievements in American literature, journalism and music. The following
are the literature winners.

1918 Ernest Poole, *His Family*
1919 Booth Tarkington,
    The Magnificent Ambersons
1920 No award
1921 Edith Wharton, *The Age of Innocence*
1922 Booth Tarkington, *Alice Adams*
1923 Willa Cather, *One of Ours*
1924 Margaret Wilson, *The Able McLaughlins*
1925 Edna Ferber, *So Big*
1926 Sinclair Lewis, *Arrowsmith*
1927 Louis Bromfield, *Early Autumn*
1928 Thornton Wilder,
    The Bridge at San Luis Rey
1929 Julia Peterkin, *Scarlet Sister Mary*
1930 Oliver La Farge, *Laughing Boy*

1931 Margaret Ayer Barnes, *Years of Grace*
1932 Pearl S. Buck, *The Good Earth*
1933 T. S. Stribling, *The Store*
1934 Caroline Miller, *Lamb in his Bosom*
1935 Josephine Winslow Johnson,
    Now in November
1936 Harold L. Davis, *Honey in the Horn*
1937 Margaret Mitchell, *Gone with the Wind*
1938 John Phillips Marquand,
    The Late George Apley
1939 Marjorie Kinnan Rawlings, *The Yearling*
1940 John Steinbeck, *The Grapes of Wrath*
1941 No award
1942 Ellen Glasgow, *In This Our Life*
1943 Upton Sinclair, *Dragon's Teeth*
1944 Martin Flavin, *Journey in the Dark*
1945 John Hersey, *A Bell for Adano*
1946 No award
1947 Robert Penn Warren, *All the King's Men*
1948 James A. Michener,
    Tales of the South Pacific
1949 James Gould Cozzens, *Guard of Honor*
1950 A. B. Guthrie Jr, *The Way West*
1951 Conrad Richter, *The Town*
1952 Herman Wouk, *The Caine Mutiny*
1953 Ernest Hemingway,
    The Old Man and the Sea
1954 No award
1955 William Faulkner, *A Fable*
1956 Mackinley Kantor, *Andersonville*
1957 No award
1958 James Agee, *A Death in the Family*
1959 Robert Lewis Taylor,
    The Travels of Jamie McPheeters
1960 Allen Drury, *Advise and Consent*
1961 Harper Lee, *To Kill a Mockingbird*
1962 Edwin O'Connor, *The Edge of Sadness*
1963 William Faulkner, *The Reivers*
1964 No award
1965 Shirley Ann Grau,
    The Keepers of the House
1966 Katherine Anne Porter, *The Collected
    Stories of Katherine Anne Porter*
1967 Bérnard Malamud, *The Fixer*
1968 William Styron,
    The Confessions of Nat Turner
1969 N. Scott Momaday, *House Made of Dawn*
1970 Jean Stafford, *Collected Stories*
1971 No award
1972 Wallace Stegner, *Angle of Repose*
1973 Eudora Welty, *The Optimist's Daughter*
1974 No award
1975 Michael Shaara, *The Killer Angels*
1976 Saul Bellow, *Humboldt's Gift*
1977 No award

1978 James Alan McPherson, *Elbow Room*
1979 John Cheever,
    The Stories of John Cheever
1980 Norman Mailer, *The Executioner's Song*
1981 John Kennedy Toole,
    A Confederacy of Dunces
1982 John Updike, *Rabbit is Rich*
1983 Alice Walker, *The Color Purple*
1984 William Kennedy, *Ironweed*
1985 Alison Lurie, *Foreign Affairs*
1986 Larry McMurtry, *Lonesome Dove*
1987 Peter Taylor, *A Summons to Memphis*
1988 Toni Morrison, *Beloved*
1989 Anne Tyler, *Breathing Lessons*
1990 Oscar Hijuelos,
    The Mambo Kings Play Songs of Love
1991 John Updike, *Rabbit at Rest*
1992 Jane Simley, *A Thousand Acres*
1993 Robert Olen Butler,
    A Good Scent from a Strange Mountain
1994 E. Annie Proulx, *The Shipping News*
1995 Carol Shields, *The Stone Diaries*
1996 Richard Ford, *Independence Day*
1997 Steven Millhauser, Martin Dressler,
    The Tale of an American Dreamer

POET LAUREATES

This is a title conferred upon a prominent
poet by the British Royal Household from
whom he or she (there never has been a
female Laureate) receives a stipend. The
origins of this title is sketchy and although
some see Samuel Jonson as the original Poet
Laureate, the first to receive the title by
letters-patent was John Dryden in 1670.

1670 John Dryden
1689 Thomas Shadwell
1692 Nahum Tate
1715 Nicholas Rowe
1718 Laurence Eusden
1730 Colley Cibber
1757 William Whitehead
1785 Thomas Warton
1790 Henry James Pye
1813 Robert Southey
1843 William Wordsworth
1850 Alfred Tennyson
1896 Alfred Austin
1913 Robert Bridges
1930 John Edward Masefield
1968 Cecil Day-Lewis
1972 John Betjeman
1984 Ted Hughes

GLOSSARY

For a term explained in the text, which does not appear in the Glossary, consult the Index.

Act A division of a play, usually marking a change in time or scene and usually further divided into scenes

Alexandrine A verse line of 12 syllables, sometimes divided into two equal groups by a caesura, predominant in French poetry since the Renaissance

Allegory A story that acts as a giant metaphor for another meaning, in the Middle Ages a Christian one, often with characters personifying abstract qualities as in Bunyan's *Pilgrim's Progress*

Alliteration A succession of words that repeat the same sound, usually the initial consonant, e.g. 'apt alliteration's artful aid'; Old Germanic (including Old English) employed alliteration rather than rhyme

Assonance An effect smilar to rhyme achieved by the repetition of a vowel sound, e.g. cold/slow/moan

Blank verse Unrhymed lines of iambic pentameters, a flexible form in English verse, especially suitable for poetic drama, as Shakespeare demonstrated

Caesura A break in a line of poetry, e.g. 'know then thyself ‖ presume not God to scan'

Canon In literature, the collection of works generally considered to be of special worth

Canto A 'chapter' of an epic or long narrative poem

Catharsis The relief or 'purging' of the emotions produced, according to Aristotle, by tragic drama

Chansons de geste ('songs of deeds'), medieval French epics celebrating the deeds of Charlemagne and other Christian heroes

Chapbook, a cheap printed book or pamphlet sold by peddlars in the 16th–18th centuries

Chorus, in Classical drama, a group of singers (also their song) who comment on the play; Shakespeare occasionally used a one-person 'chorus'

Codex An ancient book, consisting of manuscripts

Conceit A highly elaborate and ingenious verbal image, a feature of much 16th–17th century English poetry

Concrete verse Poetry that derives its effect from the way it is printed and arranged on the page, in vogue about the 1950s

Consonance The repetition of similar consonants in successive words, e.g. mud/mad/mood; see also Assonance

Couplet In verse, a pair of rhyming lines, popularised in English by Chaucer; see Heroic couplet

Dactyl In verse, a foot consisting of one long syllable and two short, e.g. skilfully

Deconstruction A controversial theory associated with the French philosopher Jacques Derrida, and popularised by scholars at Yale University since about 1970, which doubts the ability of language to convey coherent meaning

Demotic The language of the common people rather than an educated elite

Diacritic A sign over or under a letter affecting the way it sounds, e.g. é, ç ô

Dystopia An imaginary and unpleasant world, e.g. Orwell's *1984*; the opposite of utopia

Edda Collections of Icelandic Old Norse poems about gods and heroes, dating from the 9th–13th centuries.

Elegy A lyric poem lamenting the death of a particular person, or meditating on some solemn subject, e.g. Gray's Elegy . . . in a Country Churchyard

Elision The omission of a letter or syllable, often to preserve the metre, e.g. o'er, th'expence, l'homme

Ellipsis The omission from a sentence of one or more words without destroying the meaning, e.g. 'And thou [go] to Worcester'; also dots or asterisks indicating a word or words omitted

Epic A long narrative poem celebrating a legendary hero, perhaps the oldest form of literature; sometimes used more generally, e.g. 'an epic performance'

Epilogue A final chapter or summing up of a literary work

Essay A relatively short prose work, often personal in style, in which the author discusses an idea without attempting comprehensive scholarly treatment; a term originated by Montaigne

Euphuism Highly elaborate, ornamental prose style; a term deriving from Lyly's *Euphues*

Fabliaux, Short, humorous, often obscene tales in verse, popular in medieval France

Farce A variety of comedy, in which the characters are stereotypes and the humour depends mainly on frantic action

Foot A number of syllables that make up a unit of poetic metre

Free verse Poetry that does not conform to regular metre, but relies on other rhythmic devices

Heroic couplet A pair of rhyming, iambic pentameter lines, a major English verse form up to the 19th century

Holograph A document in the author's own handwriting

Iamb In verse, a foot consisting of an unstressed syllable followed by a stressed one, e.g. 'alone'

Iambic pentameter A ten-syllable line, either heroic couplets (if rhyming) or blank verse (if not)

Idiom An expression peculiar to a particular language, which therefore cannot be translated literally

Lacuna A gap, something missing, usually in a manuscript

Lipogram A text that deliberately excludes a letter of the alphabet, a notable example being *La Disparition* (1969), a novel by Georges Perec, which contains no 'e'

Lyric In ancient Greece, a song sung to a lyre; nowadays, any relatively short poem in which the poet or fictional speaker expresses personal thoughts and feelings; lyrical is sometimes used as virtually a synonym for 'poetic'

Malapropism A long or difficult word mistakenly used instead of another, similar-sounding word, after Mrs Malaprop in Sheridan's *The Rivals*, e.g. 'She's a vivacious [voracious] reader'

Masque An elaborate entertainment of royal courts in the 17th century, incorporating verse, song and elaborate costumes and scenery, an example being *Milton's Comus*

Melodrama Sensational, unsophisticated drama, similar in substance to Gothic novels, popular in the 19th century

Metafiction Fiction about fiction, specifically a novel which admits the reader to the process of its composition, e.g. John Fowles's *The French Lieutenant's Woman* (1969)

Metaphor A figure of speech which characterises someone or something with a word or phrase describing something different but suggesting a common quality, e.g. 'His wife is a cow'; see also Simile

Metre (meter) Or 'measure', the pattern formed by the regular rhythm of lines of poetry; in most English verse, it consists of regular stressed syllables within a line containing a fixed number of syllables

Mimetic Literally, imitation; in literature, the faithful reproduction (mimicking) of reality

Minimalism Reduction to an absolute minimum – of words, narrative, character, etc. – as in the later works of Beckett

Novella A work of fiction, longer than a short story but shorter than a novel

Ode An elaborate, exalted, relatively short lyric poem, deriving from Pindar, in praise of a person or entity, sometimes taking the form of regular stanzas, as in the odes of Keats

Oeuvre French 'work', the whole output of a particular writer

Onomatopeia The effect created by use of words that make a similar sound to what they describe, e.g. the buzz of bees

Oxymoron A figure of speech in which contradictory terms are combined, e.g. 'living death'

Parody A satirical imitation of the style of a particular author or type of writing

Pastiche A work that imitates another, usually earlier writers, styles or genres, but without the satiric intent of parody

Pastoral A form of writing that celebrates, romantically, the peaceful and innocent life of country people, particularly shepherds, a genre originating in ancient Greece and revived in the 16th century, e.g. in Spenser's *The Shepherd's Calender*

Pathetic fallacy The attribution of impossible characteristics to features of nature, e.g. 'weeping skies' (rain)

Pathos The quality that provokes pity and compassion in a reader

Postmodernism A rather vague term referring to experimental or avant-garde writing, mainly novels, of the past generation or so, supposedly influenced by the anar-

chic IT revolution and manifesting the collapse of conventional values

Prologue An introduction to a play or book; see also epilogue

Prosody The study of the technicalities of poetry – metre, rhyme, etc.

Protagonist The central character in a play or story, a term now preferred to hero or heroine as not all heroes are heroic

Quatrain A stanza of four lines

Recto The front of a printed sheet, hence the right-hand, odd-numbered pages in a book

Rhyme royal The seven-line stanza of iambic pentameters rhyming ababbcc, popularised by Chaucer

Romance A term now applied to various, generally non-realistic, kinds of modern novel; originally a story of gallant heroes, enchanted castles, etc. originating in legends of King Arthur

Roman-fleuve A novel sequence featuring the same characters in successive books, as in Proust or Anthony Powell

Sagas Heroic tales of history and legend in medieval Iceland, with emphasis on family histories; hence, any long story spanning the generations of a family, e.g. Galsworthy's The Forsyte Saga

Scansion Analysis of the patterns, stresses, etc. in lines of verse using symbols such as / (a stressed syllable) and ˘ (unstressed)

Simile A figure of speech comparing two different things, introduced by the word 'as' or 'like', e.g. 'a face like a pudding'; see also metaphor

Solecism Strictly, an error in grammar; also, any gross mistake revealing ignorance of correct custom or form

Soliloquy In drama, a speech delivered by a character who is alone on the stage, usually to show what he or she is thinking

Sonnet A lyric poem of 14 equal lines, iambic pentameters in English, which follows one of two rhyme schemes, the 'Petrarchian' and the less common 'English' or 'Shakespearian' sonnet

Spondee A foot consisting of two stressed syllables, in English verse only practicable as an occasional device, a line of spondees being virtually impossible

Stanza A section of a poem consisting of a fixed number of lines, the number, metre and rhyme scheme being repeated in each stanza

Structuralism An approach to literature and other aspects of culture on the basis of linguistics, deriving primarily from the theories of the Swiss philosopher Ferdinand de Saussure (1857–1913) and developed largely by French thinkers in the 1960s

Synecdoche A figure of speech in which a person or object is referred to by one characteristic aspect of the individual person or object, or by some larger group to which they belong, e.g. 'a silk' (a barrister), 'town and gown' (citizens and students)

Synonym A word having the same, or almost the same, meaning as another word

Syntax The way in which the words of a phrase or sentence are related to each other within the rules of grammar; the style of a writer is partly determined by syntax

Trochee In verse, a foot with one stressed syllable followed by one unstressed, comparatively rare in English but Longfellow's *Hiawatha* is a famous exception

Trope A figure of speech

Troubadour Originally, a poet or wandering minstrel associated particularly with Provence (southern France) in the late Middle Ages

Unreliable narrator A narrator who gives a different interpretation of events from what the reader deduces to be true, because he or she is a liar, a child or (as in Faulkner's *The Sound and the Fury*) an imbecile

Variorium edition an edition of a work or works containing explanatory notes by others, or an edition containing different versions of the original, e.g. from differing manuscripts

Vernacular The local language, e.g. French or English rather than Latin or Greek

Verse Poetry, in the sense of possessing rhythm and metre, but not necessarily implying literary worth

Villanelle A poetic form, originally French, having five three-line stanzas rhyming aba and a concluding quatrain rhyming abaa

Verso The reverse of a printed sheet, hence the left-hand page of a book; see Recto

Vulgate The version of a work in common use, usually in the vernacular rather than its original language, in particular the Bible in Latin as used by the Roman Catholic Church

Zeitgeist (German, 'spirit-time') The general mood or spirit of the age

INDEX

ACKNOWLEDGEMENTS

AKG, London: Front endpaper left, 6, 38, 56, 77, 102, 116, 117, 129, 136, 140 Bottom Right, 142, 164, 165, 168, 172, 173 / Bibliotheque Nationale, Paris 12 / British Library, London 23 / Fitzwilliam Museum, Cambridge 82 / George W. Elkins Collection, Philadelphia Museum of Art 10 / Justus Gopel 39 / Departement des Antiquites Orientales, Paris, Musee du Louvre, Erich Lessing 11 / Gutenberg Museum, Mainz, Erich Lessing 27 / Institut et Musee Voltaire, Geneva, Erich Lessing 64 / Moscow, Tretjakov Gallery 155 Top / Musee du Louvre, Paris 49 / Museo del Prado, Madrid 52 / Naples, National Museum of Archaeology 19 Bottom and top / Private Collection, Switzerland 159 / Stockholm, Moderna Museet 104 / Tretjakov Gallery, Moscow 125 left and right / Versailles, Musee du Chateau 127.

Bridgeman Art Library: Bargello, Florence 33 / British Library, London 28 / British Library, London 1, 22, 54 Bottom / Burgtheater, Vienna 15 / Casa di Dante, Florence 26 / Chris Beetles Ltd 135 / Christopher Wood Gallery 87, 100 / Dove Cottage Trust, Grasmere 81 Top / Fitzwilliam Museum, University of Cambridge 60, 79 / Galleria E Museo Estense, Modena 16 / Giraudon / Musee des Beaux-Arts 62 / Guildhall Library, Corporation of London 30 / Kunsthalle, Hamburg 74 / Paul Mellon Collection, USA 67 / Phillips, The International Fine Art Auctioneers 147 / Private Collection 20, 43, 68, 73, 107, 122, 140 Top Left / Royal Holloway and Bedford New College, Surrey 119 / Santa Costanza, Rome 17 / Stapleton Collection 94 /

By Courtesy of the Board of Trustees of the V & A 78, 89, 108 / Board of Trustees of the V & A, with permission from the Estate of Mrs G A Wyndham Lewis 149 / Walker Art Gallery, Liverpool 24, 83 / Wallace Collection, London 57.

Corbis UK Ltd: 183 Bottom / Isabel Steva Hernandez 183 Top.

Corbis / Everett: 174, 179.

Mary Evans Picture Library: 3, 13, 14, 25, 34, 35, 36, 40, 41, 44, 45, 46, 47 left, 53, 55 Top, 59, 61, 65, 70, 72, 76, 81 Centre, 85, 86, 88, 93, 95, 96, 101, 103, 105, 110, 112, 114, 131, 132, 134, 137, 146, 148, 150, 155 Bottom, 157, 162, 169, 177 / Roger Mayne 163.

Mark Gerson: 170, 171.

Getty Images: 4-5, 8-9, 32, 37, 42, 48, 50, 58, 66, 68 Background, 71, 84, 90, 92, 97, 98, 99, 106, 111, 113, 115, 118, 120, 121, 126, 128, 130, 133, 138, 144, 145, 151, 152, 156, 158, 160, 161.

National Portrait Gallery: 123.

Reed Consumer Books Ltd: front and back endpaper.

Rex Features: Guzelian 185.

The Ronald Grant Archive: 139, 175 178, 180, 181, 184 / Eon Productions 176 / Warner Bros 166.

... aur s Paul s

... mescript. et sont moult sauuage gent et ouuert
... aunes ont comme tartars. et sont en grant kaan
... nulz blez. Jesse ont thissus deleses et doulceurs. mais huter
... grant froit. Et quant len a chuenche quarante iour
... Sy treuue len la mer occeane iller cure montaignes
... ont leurs ras. car en ces montaignes ne treuue len ne
... ne beste ne oiseaue. fors vne maniere doiseaue qui sont
... de quoy les faucons se paissent il sont grans comme
... comme perpegay. et la queue comme escoudelle. et sor
... et est pour le grant froit que nul animal ny puet hab
... que kaan veult des faucons pelerins des ras. il enuoia
... les de voir que ce lieu est tant entremontaignes. que lest
... vous demeure auques a deluie denp iour. Et on y treuu
... en cel lieu. que le seignaur en a tant comme il veult. et
... eoube que les oeseurs portent en tartane quil loise au gr
... en seignaur du leuant. Or vous ay comptetou
... montaine. Or vous compteray autre